THE
POLICYOWNERS'
COMPANY

A HISTORY OF NORTHWESTERN MUTUAL, 1857 – 2007
BY JOHN GURDA

TABLE OF CONTENTS

FOREWORD

It's rare for any enterprise to last for 150 years. It's rarer still for that enterprise to remain in essentially the same business at essentially the same location for all that time. For the company to maintain, year in and year out, a consistent position of leadership in its field is practically unprecedented.

Unprecedented, and yet that's precisely the feat Northwestern Mutual has accomplished. One hundred and fifty years after its founding, Northwestern is the dominant individual life insurer in America, with 3.2 million policyowners and more than $1 trillion of coverage in force. But the company's business is not limited to life alone. Northwestern offers a full line of complementary products—from long-term care to mutual funds and from disability insurance to annuities—that help clients achieve financial security at every stage of their lives. Those clients have swelled the company's assets to $145 billion, with millions more coming in every day.

The odds against such resounding success were astronomical at the start. In 1853, an eccentric New Yorker in the twilight of his years came to frontier Wisconsin. Four years later, with more pluck than prudence, John C. Johnston launched a life insurance company. The fact that he had few friends and that a depression was under way made little difference to the old man. Johnston plowed ahead anyway, and the leaders who followed him pursued the same course, weathering internal struggles and external cataclysms to become a force in American life insurance.

It was in the 1880s, under a redoubtable figure named Henry Palmer, that Northwestern developed its abiding sense of mission. Palmer took two principles—trusteeship and mutuality—and made them the core of a culture that persists to the present day. The durability of that culture through more than a century of change is one of the most compelling stories in the history of the insurance industry.

Cultural constancy is the central theme of *The Policyowners' Company*, a book that grew out of the author's second tour of duty at Northwestern Mutual. In 1983, I wrote *The Quiet Company* for the firm's 125th anniversary. In 2006, I stepped into the same river more than twenty years downstream, finding it much the same but substantially different. So, too, are the books. *The Policyowners' Company* is not so much an update as a new telling of the same story, with more generous coverage of Northwestern's first century than *The Quiet Company* and a far richer graphic treatment.

The author had significant help in bringing the story to life. Margo O'Brien Hokanson, Mark Lucius, and Brenda Skelton shepherded the project through Northwestern channels from first day to last. Corporate archivist Stephanie Williams provided essential help in both the research and the production stages. Bob Berdan, Bill Koenig, and Jean Maier served generously and ably as official readers, and Bill Beckley and Pete Bruce supplied valuable feedback on the later chapters. Jim Price, the lead graphic designer, has once again made my words look good. Luann Boie, Tammy Landis, and Brenda Jacklin all assisted in transforming the raw manuscript to a finished book. Thanks are due, finally, to the folks on South 5, who helped make the author's home office sojourn as agreeable an experience as writing can be.

Northwestern Mutual is a towering example of the usefulness of history. Few organizations have such a lively sense of their own heritage, and fewer still try with such conspicuous success to adapt the fixed principles of their founders to the demands of a world in perpetual motion. The company in its modern form is a testament to the power of a constant faith, constantly adjusted, and in this are lessons that other businesses might take to heart. Northwestern has prospered for more than 150 years by changing and by staying the same: both, together, always.

John Gurda

Chapter 129.

PRIVATE AND LOCAL LAWS, 1857.

An Act to Incorporate the Mutual Life Insurance Company of the State of

MILLER & BREITWISCH
PHOTOGRAPHERS

FRED J. WOOD
REAL ESTATE
AND INSURANCE
MONEY TO LOAN

SSER CO. MFG. JEWELERS

4th. Such as shall have been purchased at sales upon judgments, decrees or
for such debts.

its dealings.

"THE DAY OF SMALL THINGS"

John C. Johnston was master of all he surveyed. From the back windows of his stately brick manor near Janesville, Wisconsin, the old man could look north and east to the Rock River, letting his gaze wander over some of the finest farmland in the Midwest. He owned everything he could see: 3,000 acres, or nearly five square miles—a farm of spectacular dimensions in a region still emerging from the vivid hardships of the frontier. The lord of this fiefdom had no small ambitions. Johnston raised 10,000 bushels of corn and 5,000 more of wheat in 1855, but the pride of his holdings was a herd of 260 cattle, perhaps the best in Wisconsin. His hope was to raise and sell blooded stock to farmers who wanted to improve the pedigree of their own herds. Recently arrived from New York City, of all places, Johnston was making a definite impression. "We may reasonably anticipate," wrote a Rock County chronicler in 1856, "that when he 'gets the hang of the country,' he will be considerable of a farmer."

Farming was, in fact, the fifth or sixth stop on the newcomer's long career journey. Born in about 1788, one year before George Washington became the nation's first president, John C. Johnston had spent most of his life in Catskill, New York, a picturesque village on the Hudson River, 100 miles upstream from Manhattan.

John C. Johnston, the restless Easterner who founded Northwestern Mutual in 1857

Sometimes addressed as "General" Johnston—a legacy of his days in the volunteer militia—he had at various times taught in Catskill's village school, operated a millwork factory, and sold "invalid chairs" along the Eastern seaboard. Then this restless soul discovered life insurance. The field was in its infancy as Johnston bounced from one profession to another, but here, he decided, was a product worthy of his undivided attention. Nothing in the world had such singular power to soften the blow of life's one guarantee: that it will end. With the stroke of a pen, life insurance enabled families to stay together, children to grow up without fear of want, and the elderly to end their days in comfort. A mutual company, in particular, was a "brotherhood of the provident" who pooled their funds to safeguard the welfare of their loved ones. The fact that the brothers who sold the policies could earn a very comfortable living was not lost on John Johnston. Life insurance quickly became the ruling passion of his life. In about 1850, at an age when most of his peers were either retired or deceased, he headed down the Hudson to start another career.

Johnston's destination was the Mutual Life Insurance Company of New York, a Manhattan firm founded just seven years earlier, in 1843. He did not travel alone. The zealot brought two townsmen with him: Henry H. and Henry B. Hyde, father and son. At least one had been Johnston's student in Catskill, and both had come to share his contagious enthusiasm for life insurance. Henry H. Hyde became a highly successful agent for Mutual of New York, and his son, Henry B., after a stint as the company's cashier, left in 1859 to found his own firm: the Equitable Life Assurance Society. Forty years later and shortly before his death, Henry B. Hyde wrote Northwestern Mutual "to obtain and preserve a picture of the man who had educated him in the business of life insurance." (The company sent several.) The Equitable was the largest life insurance firm in the world at the time. Even before his own career was safely launched, John C. Johnston's role as Hyde's mentor made him a significant figure in the history of American life insurance.

That role continued to grow. Passionate, persistent, and endlessly persuasive, John C. Johnston proved to be a natural insurance salesman. He and his middle-aged son, William H., established a Mutual of New York agency in Manhattan that rose rapidly in the industry rankings. It was so prosperous, in fact, that Johnston was soon a power in the firm's internal affairs. In 1853, when a lackluster figure named Joseph Collins became Mutual Life's president, business fell off so rapidly that a group of trustees resolved to unseat him. John Johnston, who knew the company's policyowners better than anyone, joined their cause, soliciting proxy votes that carried a dry goods merchant, Frederick Winston, into office by a margin of 342 votes to 330. Winston was a sound choice—he led the company for the next thirty-two years—but many insiders questioned the propriety of an agent amassing enough power to swing an election. Soon after Winston took office in 1853, John C. Johnston left the company, taking with him $30,000 in lieu of his renewal commissions— more than $750,000 in current dollars.

Newly affluent and newly at liberty, Johnston might have retired to a life of well-earned leisure. He was, after all, nearly sixty-five years old at a time when life expectancy at birth was less than forty. But the ever-restless patriarch decided that he had enough energy to begin at least one more career. "Go west, old man," an inner voice urged him, and Johnston headed to the wilds of Wisconsin. According to one local legend, he reached the new state with a wagonload of gold coins.

Janesville, Wisconsin,
the company's first home, in 1860

John Johnston's stately brick residence overlooked one of the finest farms in the state.

In November 1853, the aging tycoon began to spend his gold on a sprawling farmstead five miles northwest of Janesville, paying cash for some parcels and borrowing heavily for the rest. His creditors included Mutual of New York.

Wisconsin was a natural choice—for a younger man. As the soils of New York and New England were tilled to exhaustion, the American Northwest—that vast, fertile region north and west of the Ohio River—offered an abundance of new land to exploit. When

Wisconsin joined the Union in 1848, most of its residents were from states farther east, and New York led the list. Rock County, part of the prairie belt that straddled Wisconsin's border with Illinois, was in especially high demand. "Nature has there graded out magnificent farms," declared the *Milwaukee Sentinel* (May 22, 1851), "requiring the hand of man only to fence them in, and sow the seed, and take care of the produce of the teeming fields." Breaking the sod required significantly more effort than that, but

Rock County did attract tens of thousands of Easterners, including John Johnston. Their trading center was Janesville, a settlement that had come to life on a bend of the Rock River in the 1830s. By the time Johnston arrived, Janesville was a newly incorporated city with a population of 4,800.

The transplanted New Yorker became a highly visible presence in the community. Johnston built a "commodious brick farmhouse," as one contemporary put it, hauling his materials all the way from Milwaukee by ox cart. In 1855, he was elected a vice-president of the Rock County Agricultural Society, the group that organized the annual county fair. But Johnston never showed his livestock at that fair. There are indications, in fact, that his dreams of glory as southern Wisconsin's cattle king began to evaporate not long after he hatched them. This quixotic figure clearly had an attention span of rather limited duration. Whether the world failed to beat a path to his barn door or he simply got bored, John Johnston was doing something else by 1857. At the age of at least sixty-nine, with more hope than confidence or even common sense, he decided to start a life insurance company.

Mutual Life of Wisconsin

Some seeds fall on rock, others on sand, and the most promising come to rest on fertile ground. The seed that became Northwestern Mutual was no different, really, from scores of others sown on the frontier. Like the wheat that Yankees planted as their main cash crop, like the forms of local government they adopted, life insurance was an idea carried west from New York and New England. The company that John Johnston started was a virtual clone of Mutual Life of New York, with the same policies, the same premiums, and the same procedures as his old employer. Even the name was familiar: Mutual Life of Wisconsin. Whether it would flourish in the soil of the frontier was anyone's guess, but the signs were not propitious. Wisconsin's economy was dominated by farmers, a notoriously cash-poor class of citizens. With their money tied up in barns, livestock, and equipment, few had anything left over for life insurance: twenty other hopeful Wisconsin companies had failed by the time Johnston planted his seedling.

His first task was to recruit a board of directors—thirty-six men in all. (Women would be absent for another century.) Frontier society was extraordinarily fluid by modern

Nine of the local notables who served on Mutual Life of Wisconsin's original board

Hoel H. Camp   *James Earnest*   *Edward Dimoch*   *Joseph Sleeper*   *Simeon Mills*   *James Martin*   *Benjamin Pixley*   *John Rountree*   *Josiah Willard*

standards, and Johnston had unusual powers of persuasion. Within three years of his arrival, this complete stranger had enlisted the cream of Wisconsin society to support his bid for an insurance company. Fifteen of the original thirty-six trustees were from Janesville—by far the largest contingent—and nearly all the others lived within a 100-mile radius in southern Wisconsin. They included a United States senator, a former Wisconsin governor, the state treasurer, a former Janesville mayor, and enough bankers, lawyers, and merchants to start a chamber of commerce. The names themselves were throwbacks to colonial days: Josiah Flint Willard, John Hawkins Rountree, George Chester Northrop, James Rood Doolittle, Hoel Hinman Camp, and numerous others that might have been familiar on any village green back East. These were white Anglo-Saxon Protestants—Yankees, in the parlance of the time—who were born east of the Appalachians, took their Scripture straight from the King James Bible, and held onto social and economic power long after European immigrants had outnumbered them.

With such a formidable swarm of WASPs, Johnston had little trouble pushing his incorporation bill through the legislature. The Mutual Life Insurance Company of the State of Wisconsin was formally chartered on March 2, 1857. It was not yet, however, authorized to sell insurance. John Johnston was required to secure $200,000 of coverage before he could issue policies, and it was here that the company's bright promise began to fade perceptibly. Although support for Mutual of Wisconsin was impressively broad, it was also discouragingly shallow. Only eleven of the thirty-six charter trustees bothered to take out policies, and only five of those eleven paid their premiums for more than two years. Progress was further hampered by a severe recession that began in June 1857 and lasted for eighteen months. The Panic of 1857, one of the nineteenth century's worst downturns, depressed farm prices, dried up capital, and pushed even established companies to the wall. As both a farmer and a would-be insurance magnate, John Johnston was under considerable stress.

Policy No. 1 insured the life of John Johnston for $5,000.

Mutual of Wisconsin's first two offices in downtown Janesville

He pushed forward anyway. Johnston was listed in the 1858 Janesville city directory as "manager" of the "Mutual Life Insurance Co.," working out of a small office near the center of town. For an annual salary of $2,000—not payable until the company began to collect premiums—the old man beat the drum for life insurance in southern Wisconsin. (Although he was well past insurable age, Johnston was also promised a paid-up $5,000 policy.) One of his early brochures began on a note of morbid realism:

Now friends it is a fixed fact that all men must die; the young, the healthy, the vigorous are suddenly cut off; no time having been allowed them to accumulate a hoard; and with these, goes from their home, comfort and independence....

Let every man consider his circumstances, and make provision for his family by a life Policy, he will then have the proud satisfaction of knowing that he has performed an important duty to himself, his family and the community, and his mind will be at ease during life, and when he has been consigned to his narrow house, his grave will be hallowed with the grateful tears of his surviving relatives.

The citizens of Janesville took at least a passing interest in the new creation in their midst. The *Gazette* (July 7, 1858) reported what it felt to be significant progress:

We learn from the general manager that his success in obtaining subscriptions among our best and most reliable citizens far exceeds his most sanguine expectations.... Without going out of Main and Milwaukee streets to solicit subscribers, there has been over $250,000 subscribed.

That was an exaggeration of the wildest sort. John Johnston would ultimately bring in just over $100,000 in coverage—a task that consumed the better part of two years and required him to traipse all over southern Wisconsin. Selling a somewhat exotic product in a thoroughly depressed market, Johnston was finally obliged to seek help. His most fateful recruit, and the man who may have saved the company from an early grave, was Hiram G. Wilson of Milwaukee. Wilson was anything but an insurance expert. In 1857, he was working as a self-employed artist and the local agent for a sewing machine company. But the Ohio native was, like Johnston, a gifted salesman and, like Johnston, he developed a contagious passion for life insurance. Hiram Wilson was also alert to the advantages Milwaukee had to offer Mutual of Wisconsin. A superb harbor, first-class rail facilities, and aggressive promotion had made the city Wisconsin's commercial capital; wheat went out by the schoonerful, and returning ships brought in

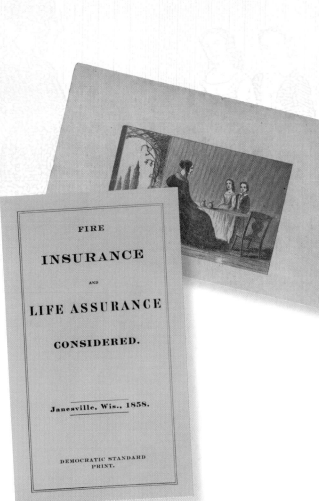

An 1858 sales pamphlet urged "every father" to "lay aside a small portion of his earnings in securing to his family a life Policy."

everything from hayrakes to harmonicas. By 1860, Milwaukee had 45,000 residents—six times more than Janesville and enough to make it the twentieth-largest city in America. Here, Hiram Wilson decided, was where Mutual of Wisconsin would find its true home.

His first step was to interest some prominent Milwaukeeans in the embryonic enterprise. By the end of 1858, Wilson had secured applications from Henry Palmer, Samuel Daggett, Dr. Erastus Wolcott, Dr. Lewis McKnight, and Charles Nash. All five were pillars of the community, and all would be closely associated with Northwestern Mutual—Mutual of Wisconsin's successor—for the rest of their lives. But Hiram Wilson wanted more than their premium dollars. Reminiscing at an agents' gathering some forty years later, Henry Palmer described what happened next:

> [Wilson] eventually came to us with the proposition to have the Company removed to Milwaukee, and they secured an amendment to the charter which authorized them to do so. After a good deal of argument, these gentlemen mentioned here [Daggett, Wolcott, and M.S. Scott], beside myself, together with a few others, agreed to go into the Company. They were to put us in the Board of Trustees and move the Company here. We entered into this arrangement with many misgivings, with doubt as to whether we should ever be able to make it a success, and we hesitated for weeks before we concluded to try the experiment.

Wilson was convinced that the move was in the company's best interests. Thanks in no small part to his own efforts, Mutual of Wisconsin had satisfied the $200,000 insurance requirement on November 25, 1858—one year and nine months after its incorporation. The company was finally in business, but it was breathing very slowly. Even the Janesville trustees—those who had bothered to stick around—saw the wisdom of relocating to a larger market. Only John Johnston demurred. The would-be cattle baron had become a full-fledged curmudgeon in his later years. Henry Palmer, the Milwaukee group's leading negotiator, described him as "a very peculiar man, [who] must have everything his own way or not at all."

In 1859, a group of leading Milwaukeeans took control of the infant enterprise: (from top) Henry Palmer, Samuel Daggett, Dr. Erastus Wolcott, Lewis McKnight, and Charles Nash.

Milwaukee was already the state's commercial capital when this bird's-eye view was created in 1858.

That view was certainly consistent with Johnston's behavior. The old man once declared that he had "got up this company at his own risk and charge," and he no doubt believed that Mutual of Wisconsin was his to run as he pleased. But the firm was already headed in an altogether different direction. On March 7, 1859—the first meeting the Milwaukee trustees attended and the last one in Janesville—the board decided that "from and after the close of this meeting the office of this company be located in the City of Milwaukee." There was a single dissenting vote: John C. Johnston's.

It is doubtful that Mutual of Wisconsin could have survived for long with Johnston at the helm, even if he had lived forever. The founder's administrative skills were open to question, and his self-interest was all too obvious. (He once requested a contract for his grandson—or any other relative of his choosing—that would have paid lifetime renewal commissions on every single policy issued up to the time of Johnston's death. The trustees, normally a tractable bunch, soundly rejected the idea.) Although he was ill-equipped to lead the company he had launched, there was an undeniable poignancy in the spectacle of this unusual character losing control of his creation. What followed was even more poignant. Johnston had acquired an enormous farm in Rock County, for which he had assumed an equally enormous debt. With the agricultural markets still depressed and

Mutual of Wisconsin in other hands, the burden proved too much for him to bear. Foreclosure proceedings began in March 1859, and the Johnston farmstead—acquired with such high hopes not even six years earlier—went to the highest bidder at a sheriff's sale. The former owner and his wife, Ruth, had moved to the capital city of Madison by that time. It was there that the patriarch died on March 23, 1860, at the approximate age of seventy-two.

The Janesville newspaper printed no notice of his passing. His biography appears in none of the standard histories of Rock County or Wisconsin or, for that matter, American life insurance. John C. Johnston faded quickly into the oblivion that awaits most of us. But Johnston was an extraordinary figure, a man who lived his life as an endless succession of possibilities, each grander and more full of promise than the last. A life insurance company proved to be the most durable of his dreams. Mutual Life of Wisconsin, later Northwestern Mutual, would reach its true potential under different leaders in a different home, but it was an eccentric wanderer from upstate New York who brought it to life. At its deepest roots, Northwestern Mutual was John C. Johnston's creation and his alone.

This early version of a copy machine pressed a finished document against a sheet of moistened tissue, creating a mirror-image duplicate.

(top) *Samuel Daggett, the firm's first Milwaukee president*

The company's "home office" was a single room, 16 by 20 feet square, on the corner of Broadway and Wisconsin Ave.

The Milwaukee delegation's first goal had been, plainly said, to save the company from its founder. With that accomplished, they tackled a substantially more imposing task: making something of the firm they had commandeered. Mutual of Wisconsin was anything but a powerhouse. When the trustees boarded the train for Milwaukee after the March 7 meeting, they carried with them a small black trunk containing all the company's tangible assets: a handful of pamphlets, a pile of blank applications, and the records of a few dozen insurance policies. The trunk was unpacked in the office Hiram Wilson was already using on the corner of Broadway and Wisconsin Avenue, near the heart of Milwaukee's modest business district. Amherst Kellogg, who joined Mutual of Wisconsin soon after the move, recalled the future giant's first home office as a single room, sixteen by twenty feet square, that contained "plenty of light, but little else."

The company's new leaders didn't give up their old jobs. Attorney Henry L. Palmer and Dr. Erastus B. Wolcott, both transplanted Easterners, served as general counsel and medical examiner, respectively, but their workloads were light and their "salaries" consisted of reduced insurance premiums. Mutual of Wisconsin's president was Samuel S. Daggett, who may have been Milwaukee's leading authority on insurance—fire insurance, that is. Born in Massachusetts, Daggett was president of the Milwaukee Mutual Fire Insurance Company and secretary of the United States Fire Insurance Company at the time of the move. He was also, appropriately enough, a loyal member and former chief of the city's fire department, an all-volunteer force. Although he would learn the life business soon enough, Samuel Daggett was a part-time president, hanging his hat at Milwaukee Mutual and visiting Mutual of Wisconsin when he needed to sign papers.

On a day-to-day basis, the transplanted company was a two-man operation, and one of them was usually on the road. The full-time home office staff consisted of Amherst Willoughby

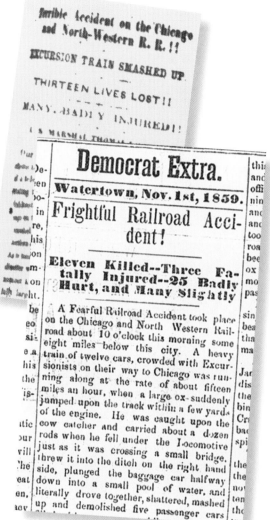

Democrat Extra.

Watertown, Nov. 1st, 1859.

Frightful Railroad Accident!

Eleven Killed--Three Fatally Injured--25 Badly Hurt, and Many Slightly

A Fearful Railroad Accident took place on the Chicago and North Western Railroad about 10 o'clock this morning some eight miles below this city. A heavy train of twelve cars, crowded with Excursionists on their way to Chicago was running along at the rate of about fifteen miles an hour, when a large ox suddenly jumped upon the track within a few yards of the engine. He was caught upon the cow catcher and carried about a dozen rods when he fell under the Locomotive just as it was crossing a small bridge, threw it into the ditch on the right hand side, plunged the baggage car halfway down into a small pool of water, and literally drove together, shattered, mashed up and demolished five passenger cars...

Kellogg, a Phi Beta Kappa graduate of Connecticut Wesleyan who had spent years in the lumber trade. Hired as Mutual of Wisconsin's secretary in April 1859, Kellogg kept the accounts, wrote the advertisements, managed the correspondence, and did whatever else the business required, all without so much as an office boy to help. When Kellogg left to run an errand, he had to lock the door. His counterpart in the field, of course, was Hiram Wilson, the man most responsible for Mutual of Wisconsin's second beginning. Wilson traveled constantly, selling insurance and recruiting agents throughout the region. By June 1, 1859—nearly three months after the move—he and his colleagues had increased the total number of policies in force to 137.

Mutual of Wisconsin was a small, vulnerable enterprise with little room for error and much less for catastrophe. When the state experienced its first serious train wreck on November 1, 1859, there was understandable anxiety among the company's leaders. Only three weeks earlier, the Chicago & North Western Railroad had completed its line between Oshkosh, Watertown, and Janesville—an extension of its service to Chicago. As part of the ongoing celebration, at least 600 Wisconsinites boarded an excursion train for a day or two of sightseeing in the Windy City. Just outside Johnson Creek, a hamlet halfway between Milwaukee and Madison, their locomotive hit a wayward ox and careened off the track, pulling five passenger cars with it. The *Milwaukee Sentinel* (November 2, 1859) described the ensuing mayhem:

On Nov. 1, 1859, a train like the one pictured above went off the tracks near Johnson Creek, Wisconsin, killing 14 passengers, among them two policyowners.

All were stove together in one confused and struggling mass of ruins. Men, women and children, were all mingled together in one common wreck of life and property. The shock was terrible, and the crash followed with irresistible power. The whole train was suddenly brought to a stand, and those who happened to be looking out of the windows could see fragments of bodies and limbs flying in all directions and lying all around.

One car, reported the *Janesville Gazette*, was driven into another "like a telescope into its case." When the dust had settled, local authorities tallied fourteen dead, including two Mutual of Wisconsin policyowners, one from Oshkosh and the other from Fond du Lac.

The death claims totaled $3,500, considerably more money than the company had on hand. Instead of panicking, Samuel Daggett and his fellow trustees saw an opportunity to benefit both the policyowners' families and their company's reputation. Waiving the usual ninety-day settlement period, they borrowed money on their own signatures and paid the claims immediately. This chivalric deed did not go unsung. Within days, the company had peppered southern Wisconsin with leaflets containing references to "the recent terrible disaster" and a pointed message from Daggett:

I allude to these sad scenes to illustrate the importance of timely Life Insurance. A small amount invested annually, while in life and health, and which can be done without inconvenience by almost any man, will, upon his death, leave to some dear friend, say a brother, sister, mother, or a companion, a present competence, and a most grateful heart.

Prompt claims settlement and savvy marketing helped the company grow, but its progress was hardly automatic. The first requirement was a network of agents to sell the firm's policies, and that was Hiram G. Wilson's responsibility. Amherst Kellogg described his peripatetic colleague as "black haired, bright eyed, active, alert, quick in movement, cordial and frank in address, ready with argument, prompt to catch the decisive turn, and withal of unbounded faith in the future of the business and of the Company, and with a contagious enthusiasm in presenting them both." Wilson exercised those qualities to become a pied piper of mutuality, practically wearing out his railroad pass in the never-ending quest for new policyowners and new agents. His travels were restricted to southern and central Wisconsin at first, but Wilson soon crossed into neighboring sections of Minnesota, Iowa, and Illinois. Recruiting on the frontier was not particularly easy duty. In 1862, Wilson fled New Ulm, Minnesota, just before a Sioux war party attacked, leaving nearly 100 settlers

Mutual of Wisconsin borrowed money to pay the claims immediately and then proclaimed the importance of "timely Life Insurance."

dead or wounded. A letter home revealed his gift for understatement: "Was in too great a rush to even attempt any business."

Conditions may have been difficult, but Hiram G. Wilson assembled a hardy band of fellow evangelists to preach the gospel of life insurance in their territories—for a ten-percent commission. Most were "local" agents, who represented Mutual of Wisconsin as a sideline to their regular pursuits. Local agents were the foundation of a well-defined hierarchy that emerged in the company's early years. They worked under "traveling" (later "special") agents, who agreed to devote their "entire time, energy and ability to soliciting applications, collecting premiums, and otherwise promoting the interests of the Company." District agents served larger territories, and general agents generally covered entire states, taking ultimate responsibility for every representative within their domains. Although commissions were highly variable in the early years, the trend was upward; by the mid-1870s, even local agents could earn twenty percent on first-year business and five percent on renewals.

The agents' stock in trade was the same product agents of every company had been selling since the beginning: level-premium, dividend-paying whole life insurance. A few variations were introduced in the 1860s, including ten-pay policies (paid up in a decade) and endowment contracts, but ordinary insurance remained the company's bread and butter for well over a century. The first policies

contained terms that seem extraordinarily restrictive by modern standards. The insured limit on a single life was $5,000 until 1864, when it climbed all the way to $10,000. Policyowners weren't allowed, on penalty of cancellation, to live within ten miles of the Mississippi or Missouri Rivers, and they couldn't even travel south of Virginia and Tennessee—for fear of malaria, among other maladies. Crossing into Canada was allowed, but California was off limits, and ocean voyages were completely out of the question. These restrictions mattered little to the great mass of policyowners in America's heartland, but a clause added in 1861 had broader implications: "[If the insured] shall become so far intemperate as to impair his health, or induce delirium tremens; or in case he shall die ... of any injury received when in a state of intoxication, then this Policy shall be null, void and of no effect." In a region rapidly rising to fame as a producer (and consumer) of beer and other libations, the temperance clause raised more than a few eyebrows, particularly when it was enforced. A memorable ruckus erupted in McGregor, Iowa, after reports reached the home office that the town's mayor had become "very intemperate." The company canceled his policies, sparking an indignant protest from McGregor residents

General agencies like Elmore & Rowe's dotted the region and ultimately the entire country.

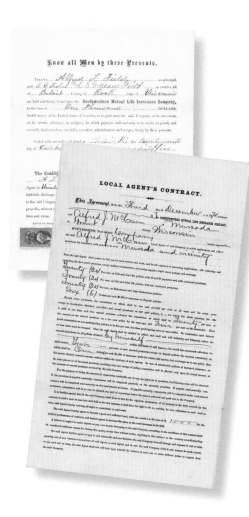

Typical agent contracts of the 1860s

who were "not strictly total abstinence men," including several policyowners who reportedly drank more than the mayor.

Mutual of Wisconsin's policy restrictions were not, in truth, radically different from those adopted by other insurers. The company was not yet ready to break from the pack; its goal, in fact, was to convince prospects that it could play in the same league as the more-established Eastern firms. In an 1861 circular, the Western upstart was careful not to claim too much for itself:

> *The Mutual Life Insurance Company of Wisconsin presents advantages in many respects equal, in some respects superior, to those of other companies doing business in the Northwest. Its rates, its plans of operations, and its basis are identical with the best companies in this country and in Europe. Its age, and consequently its accumulations, are not equal to others in amount, but in proportion to the age of its business and the amount at risk they will compare favorably with the most successful.*

The company needn't have been so modest. Although it was still practically a newborn, Mutual of Wisconsin had some natural advantages over its older competitors. Every company's performance rests on three pillars: mortality experience, investment results, and business expenses. The states of the Northwest—Ohio, Indiana, Illinois,

Michigan, Wisconsin, and northern Minnesota—were attracting settlers in the prime of their lives, people with the youth and vigor necessary to meet the abundant challenges of the frontier. "There were no old men in Milwaukee," said Peter Van Vechten, a future Northwestern Mutual trustee who arrived in 1845. "A gray-headed man was a rarity." Mutual of Wisconsin's policyowners were an unusually healthy bunch, and so was their region's investment climate. As farmers bought equipment, as settlers built houses, and as cities rose from the forests and prairies, capital was in short supply and high demand. Mutual of Wisconsin's charter permitted only two classes of investment—government bonds and mortgages on Wisconsin real estate—and mortgages quickly became the heart of the portfolio. The company routinely earned 10 percent on loans that would have drawn perhaps half that figure back East.

Superior mortality experience and superb investment returns literally came with the territory; geography made an enormous difference. Expenses, by contrast, varied widely regardless of region, and more than one firm had already spent its way into oblivion. Mutual of Wisconsin's leaders were, for the most part, seasoned businessmen who had experienced success in other fields; they were not about to throw money away. They also approached their work with a moral fervor that some modern readers might find curiously antique. The company's officers and trustees

displayed a broad Calvinist streak that was entirely consistent with their upbringings in New York and New England. These were rock-ribbed Yankees who believed that hard work, correct thinking, and upright behavior were a mark of their membership in the elect. Mutual of Wisconsin was, to some degree, a concrete expression of that outlook, one that combined old-school Calvinism with old-fashioned patriotism. The company's annual report for 1866 stated its core principles unequivocally: "It has been the aim of the managers to make this a *model* Life Insurance Company, founded on a proper basis and conducted on *equitable* principles; a *truly mutual* company managed *by* the members for the benefit of all...." Just as the Puritans had envisioned Boston as "a city on a hill," shining for all the world to see, some of their descendants might have viewed Mutual of Wisconsin as a company on a hill. One tangible result was an expense ratio that was the envy of many older firms.

Although it was not yet a power in the land, the little Milwaukee firm had a world-beating trinity. Healthy policyowners, high-yielding investments, and moderate expenses gave Mutual of Wisconsin the competitive muscle to take on any life insurance firm in America. That's precisely what the company did, beginning in its own backyard. Agents, of course, were the engines of growth; it was only through them that policyowners became policyowners. By the time Hiram G. Wilson resigned in 1864—a decision prompted by

his wife's need for a milder climate—Mutual of Wisconsin's sales network had achieved critical mass in every neighboring state and in one or two beyond. Like a child outgrowing its clothes, the company soon found its name entirely too restrictive. In December 1864, after briefly considering "The Mutual Life Insurance Company of the Northwest," the trustees decided to rename their enterprise "Northwestern Mutual Life." The change was made, they explained, "to take away any impression that the Company is merely a State institution, to identify it more thoroughly with its field of operations ... and to cause every citizen of the Northwest to feel a personal interest and a patriotic pride in its prosperity."

Although no one suggested changing it again, even the new name was soon a few sizes too small. Under John McKindley and then Heber Smith, Wilson's successors

In 1864, reflecting its rise to regional prominence, Mutual of Wisconsin decided to call itself Northwestern Mutual, a name that covered the states of the Old Northwest: Wisconsin, Illinois, Michigan, Indiana, Ohio, and part of Minnesota.

in what became the Agency Department, Northwestern Mutual continued to spread outward from its base in the heartland, opening agencies in two or three states every year. Samuel Daggett and his colleagues obviously overcame their aversion to the West Coast; in 1867, the company was licensed to sell insurance in California, Oregon, and Washington. One year later, Vermont, New Hampshire, and Maine joined Massachusetts in the fold, giving Northwestern a presence from sea to shining sea. The firm's motto, appropriately enough, was "We Spread to Protect," and it was usually printed beneath an illustration of a banyan tree. A native of tropical Asia, the banyan grows by dropping shoots from its canopy that take root and become trunks in their own right; a single tree can become a grove covering thousands of square yards. The banyan, which became the company's official symbol in 1868 after years of informal use, is also known as the strangler fig—an unofficial expression of what Northwestern hoped to do to its competitors.

A coast-to-coast presence did not mean coast-to-coast prosperity. The company was strongest in its home region, and sales in the more distant states were meager indeed. But Northwestern was making definite inroads. With the aid of a rebounding economy and the firm's stellar dividend performance, agents were finding converts to the Northwestern gospel wherever they looked. Even the Civil War couldn't slow their march. The company lost fourteen policyowners in the conflict, including one each at Gettysburg, Chickamauga, and Vicksburg, but the ranks of the insured continued to swell. Between the attack on Fort Sumter in 1861 and the surrender at Appomattox in 1865, the number of policies in force soared from 785 to 8,125—an average annual growth rate of more than 80 percent! It is not hard to detect a note of surprise in the company's report for 1866:

Commencing operations in Milwaukee less than eight years ago, without capital, the Company has overcome a wide spread prejudice against western companies, and has become not only the largest Insurance Company west of the seaboard cities, but takes rank among the foremost companies in the whole country, (only two of all the Life Companies of New York, having a larger number of members, only four a larger amount at risk, and only five larger assets), while it is confessedly the largest monied institution, (excepting railroads), in the northwest.

The banyan tree of tropical Asia provided a tangible symbol for the company's motto: "We Spread to Protect."

Such dramatic growth put intense pressure on the home office staff. After two years of solitude (and too many sixteen-hour days), Amherst Kellogg hired his first clerical assistant in 1861. The pair soon left Hiram Wilson's old quarters for a roomier suite in the Iron Block, a new landmark on Water Street and Wisconsin Avenue. In 1865, the company moved back to the intersection of Broadway and Wisconsin, buying a former millinery shop for $9,000. Within two years, a dozen clerks were hard at work under Kellogg's supervision. All were men, and all shared a single trait: superior penmanship. Every policy change, every ledger item, and every meeting record had to be entered by hand, and legibility was essential. George Austin, one of the office all-stars, earned praise as "a penman of note."

And so the David of the 1850s became a Goliath in the 1860s, relatively speaking. America's life insurance industry was still minuscule by modern standards, with just over $2 billion of coverage in force by 1870, but Northwestern was more than keeping pace with its competitors. Selling products of superior value through a devoted field force backed by an efficient home office, the company increased its insurance coverage from $1 million in 1860 to $65 million in 1870, and its assets grew from $26,000 to $9 million during the same decade. What Henry Palmer would later call "the day of small things" was rapidly fading into memory. In January, 1867, seventy-five agents, officers, and trustees of the company met at the Newhall House, Milwaukee's leading hotel, to celebrate their

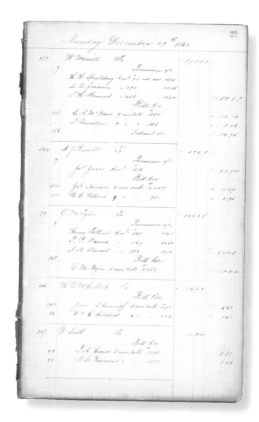

Superior penmanship was a job requirement for Northwestern's clerical staff.

Continued growth required two moves in the 1860s, the first to a suite in the Iron Block (far left) and the second to an entire building on Broadway.

Milwaukee's elegant Newhall House was the scene of an 1867 banquet that brought agents, officers, and trustees together for the first time.

success. It was the first in a series of gatherings that continue to the present day. After dining on fillets of beef larded with mushrooms and venison steak with currant jelly, the group heard a round of congratulatory speeches and a lengthy history lesson from Henry Palmer. Northwestern Mutual was all of ten years old at the time. Like everyone else present, the *Milwaukee Sentinel* reporter was struck by the company's "unexampled prosperity" after such a short time in business. "It must be a matter of great pride to all Wisconsin men," he wrote, "that a home institution should have been conducted so honorably and with such unparalleled success. But very few of our readers are aware of the magnitude of this home institution." Northwestern may have been a quiet company, but its voice was being heard throughout the land.

A Company Worth Fighting For

As it took its place among America's leading insurance firms, Northwestern Mutual became a company worth fighting for. That, unfortunately, is just what happened. The economic power and social prestige associated with the young giant attracted men of diverse gifts and sometimes divergent interests. As a result, the decade following the Civil War was marked by a lack of unanimity in the firm's direction that occasionally broke into open conflict. Northwestern continued

to make headway, but its leaders were sometimes rowing in different directions.

The discord began with a vacuum at the very top. As the company grew, Samuel Daggett gradually shifted his attention from fire to life insurance, becoming an able and devoted chief executive. He once told a friend that he considered it "glory enough for one lifetime to have been instrumental in fostering in its infancy, in nourishing its youth, and reposing in the strength of such a manhood as the Northwestern Life Insurance Company possessed." The glory was short-lived. Daggett, an ardent Republican, attended Abraham Lincoln's second inauguration on March 4, 1865, standing in the rain to hear the president proclaim "with malice toward none, with charity for all." Northwestern's leader caught a severe cold that was followed by consumption—the nineteenth-century term for tuberculosis. First housebound and then bedridden, Daggett died on May 23, 1868.

Succession planning had not been the company's greatest strength. The race for Daggett's seat was wide open and hotly contested, with two strong candidates squaring off: Lester Sexton, Milwaukee's leading wholesaler of dry goods, and S.D. Hastings, Wisconsin's state treasurer. The first ballot was so close—fourteen trustees voting for Sexton and thirteen for Hastings—that a final decision was postponed for six months. Some aggressive politicking took place in the interim. Although Northwestern's charter allowed policyowners to vote for trustees by proxy, the practice was seldom used until the next election. Agents, of course, were much closer to their clients than anyone in the home office, and Heber Smith, the company's general agent since 1867, apparently led the campaign to gather proxies from the field. A total of 271 votes had been cast in the 1868 board election. Swollen by proxies, the number exploded to 7,684 in 1869, and nearly all endorsed the ticket headed by Lester Sexton. The luckless S.D. Hastings received only ten votes, ending his tenure on the board and leaving the presidency to Sexton. In a related development, Heber Smith became a trustee and Northwestern's vice-president.

As one of the original Milwaukee board members and a notably successful businessman, Lester Sexton might have been a fine president, but he barely had time to warm his chair. On March 12, 1869, less than two months after the election, Sexton finished the noonday meal with his family, pushed back from the table, and suffered a fatal stroke. The company was once again without a leader, but not for long. This time the gavel passed without serious incident to John Van Dyke, a prominent lawyer, well-known art patron, and Northwestern trustee since 1862.

However calmly it began, Van Dyke's five-year tenure would prove to be the stormiest in the company's history. At least a few trustees were annoyed when the new president practically forced them to raise his salary from $6,000 to $10,000—about $150,000 in current dollars. There were also the first signs of open friction between the trustees and the agents. In 1870, the board declared that any agent working for the defeat of regularly nominated trustees—a not-so-subtle reference to the previous year's proxy campaign—was "unworthy of a position in the Company." The agents responded in kind, labeling the resolution an "insult" advanced by "a few members of the board" who were devoted to "their own selfish purposes." Both sides tried to restore harmony, forming a joint committee to choose the 1871 board slate, but it was obvious that a breach had opened.

The tensions were aggravated by a serious accounting mistake. Edward Ilsley, who was an actuary in name only, forgot to include prepaid premiums as a liability in his 1869 dividend calculations—a blunder that led to a serious overstatement of the surplus available for distribution to policyowners. After fielding a host of complaints from both agents and trustees, John Van Dyke turned for help to Elizur Wright, the insurance commissioner of Massachusetts and perhaps the most respected figure in American life insurance. Wright looked beyond the immediate problem, recommending that, for absolute safety, Northwestern lower its reserve rate—the

The arithmeter was a rotary slide rule that actuaries used for their most complex calculations.

President Lester Sexton died in 1869 after less than two months in office.

His successor was John Van Dyke, a prominent lawyer and company trustee.

assumed return on its investments—from 4.5 to 4 percent. After some initial reluctance, the board endorsed the move. Because a lower rate reduced the available surplus, the company had to inform its policyowners that there would be no dividend in 1870.

Suddenly no one was happy. After years of trumpeting their company's superior dividend performance, the agents were embarrassed and open to attack from their competitors. Policyowners were similarly exposed. Most had purchased their insurance with a combination of cash and premium notes—7-percent loans their annual dividends were supposed to cover. With dividends suspended, even for a year, there was a rash of lapsed policies; between 1870 and 1871, the company's insurance in force dropped 4 percent while the entire industry's grew by the same amount. The trustees faced a thorny personnel problem as well. They wanted to fire actuary Edward Ilsley, a move complicated by the fact that his son, banker Charles Ilsley, was a prominent board member. When Charles failed to win re-election in 1871, the way was clear. Northwestern hired Emory McClintock, an accomplished actuary who would stay for the next eighteen years. The whole imbroglio prompted the trustees to pay closer attention to the details of the business. In 1871, they established an Examining Committee whose sole job was to scrutinize the company's books every year. That body

would evolve, over time, into the Policyowners' Examining Committee of the present day.

Northwestern Mutual had been growing all the while. In 1868, after years in one hand-me-down headquarters after another, the company decided to build a new home office that reflected its rising fortunes. The corner was familiar—Broadway and Wisconsin—and the architect was Milwaukee's favorite: Edward Townsend Mix. A Victorian master, Mix created a five-story landmark "in the French style," with a mansard roof and dozens of arched windows. The company took occupancy in April 1870 (two weeks after passing its annual dividend), and a Chicago critic pronounced the new building "a model of taste, convenience and solidity." Northwestern Mutual was America's eighth-largest insurance firm at the time, with $65 million of coverage in force. The dividend debacle slowed the company down temporarily, but John Van Dyke and his associates were certain that new business would soon return to a growth pattern worthy of the company's new home.

Agents remained the primary engine of growth, and their numbers and influence both swelled in the post-Civil War decade. Between 1865 and 1875, the number of states in the Northwestern orbit soared from ten to thirty-five, with each developing its own version of the company's agent hierarchy: general, district, special (or traveling), and local. The field was overwhelmingly a male domain at all levels, but never exclusively. In 1872, a traveling agent identified only as "Mrs. Dudley" made the rounds of southern Wisconsin. "She is a very worthy lady," reported the *Fond du Lac Commonwealth* (September 11, 1872), "and richly deserves the success she is meeting with. Then, too, the Northwestern is one of the very best companies in existence." The home office did its best to keep Mrs. Dudley and her counterparts motivated. Agents competed for suits and pocket watches every year, and even modest producers could earn "extra compensation for extra effort"—up to two dollars for every $1,000 of insurance they sold beyond a $50,000 minimum.

Heber Smith, the man behind the bonuses, emerged as a central figure of the period. Born in Bastard, Ontario, he began his Northwestern career as an agent in Watertown, Wisconsin, then moved on to the more lucrative Chicago market and finally the home office. As head of the field force, Smith became the agents' coach, counselor, and chief advocate, promoting virtually any course of action that would make it easier for them to sell insurance. Some of the harsher contract provisions were gradually softened— travel restrictions were largely gone by 1870—and there was a steady blurring of the line between insurance and investments. Mortgage loans on Midwestern real estate remained the company's investment of choice, with no shortage of applicants even at 10 percent. Those applicants represented

Northwestern's new home office, built in "the French style," was an instant landmark when it was completed in 1870.

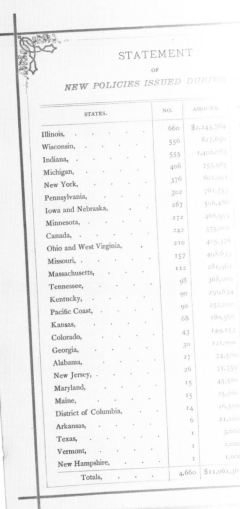

Agency superintendent Heber Smith directed the firm's expansion into 35 states, but he was also the central figure in a fierce power struggle.

a golden sales opportunity. Northwestern moved by degrees to a policy of "compulsory insurance"—a sort of buy-to-borrow plan that made an insurance contract part of every loan package. The system had its detractors, notably John Van Dyke, but Heber Smith argued that it was good for the company and good for the agents.

Smith did not bow to every request from the field. In 1872, when a new agent asked for money to furnish his office, he found himself on the receiving end of a stern letter from his vice-president: "Our low ratio of expense is brought about by pursuing the conservative course and by avoiding all extravagances of any nature. In a mutual company like the Northwestern, we do not believe the officers have any right to expend the funds of the company in expensive experiments." Although Heber Smith could stand up for Northwestern principles, he also stood up for Heber Smith. By the strength of his personality—and his demonstrated ability to control proxy votes—Smith became a force in Northwestern's affairs, much as John C. Johnston had twenty years earlier at Mutual of New York. As both a trustee and the company's vice-president,

he was already the highest-ranking former agent since Johnston himself, and Smith could easily envision himself in an even higher post.

It was clear that he had no particular regard for John Van Dyke. The two men were on opposite sides of the buy-to-borrow question, and their personal relationship was decidedly lacking in warmth. The increasingly open conflict reached its climax at the board meeting of January 27, 1874, a five-hour marathon dominated by remarks "of a personal character" from Smith and a vigorous response from Van Dyke. Heber Smith would have the last word. At the annual election of trustees, held the very next day, 12,407 votes were cast, nearly all of them proxies. John Van Dyke received a total of 194. His term on the board and therefore his presidency were at a sudden and ignominious end, and Smith prepared for his triumphal march into the executive suite.

Not so fast, said the other trustees. There had always been an anti-Smith bloc on the board—he barely won the vice-presidency in 1869—and now the ranks of the disaffected swelled. Some trustees resented the summary dismissal of their president; others resisted the idea of anyone ruling by proxy. In the

few hours between Van Dyke's defeat
and the scheduled election of officers, a
majority of the trustees decided to find a new
president. Their choice was Henry Palmer,
Northwestern's long-time general counsel
and a pillar of the company since its move
from Janesville. Palmer himself recounted
the details more than forty years later:

> *While I was engaged as counsel of the
> company in preparing the returns of the
> inspectors of election, a message came to
> me that I was wanted in my own office. I
> went up there and found a majority of the
> Board of Trustees assembled there, who
> then announced to me that they desired
> me to take the place of president. That is
> the first information I had about it…. The
> position came to me entirely unsought
> and entirely unexpected. I did not know
> for two hours before the election took
> place that it was contemplated at all.*

After so much intrigue, the election
itself was almost anti-climactic. Henry
Palmer trounced Heber Smith in the
voting for president, eighteen to ten, and
then Smith lost the vice-presidency—his
old job—by a similar margin. Instantly
unemployed, he was forced to leave
the company. Ten years of drama and
discord were over; the forces of tradition
and trusteeship had prevailed. 🌱

*The election of Henry Palmer
restored peace and marked the
beginning of a new stage in
Northwestern's evolution.*

"PRE-EMINENTLY THE POLICY-HOLDERS COMPANY"

With the ascendancy of Henry Palmer, Northwestern Mutual entered a period of calm that lasted for thirty-four years—the duration of Palmer's remarkable presidency. The American economy swelled and contracted. Electric motors took the place of steam engines. Horses gave way to streetcars, and the first automobiles appeared on the nation's streets. America went to war with Spain and came home again. Through it all, Northwestern stayed the course. Year after year, then decade after decade, Palmer followed the same policies, upheld the same standards, and refined the same winning formula. It would be too much to say that he reinvented Northwestern Mutual—the underlying instincts were already in place—but he codified those instincts, transforming them into a body of beliefs that still constitute the company's core. Palmer's role was so pivotal that he might be considered Northwestern's second founder.

Henry Palmer was a small man in an age of small men, at least by current standards. According to his 1858 insurance application, the new president carried only 126 pounds on a five-foot, nine-inch frame. (The examiner described him as "spare but well-proportioned.") But this diminutive figure became a towering presence in his adopted hometown as well as his company. Like so many Milwaukeeans

Henry Palmer, whose 34 years at the helm shaped Northwestern's course in ways that are still evident

was nearly as prominent in the political arena. An ardent Democrat, Palmer won multiple terms in the Wisconsin Assembly, the state Senate, and on the Milwaukee School Board.

He was a natural leader, chosen by his peers as speaker of the Assembly and president of the School Board, but this was no ordinary politician. Henry Palmer was neither a stereotypical back-slapper nor a vicious partisan, and he earned respect from both sides of the political aisle. Even the *Milwaukee Sentinel,* a fiercely Republican paper, offered grudging praise, opining that Palmer, "while tainted with a certain portion of political depravity, possesses evidences of personal honesty." The Democrat approached even the most divisive issues with a decidedly judicial outlook. His last elective office, in fact, was as a Milwaukee County judge. Palmer took the bench on January 5, 1874, and stepped down after Northwestern drafted him on January 28. Although his tenure lasted less than a month, the president was known forever after as "Judge Palmer."

His election may have restored the company's equilibrium, but taking charge in early 1874 was like taking the helm of a schooner in a gale. The Panic of 1873 had started a few months earlier, and with it came the longest sustained slide in American history. The economy contracted for more than five years without a single uptick, settling to its low point in early 1879. Virtually every business was affected, including life insurance.

of his era, Palmer was a Yankee who looked back to roots in the East. Born in Pennsylvania in 1819, he moved to the frontier at the age of thirty, starting a law practice in Milwaukee when the city was only three years old. Although the law was his livelihood, the newcomer had no shortage of outside interests. Rising by degrees, he became one of the highest-ranking Masons in the region, and he

Northwestern's sales were cut precisely in half between 1872 and 1878, dropping from $13.2 million to just $6.6 million. New premium dollars were so scarce that the company's expenses actually exceeded its income in 1878—a problem that didn't occur even during the better-known depression of the 1930s. The skies were just as dark on the investment side. As borrowers defaulted on their loans, Northwestern became the unwilling owner of more than $1.5 million in "special real estate"—an amount equal to the company's entire investable surplus of a few years earlier. The board's Examining Committee described these distressed properties as "standing stigmas of great detriment to the Company," and in 1880 Northwestern launched a Special Real Estate Department to pare down the portfolio "as speedily as possible."

Reflecting both the tenor of the times and the dictates of his own temperament, Henry Palmer adopted a policy that can be described in a single word: retrenchment. On virtually every front—field relations, underwriting, investments, home office operations—Northwestern took the safer, steadier, more conservative path. Not that the company had been reckless in previous years. In 1873, before Henry Palmer took charge, James Skinner, the corporate secretary, offered a concise statement of Northwestern's primary goal: "The object of this Company is to furnish <u>safe</u> insurance and to furnish it at the lowest possible cost."

What changed under Henry Palmer was the degree of emphasis: "safe" became ultra-safe, and Northwestern tried to reduce its risks to the absolute acceptable minimum.

Those risks might have included another palace rebellion. In the aftermath of Heber Smith's abortive coup, the company abandoned, for the time being, its traditional general agency system. By 1879, 460 of Northwestern's 600 agents reported directly to the home office. Matthew Keenan, who replaced Smith as the field general in 1874, was hardly a dictator—one agent recalled him fondly as "a real Irish gentleman"—but he labored to instill a greater sense of shared purpose in a group that had shown a definite tendency to wander. Keenan had the full support of Palmer and the

The Panic of 1873 made Northwestern the unwilling owner of thousands of acres of foreclosed farmland, primarily in the upper Midwest.

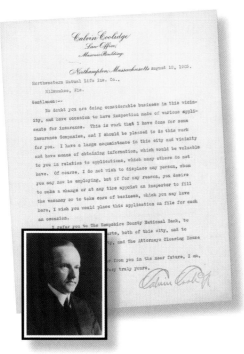

In 1905, 18 years before he entered the White House, attorney Calvin Coolidge offered to help Northwestern investigate its insurance risks.

The Medical Department enforced some of the strictest underwriting standards in the industry: (l. to r.) Drs. John Fisher, Charles Albright, and Lewis McKnight.

Board of Trustees, whose members included a returning veteran: John Van Dyke. Within months of his unceremonious ouster, Van Dyke had been re-elected to both the board and its influential Executive Committee.

Palmer's retrenchment applied to insurance risks as well. Agents were withdrawn from sections of the South deemed particularly "unhealthy." Women were no longer insured after 1876, following a determination that the hazards of childbirth made them poorer mortality risks than men. All applicants were subjected to more searching examinations. Methods of the previous period had been somewhat slapdash: every prospect was required to have a "certificate of health" filled out by the Northwestern-appointed doctor

in his town—"or if he is not at home by some other responsible physician." The system was tightened considerably after 1874, and applicants were turned down for any number of reasons: "overweight," "light weight," "family record," "want of vigor," or—the most telling disqualification—"not up to our standard."

The company's criteria were not exclusively physical. Like its competitors, Northwestern developed a national network of free-lance investigators who examined the backgrounds of prospective policyowners. (Calvin Coolidge, when he was still a small-town lawyer, offered to evaluate the risks in his corner of Massachusetts, promising "means of obtaining information ... which many others do not have.") In 1878, Northwestern raised the bar significantly, establishing an Inquiry Department whose sole job was to investigate the "moral hazard" of both applicants and insureds. Intemperance remained the quickest route to rejection or cancellation. As the tide of Prohibition rose around the country, Northwestern Mutual was on the leading wave. "Periodical drinkers and reformed drunkards are not insurable," declared Dr. John Fisher, the company's medical director in the late 1800s. "Constant free indulgers in beer or spirituous liquors are not desirable risks," he added, "although they may not use such to intoxication." Any applicant who admitted drinking to excess was required to submit "a detailed statement ... concerning his overindulgence, how long continued and when last intoxicated."

It is doubtful that Henry Palmer himself would have passed muster with the Inquiry Department. Although he was anything but a libertine, Palmer did pay twice-daily visits to a nearby saloon, where he and Charles Dyer, the general counsel, each downed a single whiskey, neat, and then returned to the home office. Critics might have complained of hypocrisy in high places, but Northwestern's hard-nosed underwriting did produce one of the lowest mortality ratios in the industry. It also fostered a sense of corporate pride: by the simple act of qualifying for insurance, every policyowner felt that he was joining an elite fraternity. "The institution is *not cosmopolitan*," said a Syracuse agent, "but is the most exclusive life Company on the continent"—something he considered a definite selling point.

The same self-willed elitism applied to investments. One of Henry Palmer's first moves as president was to end the buy-to-borrow policy of his predecessors. "I made a radical change in that system then and there," he recalled in 1906, "and it has continued ever since." Palmer believed that mingling investments with insurance had resulted in bad loans as well as bad underwriting. He scrupulously separated the two sides, assigning the mortgage operation to salaried loan agents rather than commissioned sales agents. Northwestern's mortgage specialists still looked for superior real estate loans in the upper Midwest, but there was a steady shift from rural to urban properties. The

applicants approved in 1886 included St. Hedwig's Church of Milwaukee; the Deutscher Verein of LaCrosse, Wisconsin; a Civil War veterans' group in Minnesota; a Congregational church in Lincoln, Nebraska; the Minerva Furnace Company of Milwaukee; and the Catholic diocese of Fort Wayne, Indiana. Although mortgage loans were the backbone of its portfolio, Northwestern continued to invest in government securities. An 1887 purchase marked a return to the company's roots: $40,000 of bonds issued by the City of Janesville, Wisconsin.

Under Henry Palmer's watchful eye, the company picked its investments as carefully as it selected its policyowners—something of a departure from past practice. In 1879, the board's Examining Committee noted "a lack of requisite care in this regard some years ago" and praised Palmer's administration for "a great improvement in the character of our loans in every respect." William McLaren, the Scotsman who headed the company's investment side, sounded a refrain that might have described the entire company after 1874:

It is sometimes said that the North-western is too particular in its methods, and if it was not so particular, it would make more loans…. We do not deny that we are conservative, and that our first consideration is always the security of our loans. With this constantly and prominently in view, it is no doubt true

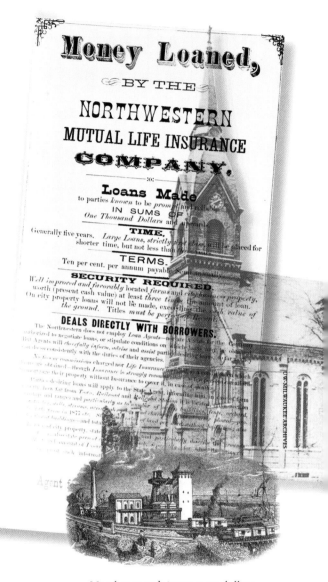

Northwestern's investment dollars financed the development of everything from Catholic churches to blast furnaces. These Milwaukee landmarks are St. Hedwig's Church and the Minerva Furnace.

It was probably in the home office—his personal domain—that Henry Palmer's "judicious management" was most strongly felt. He had a commanding grasp of the big picture, but Palmer was every bit as interested in the day-to-day minutiae of the business. It was on a solid foundation of details, he believed, that the success of the larger enterprise rested. Frederick Winkler, his fellow trustee and former law clerk, described Palmer as "pre-eminently a man of business," a self-contained and somewhat severe chief executive who carried himself with "an impalpable air of decision." The president, wrote Winkler, knew precisely what he wanted from his subordinates:

Henry Palmer's office was Northwestern Mutual's nerve center. His principled passion set the tone for the entire enterprise.

He did not need to preach or to proclaim it, his very presence, his mere look, denoted to every officer, agent and employee that he was expected to do his duty. There was no room for idlers about the establishment of which Judge Palmer was the head. Punctual himself, punctual to the minute, the strictest punctuality was the ruling discipline of every department.

that we sometimes decline to make loans which would ultimately prove safe, just as the Company may decline some insurance risks that would probably be good.... They may be, but if they are the only mistakes made by the Company, arising out of judicious management and conservative methods, its record and results will continue to command the satisfaction of its policy holders, and the respect of every intelligent business man.

Northwestern's boss led by example. Even in the twilight of his career, not a single death benefit or loan disbursement left the home office without crossing Palmer's desk. He worked so hard that the board more than once granted him a lengthy vacation and then designated a committee "to see that the full time is taken." (It rarely was.) But hard work alone was hardly enough. Henry Palmer was, in modern terms, a systems specialist: he developed tools and techniques that ensured the proper endorsement of every bond, the careful filing of every property abstract, the utmost accuracy of every ledger. If new technologies could help, Palmer embraced them. The first home office telephone appeared in 1880 and the first typewriter—a Milwaukee invention—in 1887. (There is a persistent legend that Henry Palmer turned down an earlier proposal from the typewriter's creator, Christopher Latham Sholes—an assertion for which there is no support in the historical record.) In 1891, Northwestern became one of the industry's first firms to copy insurance applications photographically, ending

decades of hand-cramping drudgery. Palmer also allowed (single) women into what had traditionally been an all-male domain. The first female employee, a former small-town school principal named Frances Lillian Madden, took a job in the collections division in 1880. By 1889, there were at least seven women working at Northwestern; by 1908, there were sixty-four.

What Henry Palmer created in the home office was a well-oiled machine. The board's 1889 Examining Committee described the company as "a perfect and ponderous thing," an organism that was "conscious of its strength" in every phase of its operations. Northwestern's nerve center was undoubtedly Henry Palmer's suite. The 1895 Examining Committee highlighted "the loyal and unflagging devotion of the officers of the Company," starting with Palmer himself. "This devotion," continued the report, "asserts itself not only in the officers, but also in the employees, who by force of example are impressed with the sacredness of the trust confided to them." Managing with economy and efficiency in mind, Northwestern kept an important competitive edge, but the firm also kept an uncommon fidelity to its mission. "In this fidelity," concluded the 1895 trustees' report, "rests the security of the policy holders, and the future of the Company."

Francis Madden, a former school principal, became Northwestern's first female employee in 1880.

Telephones and typewriters began to appear in the home office in the 1880s.

The Board of Trustees demonstrated the same commitment. Northwestern attracted a blue-ribbon board befitting its status as America's seventh-largest life insurance company—a ranking it achieved in 1880. Trustees of the Palmer era included a U.S. Supreme Court justice (David Brewer), a sitting Wisconsin governor (William Smith), a growing contingent of East Coast luminaries, and the very cream of Wisconsin society, a group that included capitalist Alexander Mitchell, industrialists Edward P. Allis and J.I. Case, meat-packer John Plankinton, railroad magnate S.S. Merrill, tanner Guido Pfister, and—perhaps the most surprising addition, given the company's views on alcohol—brewer Emil Schandein, Frederick Pabst's brother-in-law. As a group, the board showed impressive continuity. Terms were generally long, and board seats sometimes passed from fathers to sons: Alexander Mitchell to John, John Van Dyke to William. Although the board represented a fairly narrow social and economic spectrum, there was an attempt at geographic diversity. When trustees from Baltimore, Cincinnati, and Richmond stepped down, they were replaced by prominent citizens from Baltimore, Cincinnati, and Richmond.

These were all busy men, but there were no figureheads on the Northwestern Mutual board. The full group convened quarterly, and committees met often in the interim—a practice that put the greatest pressure (and conferred the greatest power) on trustees who lived in Milwaukee. The Executive Committee acted for the whole board when it was not in session, often meeting once or twice a week. The Finance Committee assembled each Monday, Wednesday, and Friday afternoon to vote on every one of the

Northwestern's board attracted some titans of industry in the late 1800s, among them (l. to r.) manufacturer Edward Allis, capitalist Alexander Mitchell, and meat-packer John Plankinton.

thousands of loans made during the course of the year. Its members gathered 168 times in 1888 alone, and the Insurance and Bond Committees kept a similar pace. Although its work was more episodic, the Examining Committee may have been the hardest-working of the bunch. Its members were charged with a twice-annual review of the company's books and general business—an excruciatingly detailed task that involved counting bonds, sampling loan entries, and making sure canceled checks corresponded with their ledger entries. Operating, in effect, as internal auditors, the 1896 team put in six hours a day for twenty-five days. Although their work was demanding, Examining Committee members had the closest possible look at Northwestern's affairs, and the view was always reassuring. The 1905 team paid particular tribute to Henry Palmer's administration:

> *How eloquent of faithful, successful effort, loyally and ably assisted, and how hopeful of future growth and strength, when we realize, as those who examine the Company must realize, how thoroughly honest and skillfully prudent the management of the Company has been and how strongly it has impressed upon every department of the business its own rugged and unflinching personality.*

Products, a Proposition, and Principles

Henry Palmer may have been an unflinching conservative, but he had no desire to return to the Dark Ages. His policy of retrenchment applied to Northwestern's inner workings—its field relations, underwriting policies, investment decisions, and home office operations. In dealing with the outside world, Palmer was entirely willing to bend. The choice, in truth, was hardly his alone. The last quarter of the nineteenth century was a period of sweeping technological and social change in American society. The nation moved from the Steam Age to the Electric Age, and from the rigors of the Civil War and Reconstruction to a period of high-flying materialism Mark Twain dubbed the Gilded Age. Any business that failed to keep pace with the times was courting extinction.

Palmer's openness to change was expressed most clearly in the products Northwestern offered the insurance-buying public. As long as its well-advertised concern for safety was never compromised, the company was quite willing to respond to the changing desires of the market—desires communicated most forcefully by Northwestern's own agents. Provisions that had seemed ironclad just a decade or two earlier were jettisoned in a slow but steady process of liberalization. In 1884, virtually all restrictions on occupation, residence, and travel were lifted after a policy had been in force for three years.

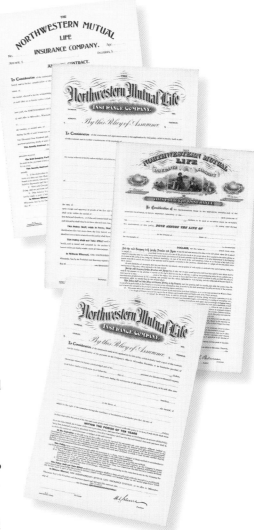

A sampling of insurance policies from the late 1800s

Even suicide fell under the three-year rule, but policyowners still faced cancellation if they became "habitually intemperate" within five years. The incontestability period for most conditions (except intemperance) continued to shrink—down to two years in 1892 and one in 1905—and more generous non-forfeiture provisions protected a policyowner's investment in case of lapse. The single-life limit was raised to $50,000 in 1888, but medical examiners were warned to exercise "very great caution" with this "large class of policies." Old clients were never forgotten, a principle articulated in Northwestern's 1896 annual report: "Whenever the policy contract of the Company has been liberalized or new features adopted, the same privileges have also been extended to the old members, so far as could consistently be done under the terms of their contracts."

As Northwestern's policy terms were liberalized, there was a corresponding proliferation of policy types. New products of the Palmer era included term insurance (limited, renewable, and convertible), annuities (immediate and deferred), semi-endowments, partnership insurance, and a variety of modified life contracts (for substandard risks). One new contract—addition life—was a precursor of things to come. It blended two-thirds ordinary insurance with one-third term, and the ordinary dividends were applied to the term premiums. Although Northwestern's product line remained one of the industry's simplest, the company offered so many policies in so many variations that by 1903 the agents' rate book had swelled to 312 pages. Speaking in 1895, veteran agent Alonzo Kimball marveled at the changes he had witnessed:

Thirty years ago the whole scheme of life insurance was simply this: You pay so much until you die, and the company will pay so much when you die. Now, the functions and elasticity of a life insurance contract are so multiform, complex and ramifying, that we are led to think of the new machine patented by a live Yankee down in Brother Moody's field, which would saw, split and pile the wood, cut the grass, weed the onions, milk the cow and spank the children.

One wonders how Kimball would have greeted the truly "multiform" insurance policies of the computer era.

Of all the products unveiled during Henry Palmer's presidency, by far the most important was tontine insurance. Named for Lorenzo Tonti, an Italian banker of the seventeenth century, the tontine plan was, in essence, a longevity lottery. The owners of ordinary whole-life policies agreed to defer their dividends for a period of ten, fifteen, or twenty years. If they died or let their policies lapse before the term expired, every dollar of their accumulated dividends was forfeited to those still alive and still insured at the tontine

Veteran agent Alonzo Kimball was considered "the orator par excellence among the Northwestern men of his day."

period's end. Equitable Life Assurance—Henry B. Hyde's firm—introduced the tontine plan to America in 1867. After much initial hesitation, Northwestern Mutual followed with its own version in 1881, but the policy soon gave way to semi-tontine insurance, which guaranteed a cash surrender value in case of lapse. The new plan, according to Northwestern, offered the best of both worlds: it enabled clients "to protect their dependents by the life insurance policy, and to protect themselves by providing a fund available in case they should survive." The entire industry was in the doldrums for years after the Panic of 1873, and Palmer and his colleagues hoped the product would help put wind in the company's sails again. They weren't disappointed. New business rebounded nicely, and its source was no secret: by 1893, semi-tontine policies accounted for 60 percent of Northwestern's insurance in force.

Whatever policies its agents sold—tontine, term, or traditional whole life—the company behind the policies was utterly consistent. The overriding goal of Henry Palmer's retrenchment campaign was to maximize Northwestern's focus on the things it was already doing well: the familiar trinity of low mortality, high investment returns, and modest expenses. The company became more selective in all three areas, and the result was a distinctive proposition: low net cost. Northwestern's premium rates were never the industry's lowest, and never intended to be, but its exceptional dividend performance—the result of its superior mortality, investments, and expenses—made the company's insurance, over time, an excellent buy. If you were healthy enough to qualify for a Northwestern policy and disciplined enough to keep it, no firm in America offered better value.

Underlying the proposition of low net cost was an equally distinctive principle: trusteeship. Henry Palmer used one word with particular frequency in his speeches and writings, and that word was "trust." Year after year, Palmer hammered home the theme that Northwestern's assets were "a trust fund" managed by "trustees in the truest legal sense of the term" who were "entrusted" with an awesome responsibility. The president's statement to an 1893 gathering of agents was typical:

I think all the Officers of this Company realize and appreciate that the care and management of the financial affairs of the North-western Mutual Life Insurance Company is a great trust which ought at all times to be in the safest possible hands. We understand, I think, the duties of a Trustee. We know what the law is in regard to what a Trustee may and may not do with that which is placed in his hands as a sacred trust. We know that it is not our fund we are handling, and that we are bound to the exercise of the highest degree of diligence in every investment we make of it, in every turn we make of it, in everything we do with it.

Agent Percy Teeple of Marquette, Michigan, kept track of his prospects in a well-organized card file.

When the trustees filed their report for 1888, little did they realize that their ringing statement of purpose—to be "pre-eminently the policy-holders Company"—would remain Northwestern's credo to the present day.

The natural corollary of trusteeship was mutuality: if Northwestern assumed responsibility for the welfare of its policyowners, it assumed that responsibility for all of them, and all of them equally. On one level, trusteeship and mutuality imposed a legal obligation that Palmer, as a career lawyer and former judge, understood perfectly. But the principles assumed a potent moral dimension as well. It was in the 1880s, a time of market recovery and rapid growth, that Northwestern Mutual found its still center, the sustaining body of beliefs that has underpinned its identity ever since. There is no better summary of those beliefs than the Executive Committee statement of 1888. Looking back on

thirty years in the insurance business, the trustees adopted a declaration that rose to the eloquence of a credo:

The ambition of the Northwestern has been less to be large than to be safe; its aim is to rank first in benefits to policy-holders rather than first in size. Valuing quality above quantity it has preferred to secure its business under certain salutary restrictions and limitations rather than to write a much larger business at the possible sacrifice of those valuable points which have made the Northwestern pre-eminently the policy-holders Company. A higher interest and a lower death rate than secured by its competitors, added to wise and economical management, have made the Northwestern not the largest life insurance company—but in all points of real and substantial benefit to policy-holders, unquestionably the most successful life insurance company in the world.

As a declaration of purpose that blends humility and pride, principles and practicality, the 1888 statement is a landmark in the literature of American life insurance. Where had it come from? The statement was, at least in part, a reflection of Henry Palmer's own personality. One of his great gifts was the grace to realize that it wasn't about him. Palmer had not sought the presidency, and he was not consumed by its pay or its perquisites. He ran his company with a stern collegiality that always focused on the task at hand rather than the person in charge. Addressing the agents in 1901, near the end of his career, the president took pains to deflect attention from himself:

> *No one man built the Northwestern. No one man controls its business today, but the primary source of the governing power of the Company is in the member-ship, the policy-holders of the Company.... I wish the agents of this Company, our force in the field, to understand that no one of us claims that he is the almighty power which controls the interests of the Northwestern Mutual Life Insurance Company.*

If the company mirrored the personality of its president—strong-willed but self-effacing—it also reflected the culture of the larger leadership group. Northwestern was slowly becoming less monolithic, but the home office remained a bastion of blue-blooded Yankee Protestants. Even as the outside world grew more and more secular, many insiders, Palmer included, still lived and breathed the old Calvinist ethic of hard work and careful husbandry. Officers and trustees alike were animated by a simple common belief: it's not our money. In their public statements, and even more convincingly in their internal communications, Northwestern's leaders saw themselves as stewards, called to protect and multiply the resources entrusted to them. They managed the business as if lives depended on it—which, of course, they did: the lives of every survivor exposed to want when a policyowner died.

The result was an unmistakable sense of mission that permeated the entire organization. The profit motive is conspicuously absent in a mutual company; Palmer and his colleagues weren't laboring to enrich investors, earn bonuses, or attract more stockholders. Their goal was to make Northwestern Mutual the best life insurance that money could buy. And what,

A seasoned executive team kept the company moving forward under "certain salutary restrictions."

beyond their own salaries, was in it for them? Protecting families from ruin was a compelling motivator. Higher social standing was another, as well as the satisfaction of beating older and better-known competitors at their own game. But the greatest reward for Northwestern's leaders may have been something even simpler: a feeling of intense pride at being part of a beneficent body much larger than themselves.

Virtue is too often its own reward, but Northwestern Mutual reaped a more substantial harvest. The company's proposition—low net cost—and its underlying principle—trusteeship—proved to be a winning combination, igniting some of the most explosive growth in the industry. From their low point of $6.6 million in 1878, insurance sales soared to a new peak of $28.1 million in 1886 and kept on climbing to $40.3 million in 1888 and $66.6 million in 1892. That was a tenfold increase in just fourteen years—twice the average for all companies selling ordinary policies. Northwestern's insurance in force showed corresponding growth, ballooning from $61.4 million in 1878 to $312.5 million in 1892. The company trailed only five others in America—Equitable, New York Life, Mutual of New York, Metropolitan, and Prudential—and the last two served a completely different market, selling low-cost, low-coverage "industrial" insurance to working-class families. Northwestern was indeed running with the leaders.

Such dramatic growth put enormous pressure on the home office staff. In 1885, after fifteen years in the company's "French style" headquarters on Broadway and Wisconsin, Henry Palmer complained that his employees were "inconveniently crowded" and the vaults were filled to overflowing—even after Northwestern took over the back rooms of an adjoining cigar store. The firm decided to move all of one block south, to the corner of Broadway and Michigan. The elegant Newhall House—the scene of Northwestern's sumptuous 1867 banquet—had dominated the intersection for years, but it burned to the ground in 1883, with the loss of at least seventy-five lives. The company bought the cleared site for $90,000, finding it "best for the convenient transaction of the Company's large and constantly increasing business, and for its income producing power." Northwestern hired S.S. Beman, a prominent Chicago architect, to design the new home office. Beman produced a building that was more Roman than French, with graceful limestone arches, inlaid tile floors, and a spectacular central atrium. Palmer and his co-workers moved down the hill in the summer of 1886, but they occupied only one of the structure's six floors; the rest were rented for stores and offices. Reflecting its emphasis on economy, Northwestern had fewer than fifty employees at the time of the move, all of them overworked. By the time Henry Palmer left the building, there would be 422, and the company would be forced to rent overflow space in the building next door.

From the ruins of the old Newhall House …

... rose a magnificent new home office in the Romanesque style. Completed in 1886,

the landmark stood all of one block from Northwestern's previous headquarters in downtown Milwaukee.

Supply

Agency

Actuarial

Law

The focal point of the building's interior was a skylit atrium surrounded by the full complement of insurance departments.

Cultivating the Field

Northwestern's agents remained the key to growth, a fact gratefully acknowledged by the board's Examining Committee in 1879: "Agents are the channels through which the Company derives its sustenance. Anything that cripples or disheartens them impairs the business, progress, and prosperity of the Company." The home office worked diligently to keep its channels to the field wide open. Whatever rancor lingered from the Heber Smith years had dissipated quickly under Matthew Keenan. Although he replaced the malcontents and put most of the remaining agents under direct contract, Keenan proved adept at rebuilding trust. His successor, Willard Merrill, took the next logical step: rebuilding the general agency system. Within a decade of Merrill's 1881 appointment, Northwestern was working exclusively through general agents, who recruited and supervised their own district, special, and soliciting agents. The company adhered strictly to what it called a "civil service rule": general agents were nearly always drawn from the ranks of the most successful field agents.

Willard Merrill was an important figure of the Palmer era. Born in upstate New York and trained as a lawyer, he opened a practice in Janesville in 1860—not long after John C. Johnston had left town. Like many another small-city attorney, Merrill spent his evening hours selling insurance, and he was uncommonly good at it. Convinced that life insurance was "the grandest beneficence on the face of the earth," the young man sold 550 Northwestern policies in and around Janesville—a healthy share of the district's population. Merrill also found time for politics, serving in the same session of the Wisconsin legislature as Matthew Keenan. (He was a Republican, and Keenan, like Henry Palmer, was a Democrat.) Called to the home office in 1873, Merrill quickly became a member of Palmer's inner circle. The two were cut from the same Yankee cloth, but they had differences that extended beyond their political affiliations. Willard Merrill was a confirmed teetotaler and probably a prohibitionist. Addressing a "union temperance meeting" at Immanuel Presbyterian Church in 1874, Merrill stated that he would rather have smallpox in his family than a moderate drinker, "for smallpox would kill or be cured, but the other affliction was so subtle in its effects that it contaminated everything within its reach, and is rarely detected until too late." The fact that he could work, and work closely, with a moderate drinker like Henry Palmer indicated that there was room for a certain diversity of viewpoints within the corporate fold.

Merrill's twenty-four-year tenure as head of the Agency Department, lasting from 1881

Willard Merrill, a former agent himself, directed the Agency Department for twenty-four years, earning the deep and undivided loyalty of the field.

His charges included this group of Iowa agents.

In 1877, the Association of Agents was created to "form a more perfect union" among Northwestern's representatives. The group's early annual meetings were held in a makeshift tent on the home office roof.

and Trustees of the Company, and with its resources and methods, and the best manner of using these to secure business." The Association of Agents became the voice of the field at Northwestern Mutual Life. Its signature event was, and is, an annual meeting that institutionalized the practice of informal gatherings started in 1867. Held in Milwaukee every January until 1882 and every July thereafter, the annual meeting was a busy blend of education, politics, and old-fashioned fellowship. Although every agent was welcome to attend, Northwestern paid the expenses of anyone who sold at least $50,000 of insurance in the previous year–$150,000 by the late 1890s. In the early years, when attendance rarely exceeded two or three dozen, there was room for everyone inside the home office, but the event's growing popularity forced a change of venue. For many years, the agents met on the home office roof in what one reporter described as "a capacious structure of wood and canvas, with plenty of windows on all sides to admit the cooling breezes of Lake Michigan and the cheerful sunlight." The temporary structure was "gracefully festooned with the colors of our national banner" and "brilliantly lighted by pendant incandescent electric lights" in the evening. Attendance frequently topped 200 in the early 1890s—relatively few in comparison with today's extravaganzas but quite an assembly at the time.

until shortly before his death in 1905, fell entirely within Palmer's presidency, and it brought a similar stability to relations with the field. The agents formed an association of their own in 1877, borrowing language from a more famous constitution to articulate their aims: "In order to form a more perfect union among the agents, to become better acquainted with one another, with the Officers

The point of getting together was, first of all, simply to get together. There are famously few shrinking violets in any gathering of insurance agents, and Northwestern's annual affairs encouraged a lively sense of fraternity among the company's far-flung representatives. They also provided a forum for recognition. Beginning in 1881, the Association of Agents gave the year's sales leader an ordinary straw broom festooned with ribbons as an award for "sweeping the field." By 1884, the top prize was a gold medal with a tiny gold broom attached. George Pick of Milwaukee won it for eleven years in a row, beginning in 1893, generally on volume exceeding $1 million a year—roughly $25 million in current dollars. Pick attributed his success to the rightness of his cause and the rightness of his company. Too many agents, he declared, asked themselves, "Does the man want what I have to sell?," while the most successful asked, "Ought the man to be insured, and how can I conscientiously insure him?" If insurance made sense—and when did it not?—Northwestern insurance was the clear choice. "A Northwestern agent," Pick told his peers in 1900, "can hereafter regard his competitors as his allies, because they will create the demand for insurance which he, because of his company's superiority, will write."

Presentations like Pick's were the meat of the meeting. Every gathering featured a full round of talks—motivational, technical, even historical—designed to send the agents home informed, uplifted, and energized. Topics ranged from meeting competitive threats to managing office expenses, and the presenters were usually other agents. They conformed to a rhetorical standard notably different from the twenty-first century's: florid and fustian, replete with citations from Homer, Shakespeare, and the Bible. John Bristol, Northwestern's general agent in New York City, pulled out all the stops in 1905, apparently urging his colleagues to keep up with the times:

> With every recurring year, as the mighty pendulum of Time ticks off the passing centuries—those drops from the ocean of the Present that are ever descending the falls of Eternity—Progress is writing its enduring record in the minds of men and upon the open pages of Nature's bible. The man that is not progressive, belongs to a past age—the century's telephone of grand achievement cannot call him up, and the wireless pulsations of the widely disseminated thoughts of mighty minds are not for him.

The agents also made time for play. The program typically included character sketches, minstrel acts, and musical numbers—all performed by association members—as well as more serious fare. There were sightseeing excursions to Pabst's Whitefish Bay Resort, the National Soldiers Home, the Alexander Mitchell mansion (now the Wisconsin Club), and other points of interest, and wives and

One highlight of each gathering was the presentation of a broom—first real and then symbolic—to the agent who "swept the field" as top producer.

No annual meeting was complete without excursions to Pabst's Whitefish Bay Resort and intramural baseball games.

SCENES AT WHITEFISH BAY, ANNUAL MEETING JULY 18TH 1905.

the 1880s: "We had a parade afterwards at the hotel and I will not tell how many beers it cost the victor to properly wet that broom."

It is safe to assume that Henry Palmer never swung a bat or lifted a stein with the visiting agents, but Northwestern's officers and trustees were much in evidence at the annual meetings. Palmer was a regular speaker, and the program always included remarks by Willard Merrill on "Anything he has to say to the Boys." Agents relished the opportunity to rub shoulders with the home-office brass, both to lobby for fast and favorable action on their own insurance cases and to share their views on the direction of the company. Every meeting featured free-wheeling discussions of the issues of the day: insuring women, the temperance clause, single-life limits, brokerage business, and a host of others. The agents, understandably, argued for more liberal provisions on every front, while Palmer, just as understandably, promised only that the association's resolutions would be "duly, candidly and carefully considered." Management's response was rarely expeditious. Daniel Murphy, the company's general agent for northern Wisconsin and upper Michigan, chided his home office colleagues in 1896: "Do not forget that in the past you have been very slow to grant us new features.... The new features will no doubt come now too, as usual, but we hope to have them before they are no longer new." There was, at the same time, an awareness that the

girlfriends were encouraged to attend. Baseball games between the eastern and western regions were popular at the turn of the century, including one contest played on a vacant lot at the corner of Mason and Jefferson Streets—only a block away from the present home office. The regions were generally well-matched, but in 1906 the East took a 16-0 pounding from the West's "aggregation of brawny ballists." There were unscheduled diversions as well. After the gavel had come down on the day's official sessions, many agents sought out the beverage that had made Milwaukee famous. George Reynolds, a Pennsylvania general agent, described how association members celebrated their volume leader's success in company's caution was often salutary. In 1892, New York agent Edward Stone praised "the stern, uncompromising, unflinching honesty of the home office management."

The policy discussions underlined the together-and-apart nature of home office and field. Although they were complementary components of a single enterprise, there was not an automatic unity of interests between the two; the relationship was rather one of creative tension. The home office certainly did more than make its insurance products available to the field. The company advertised broadly, if exclusively. Trustee John Johnston, a Milwaukee banker, described the prevailing policy in 1898:

Even in the matter of advertising the advantages of our Company, we have felt that certain dignity and decorum are always to be maintained. We advertise as our great banks advertise, and avoid all catchpenny clap-trap. We are not in the patent medicine or soap business, and our placards will not be seen on every bill-board from the Hebrides to Constantinople.

Northwestern also tried to keep its agents informed and motivated. In 1901, the company published its first issue of *Field Notes*, "a medium of occasional communication between the Home Office and the Field on subjects of use in the vigorous campaign you are carrying forward." The monthly missive has continued in one

form or another for more than a century. And there were the beginnings, at least, of a training program. In 1904, Northwestern unveiled its "Educational Series," a series of eight slim pamphlets deemed "sufficient to the requirements of success." The collection included "Why Should I Be a Life Insurance Agent?" and "The Northwestern: Its Past, Present and Future."

Although the home office provided significant help, the agents were largely on their own: independent contractors rather than paid employees. As a group, they were extraordinarily diverse. The company's leading agents included Jews and Catholics, Southerners and Easterners as well as the standard-issue Yankees of Northwestern tradition. They also served a remarkable range of markets. One Oregon agent told of riding across 100 miles of back country, changing horses twice, just to get five insurance applications. Other agents built lucrative practices within a few square blocks of downtown Manhattan. Whatever their backgrounds, the profit motive applied to all—the more they sold, the more they earned—but the company's agents eagerly followed their president to higher ground. They made Northwestern's aim to be "pre-eminently the policy-holders Company" entirely their own, and it was in pursuit of that goal that

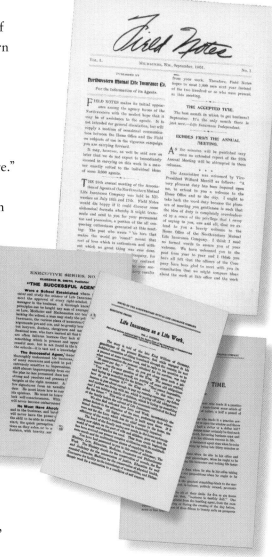

Field Notes *debuted in 1901 as a link between home office and field. A rudimentary correspondence course for agents followed three years later.*

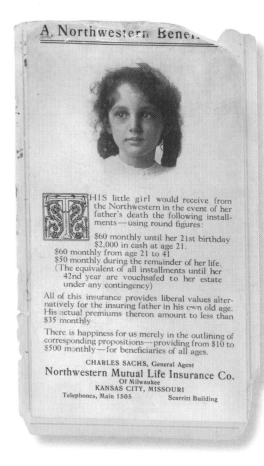

Northwestern appealed to the parental instincts of potential customers in this circa-1905 advertisement.

this diverse group found its ultimate unity. One agent declared that Northwestern had "a corner on the conscience of the country." Another described his comrades as "home missionaries." "There is no loyalty in life insurance like the loyalty of Northwestern agents," wrote Alonzo Kimball in 1891. "Next to your God, your country, and your family, *there is the Company.*" Addressing the 1903 annual meeting, an Illinois agent concurred: "Gentlemen, my life is so completely interwoven with the Northwestern that it seems to me without it I could scarcely live." All the high-flown sentiments came together in *The Northwestern Agent's Song,* whose homemade lyrics were grafted onto a more familiar patriotic melody:

> *Northwestern 'tis of thee,*
> *Champion of equity,*
>   *Of thee I sing.*
> *While rivals snarl and fight,*
> *Thy name is pure and bright,*
> *Sure that thy course is right,*
>   *To thee I cling.*
>
> *Thy plans are clear and just,*
> *Guarding a sacred trust.*
>   *I premiums bring.*
> *Promptly is paid each claim –*
> *Lustrous by deeds thy name,*
> *Echoing well-earned fame,*
>   *Gladly I sing.*

The higher moral ground proved to be the higher marketing ground as well. Northwestern's principles—and the performance they supported—helped set the firm apart from its more earthbound competitors, and the agents were only too glad to assert their moral as well as their net-cost superiority. Small wonder that the company's representatives were the subject of a standard industry joke: "You can tell an Equitable agent by his checkered vest, a Prudential agent by his kit, and a Northwestern Mutual agent by his halo."

Under A Microscope

Whether they sported haloes or more pedestrian headwear, Northwestern's agents found themselves in an all-out war for new business in the waning years of the nineteenth century. For reasons that had much more to do with ego than economics, each of the Big Three—Equitable, Mutual of New York, and New York Life—was determined to be the Big One. The result was intense, even ruthless competition that made every other firm run just to keep up. Known as "the racing companies" or simply "the racers," the Big Three dipped into their huge tontine surpluses to fund no-holds-barred expansion campaigns. Marketing expenses went through the roof, regularly exceeding 100 percent of premiums. Raids on rival field forces were common, with one company promising agents higher commissions and larger advances than the next. Brokerage business reached new heights. Overseas branches opened in every major city from Melbourne to Madrid. Domestic agents engaged in practices that were, at a minimum, destabilizing. The most serious were "twisting"—persuading clients to drop a competitor's insurance for theirs—and rebating—giving new policyowners a portion of their commissions to stimulate sales.

Northwestern Mutual, which ranked a distant fourth among the companies selling ordinary policies, proceeded cautiously in this supercharged competitive atmosphere. Brokers had been selling Northwestern policies for years, although never in significant volume, and full-time agents regularly provided rebates on their commissions rather than risk losing clients. After long discussions with its field representatives, the company decided to end both practices. A no-brokerage rule was adopted in 1897 "as a protection to the company and as a guarantee that the loyal agents of the company shall not be deprived of the fruits of their labor." Rebating was banned even earlier. In 1891, Alonzo Kimball, who was then in charge of the Agency Department's western region, blasted rebating as "the prostitution of this great and most beneficent business of life insurance to the greed and cupidity of men trying to get advantage of each other and of companies trying to beat one another in a race." Northwestern outlawed the practice in 1893, not only because it reduced

agent incomes but also because it tended to make life insurance a commodity, as vulnerable to price cuts as pork chops or hay. The agents adopted a crystal-clear resolution at their 1893 annual meeting: "We hereby, upon our honor as men, pledge our loyalty and fidelity to the principle that Northwestern policies shall bear but one price wherever sold, and that price PAR, from Maine to Texas, from Massachusetts to California."

The company preferred to pursue its own, more traditional path in the competitive melee, and no one could argue with its double-digit annual growth. As sales reached new heights every year, competitors paid Northwestern the considerable compliment of direct attack. Equitable, Mutual of New York, New York Life, and other Eastern firms published circulars questioning the firm's dividend performance, loan security, and claims policy—all of which the company was able to answer without undue difficulty. Demonstrating the restraint so typical of Henry Palmer, Northwestern refused to reply in kind.

The Panic of 1893 only made things worse. As more agents fought for their share of a smaller pie, competitive pressures intensified. Northwestern's new business plummeted from $66.6 million in 1892 to $48.7 million a year later—a 27-percent drop—and

This postal scale saw heavy use in the home office.

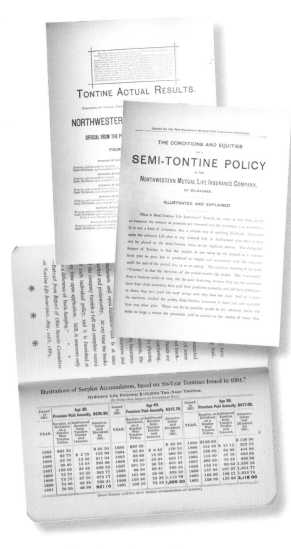

Although Northwestern's semi-tontine policies outperformed the competition's, the product fell into disrepute by the late 1800s, partly because some firms abused the huge tontine surpluses.

Minneapolis agent Isaac Kaufmann, one of the company's leading producers, expressed alarm: "I doubt if there has ever been a time in the history of this country when an era of prosperity, and of new business ventures, and of general abundance, was so suddenly and completely transformed into a period of poverty, of distrust and general stagnation...." The silver lining, said Kaufmann, was a heightened awareness of the need for security, but it would take two or three years for sales to rebound. Semi-tontine insurance, in the meantime, fell decidedly out of favor. Sinking interest rates and rising life expectancies made the rosy illustrations of the 1880s seem like pipe dreams in the 1890s; the longevity lottery had so many winners that individual shares of the final surplus were modest indeed. Northwestern's performance exceeded the industry average by a substantial margin, but "deferred dividend" insurance steadily gave way to the annual variety. Another development was more popular. In 1894, the company allowed policyowners to borrow up to 90 percent of their cash surrender values, using the policies themselves as collateral. Some home-office traditionalists worried that policy loans would cause a spike in lapse rates, but consumers undoubtedly welcomed a source of ready cash during the continuing hard times. By 1897, the policy loan account had reached $5.5 million—more than 5 percent of Northwestern's assets.

When the clouds of the financial panic began to lift in 1897, the competitive free-for-all resumed with all its earlier nastiness. The outrageous behavior of the Big Three had been generating bad press for years, and the drumbeat of public criticism became more insistent through the turn of the century. It was not until 1905, however, that the racers found themselves caught in a full-blown scandal. A pitched battle for control of the Equitable was front-page news for months, and the allegations of wrongdoing were so ripe that the New York legislature was compelled to launch an investigation. Chaired by Sen. William Armstrong, the joint legislative panel met dozens of times in late 1905, generating 6,483 pages of reports, and its dragnet took in Mutual of New York and New York Life as well as the Equitable. Under the relentless grilling of Charles Evans Hughes, who would finish his career as chief justice of the U.S. Supreme Court, Big Three witnesses made one sensational disclosure after another. Ruthless marketing practices were the least of it; the Armstrong Committee uncovered a bottomless pit of Gilded Age excesses. Chief counsel Hughes concluded that the racing companies were run by family dynasties who operated in shameless collusion with the great investment banking houses of New York. Their accounting practices varied from lax to illegal. Exorbitant executive salaries funded extravagant lifestyles. Insider trading, self-dealing, influence-buying, and price-fixing were all standard procedures.

The disclosures would have been damaging enough if they had involved railroads or oil companies, but these were life insurance firms, pledged to protect the welfare of widows and orphans. Public outrage knew no bounds. In the short term, the Big Three's senior executives resigned en masse, their agency systems came unglued, and sales dropped catastrophically. The long-term repercussions were even more serious. Life insurance has always been subject to state rather than federal regulation, and New York has traditionally been first among equals—the bellwether state that tends to set the tone for the rest of the Union. In the wake of the Armstrong hearings, New York adopted an entire canon of new regulations that changed forever the way American insurers conducted themselves. New business was limited to a fixed percentage of each company's insurance in force, bringing to an end the era of break-neck growth. Tontine insurance, whose surpluses had proved such a temptation, was outlawed. Marketing expenses were severely limited, and sales bonuses and awards were banned altogether. Rebating, permanent proxies, investments in corporate stocks, political contributions of any kind, and improvised accounting practices—all were consigned to the trash heap.

The shock waves from the Armstrong investigation did not cause the earth to shift in Milwaukee. Northwestern Mutual, in fact, was forced to make very few changes of

any kind. Deferred-dividend insurance had been dropped months before the inquiry started, and the tontine surpluses were all carefully tabulated and assigned. Although commissions had to be reduced slightly, the company's gross selling expenses were already well below the new Armstrong limits, as were executive salaries. Mutual of New York paid its president $150,000 a year; Henry Palmer never earned more than $25,000 (about $540,000 in current dollars). The company had not made a single political contribution in its history, and there was not a single share of corporate stock in its portfolio.

Industry excesses were pilloried in this 1905 cartoon. New York's Armstrong Committee made sure that "Crooked Life Insurance Officials" would never again ride "Greed" in the service of "Graft."

Charles Evans Hughes was chief counsel of the Armstrong Committee and later chief justice of the U.S. Supreme Court.

The behavior of the Big Three had thrown Northwestern's practices into vivid relief. Now the points of difference became a competitive advantage that Palmer and his colleagues were not afraid to exploit. In a development that might have surprised Sen. Armstrong, they began to describe the New York investigation as not only an exoneration but an endorsement. *Field Notes* (January 1907) declared that the post-Armstrong laws "virtually made mandatory the business policy of the Northwestern"—for *all* insurance companies. At their 1906 annual meeting, the agents adopted a resolution praising Henry Palmer for keeping the enterprise "simply a clean American company doing a clean American business." Henry Norris, who succeeded Willard Merrill as head of the field force in 1905, exhorted his agents to make hay while the sun of public approval shone on their firm:

> *No company during the whole history of the business ever stood out so prominently before the public as an example of what is best in life insurance as the Northwestern does to-day and there was never a time when the public were turning to any particular company for insurance as they do to the Northwestern right now, never a time when any company was so generally and universally recognized as the best. You do not have to waste time talking company…. All you have to do is to talk life insurance and you will get the business.*

Norris reminded the sometimes-impatient agents that Northwestern's slow and steady ways were winning the race: "Some of the fellows who used to laugh at you for working for 'that old conservative moss-back company' would give their left hands to be in your place now."

As its largest competitors struggled to pull themselves out of the mud, Northwestern Mutual kept moving forward on the high road. The company did not, however, escape the unpleasantness of official inquiry, and the investigation began in its own backyard. The company had already felt the sting of aggressive regulation in Wisconsin, fighting and losing an 1899 battle to prevent what it considered excessive taxation. (When Henry Palmer was told that greasing a few palms would help Northwestern's cause, he issued a memorable reply: "I will see the whole institution burned to the ground before I will consent to paying a single dollar of the money of the Company to any member of the legislature.") But Palmer and his colleagues had no reason to fear an inquisition from their elected representatives. As recently as March 1905, the state's Insurance Commission had examined the firm and found its performance exemplary. "The policyholders of the Company," reported commissioner Zeno Host, "and the people of the state of Wisconsin may well feel proud of the company's condition and record, especially at this time when so much criticism prevails concerning the management of some companies."

That was before the legislature got involved. The Progressive wing of the Republican Party, headed by Gov. Robert La Follette, had taken control of state government in 1900, and more than a few Progressives found something unnatural, perhaps even immoral, about any concentration of capital—even if it existed for the benefit of widows and orphans. Taking their cue from the Armstrong Committee, Wisconsin's legislators launched an investigation of their own. The joint committee's hearings stretched from April through June of 1906, and Northwestern Mutual was the center of attention. As the deliberations began, Henry Palmer was the picture of confidence:

> *The management of the Company has no fear as to the outcome. It courts the fullest investigation of its policy and methods, and the committee is being aided in every possible way. The Northwestern Mutual Life Insurance Company has nothing to conceal and its members may feel secure in the promise of their officers that no scandals are to be uncovered by any possible investigation, because none exist.*

There were no scandals, to be sure, but the committee did find some nits to pick. Its counsel charged that, because only board-approved slates were nominated for election each year, the Board of Trustees tended to be self-perpetuating—hardly a revelation. The Inquiry Department, whose sleuths assessed the "moral hazard" of prospects and policyowners, came in for its share of criticism.

Some committee members wondered aloud why Northwestern didn't make more Wisconsin farm loans. Rebating, it appeared, was not yet extinct, despite the company's 1893 ban, but the most embarrassing disclosures involved policy loans. Because the true value of a semi-tontine policy was not calculated until the tontine period's end, the company couldn't lend money on deferred-dividend contracts. Policyowners could, however, take advantage of private loans on the same policies made by Northwestern's officers, trustees, and their spouses and friends. The company defended the practice as a win-win proposition, providing ready cash for policyowners and a safe investment for lenders, but the legislative committee found it discriminatory, particularly in cases where the lenders paid to keep lapsed policies in force.

The company's halo might have slipped a notch or two, but Northwestern survived the most microscopic scrutiny with no lasting damage to its reputation. The investigation had been surprisingly hostile, given the firm's standing in the state, and the same tone characterized a series of laws passed by the 1907 Wisconsin legislature. The measures, which capped expenses, limited premiums, and mandated specific investments, were

The Progressives of Wisconsin, led by Gov. "Fighting Bob" La Follette, launched a legislative investigation of their own in 1906, and Northwestern was the center of attention.

so harsh that nearly two dozen insurance companies, including all of the leaders, left the state. All of the leaders, that is, except Northwestern Mutual, whose roots were too deep to disturb. Ever insistent on the high road, the company did not exploit the resulting competitive vacuum; Henry Norris instructed his Wisconsin agents "to impress upon every policyholder of every one of these companies that his policy is just as good as it was before the withdrawal of the companies."

The Wisconsin investigation was time-consuming, mildly embarrassing, and more than a little aggravating, but it was in some ways beneficial. Although Northwestern did not escape criticism, it emerged with what amounted to a clean bill of health—particularly in comparison with the cancers exposed by the Armstrong Committee. The public expressed its approval with a resounding increase in sales. New business soared from $73.4 million in 1904 to $93.9 million in 1906—a 28-percent increase in two years—at the same time that industry-wide sales of ordinary insurance dropped 19 percent. Those were record-setting results. Northwestern's annual report for 1906 noted that "the increase in the business in force was greater than that of any other company in the world." Nor did the agents desert the flag. Although the Armstrong laws banned expenses-paid trips of any kind, more than 200 attended the 1907 annual meeting—normal attendance for the event. Henry Norris praised the turnout as "evidence of your loyalty and your love for the institution that you could not have furnished under any other system." The agents paid their own way, and they've been doing so ever since.

With the investigations over and calm finally returning to a cleaner, more responsible insurance industry, Henry Palmer could, at long last, retire. He had announced his desire to step down at the 1906 annual meeting, in remarks that had the unmistakable air of a valedictory:

I have reached that point when I begin to think, and can not help but think, that if there is to be any rest in this world for me before the final summons, it is about time it came. Having passed the limit usually accepted as the extreme limit of human life, four score years, by almost a decade, I feel that the time when I must lay down work is not far distant, and it can not come too soon to suit me. But while I remain in the service of this Company I shall endeavor to give to it as conscientiously as possible the service which it requires at my hands.

Henry Palmer had become an eminence by the early 1900s, the last living link with the company's deepest roots.

The president was nearly eighty-seven at the time—an unheard-of age for a life insurance executive, then or now. It was only the climate of uncertainty created by the legislative investigations, first in New York and then in Wisconsin, that had convinced him to stay. By 1908, his hand-picked successor, George Markham, was ready to take the reins, and Palmer retired in July, three months before his eighty-ninth birthday. From the day he and a handful of others, all of them long dead, had carried the company's belongings from Janesville to Milwaukee in a small black trunk, fifty years had elapsed.

There were probably some Northwesterners, in both home office and field, who had thought Henry Palmer would live and reign forever. He had become, over the decades, an eminence, the last living link with Northwestern's beginnings, revered by his peers and practically venerated by his subordinates. But it was not his longevity that elevated Palmer to such an important place in the company's history. He made his most significant contribution as the primary author of an enduring corporate culture. That culture married performance and principle, and its hallmarks—competitive excellence and an uncompromising commitment to trusteeship—have not changed, in their essentials, since Palmer's last day in office. The patriarch did something absolutely extraordinary: he took Northwestern out of time. Palmer wasn't looking for a good

quarter or a good year; he was looking for a good eternity. There are some principles, he believed, that never go out of fashion, some values too important to change. Under his guidance, Northwestern Mutual became a great gray ship, plowing through the high seas in every weather, alert to the smallest details but supremely confident of its ultimate course.

Of all the tributes and testimonials that crowned Palmer's last year in office, agency superintendent Henry Norris offered one of the most perceptive. "The Northwestern is great, and strong, and honest," wrote Norris, "because Henry L. Palmer all these years has been great, and strong, and honest. The personality of that grand man, more than any other, is represented in the character of the Company." Norris's assessment was on the mark. When Palmer accepted Northwestern's presidency in 1874, the company had a personality. When he left, thirty-four momentous years later, it had a character—ageless, adaptable, and with a staying power that continues to amaze.

When Palmer finally retired in 1908, at the age of 88, he was lauded as Northwestern's second founder— the creator of its culture and the chief architect of its character.

FIELD NOTES

rthwestern Mutual Life
surance Company

BELIEVES

ness of life insurance is one of trusteeship, and that com

uality of obligation, benefit and service to each policyh
ship between policyholder and Company and is enjoine
e states;

e standards of selection should be applied to all appl
and equality are to be preserved. To require a medical e
d not of others, without segregation, violates this a
does not, and will not, do a non-m

t year i
re curre
certain

t made health
nd at lea
is still
to the h
ble inv

"THE COURAGE TO SAY 'NO'"

George Markham represented, at sixty-five, a youth movement in the stately halls of Northwestern Mutual. Nearly twenty-five years younger than his predecessor, the new president might have been expected to bring some new ideas, relatively speaking, to the management of America's sixth-largest life insurance company. Markham, it soon became clear, had no such intentions, and his successors—William Van Dyke and Michael Cleary—showed the same fidelity to tradition. The three presidents, all of them lawyers, made a principled conservatism Northwestern's dominant theme between 1908 and 1947.

That was no easy task in a period distinguished by its volatility. The life insurance business went from boom to bust and back again over four decades, and nearly everyone alive felt the impact of two world wars and the Depression. Despite the ups and downs in its industry and the epic catastrophes in the world outside, Northwestern held its course, bending before the wind but never losing its bearings. As other firms departed radically from past practice, continuity remained Northwestern's keynote. The company became, as a result, a de facto specialist in what one officer described as "classical coverage."

George Markham, the

single-minded autocrat who led

Northwestern from 1908 to 1918

The Markham Years

George Markham sounded the period's theme at the very start of his tenure. Addressing Northwestern's agents on July 16, 1908, one day after his election, the president assured his listeners that "there will be no radical changes." "In fact," he continued, "I today do not conceive the necessity for any changes whatever." Markham offered a warm tribute to Henry Palmer and a pledge of allegiance to the second founder's principles:

> *All I can promise you, gentlemen, is that so far as the power lies in me, I shall endeavor to carry out the precept and example set before me by my distinguished predecessor. This Company has been built up by, and present growth of the Company is due almost entirely to, his conservatism. The President believed, and I believe, that it is far better that we have the best and safest company in the world rather than the largest.*

The new president had a great deal in common with the man he followed. Both were Yankees with roots in the East; Markham was born in 1843 in upstate New York, Palmer in 1819 in Pennsylvania. Both entered the bar at home and came to Wisconsin as seasoned lawyers, Markham at twenty-seven, Palmer at thirty. Both became pillars of Milwaukee society, frequenting the same clubs and moving in the same social circles. In 1895, when Northwestern had a board seat to fill, George Markham was a natural choice. He was a prominent attorney with substantial holdings in Milwaukee real estate, and his business skills proved a real asset to the company. In 1901, after a stint on the Executive Committee, Markham moved from trustee to employee, becoming a vice-president with responsibility for Northwestern's real estate investments. At fifty-eight, he also became Henry Palmer's protégé and helpmate, assuming much of the old man's burden as he finally began to lay it down. When Palmer retired in 1908, George Markham's election was a foregone conclusion.

Although their backgrounds were nearly identical, the new president was by no means a clone of his predecessor. While Palmer had spent years as a Democratic warhorse, George Markham showed little patience for political life; more than once he railed against "professional politicians" who made "unjust assaults" on the business establishment. Patience of any sort was not one of Markham's virtues. Both he and Henry Palmer were famously plain-spoken, but Markham tended to be brusque and autocratic where Palmer was forceful and direct. Henry Tyrrell, Northwestern's full-time lobbyist and part-time historian, struggled to find something nice to say about his old boss in a 1933 account:

He was a man of strong convictions, and he was not always diplomatic in their expression. Because inflexible in his opinions, he appeared arbitrary at times, but when business proceeded un-ruffled, he was a kind, considerate gentleman. The arbitrary rules required by modern methods irked him, and there were times when he was disregardful perhaps of those exact amenities which are expected from a diffusion of responsibilities in a corporation.

Perhaps the biggest difference between Palmer and Markham was not so much temperamental as environmental. George Markham took office in a climate far different from the gale that had greeted his mentor in 1874. Henry Palmer was elected in the wake of a bitter power struggle and at the start of a severe recession. The company he passed on to Markham was the picture of stability, its character fixed and its course determined. Northwestern Mutual was still riding the winds of public approval that had filled its sails after the public investigations of 1905-1906. Some major competitors had been practically blown off the sea—their favorite practices banned by legislative fiat, their agency systems in tatters, their reputations ruined—while Northwestern continued to offer the same products with the same guarantees through the same exclusive field force.

The flood of new laws that followed the investigations did not leave the company untouched. George Markham's salary was capped at $25,000 until 1915, when policyowners approved a raise to $40,000. Agents continued to pay their way to the annual meeting, competing for prizes that had no monetary value but carried something even more precious: the esteem of their peers. Wisconsin remained, for a time, surprisingly hostile to the largest financial institution within the state's borders. James O'Connor, chief counsel for the 1906 investigating committee, proposed that ballots for every Northwestern board election include one "administration" ticket and a second "policy holder" slate, as if the two classes were somehow opposed. O'Connor himself ran for the board as an independent in 1908—and lost in a landslide.

The company had already taken an important step toward greater transparency. Every year since 1871, the board's Examining Committee had probed the company's inner workings in minute detail. In 1907, responding to calls for broader participation, the company invited non-trustees to do the probing. A committee of three (later five) policyowners, suggested by the general agents and chosen by senior management, was given the run of the home office, with freedom to interview officers, open the books, and hire auditors. Thus was born the Policyowners' Examining Committee, still a

A handful of the 4,500 agents who lifted their company's insurance in force past the billion-dollar mark in 1909

THE DISABILITY CLAUSE

REPRINTED FROM
"THE ADJUSTER"
OF SAN FRANCISCO

Issued by
THE NORTHWESTERN MUTUAL LIFE
INSURANCE COMPANY
of Milwaukee

Northwestern's aversion to disability insurance and the double-indemnity clause was well-documented.

proud Northwestern tradition. The Examining Committee provided a welcome source of external feedback and, as it developed, a deep pool of potential board candidates as well. No competitor saw fit to follow the firm's example, enhancing Northwestern's reputation as "pre-eminently the policy-holders company."

Although the public investigations changed the industry's operating rules permanently, the misdeeds of a few had not diminished the importance of life insurance for the many. People still died, and their survivors still needed the financial security that only life insurance could provide. As the storm passed and the air cleared, the industry revived—better-managed and better-regulated, but every bit as competitive as it had been before the scandals broke. A generally robust economy encouraged new companies to enter the waters, and the roster of American life insurance firms swelled from 190 in 1908 to 295 in 1918—a 55-percent increase in a single decade. As always, competition encouraged experimentation. An increasingly crowded field led some companies to break away from the pack, offering new products and variations on old ones that promised to give them an edge in the marketplace. The most important of them were group policies, disability insurance, and the double indemnity clause, all of which began to appear in their modern forms not long after 1907. The limited menu of the nineteenth century was becoming a smorgasbord in the twentieth.

Northwestern would have none of it. Group insurance, sold wholesale and without medical examinations, was anathema. Disability income contracts, which guaranteed monthly payments to policyowners who had suffered total and permanent disabilities, were nearly as abhorrent; the only total and permanent disability Northwestern recognized was death. The double-indemnity feature, which paid twice the face amount of a policy in cases of accidental death, was dismissed as a sales gimmick, and even term insurance—a product Northwestern sold—was suspect. In 1909, the company offered its agents a $25 prize for the best essay exposing the pitfalls of "makeshift" and "temporary" term contracts. A St. Louis agent, R.H. Calkins, took home the cash with a treatise blasting term insurance as a hazard to an agent's very soul: "Yielding to the temptation to write 'easy' business, his moral fibre weakens, and he becomes less of a man, and less of an agent—injured morally and financially." Ten years later, the company's Syracuse general agent, Henry Phillips, made a hopeful (and thoroughly mistaken) prediction: "Renewable term has at least had its day and another five years will probably witness its complete demise."

What Northwestern Mutual emphasized was the product that had been its bedrock since the very beginning: whole life insurance sold by career agents to a select population of individuals. Anything else was somehow tainted and inferior. Multiple lines were inconsistent with Northwestern's insistence on simplicity of operations; the company's low expense ratios were due in large part to its limited product offerings. Group insurance, in particular, was completely incompatible with Northwestern's emphasis on select risks. The company never stopped trying to perfect its selection process. In the early 1900s, medical director Dr. John Fisher became fascinated with a new diagnostic tool: the sphygmomanometer, or blood pressure cuff. Careful scientific studies convinced him that there was a causal link between high blood pressure and higher-than-average mortality. In 1907, Northwestern made the pressure test mandatory for every applicant over the age of forty, and it was eventually required of everyone who wanted insurance. John Fisher's insistence on high-quality risk selection made Northwestern Mutual the pioneer in a practice that became the industry standard.

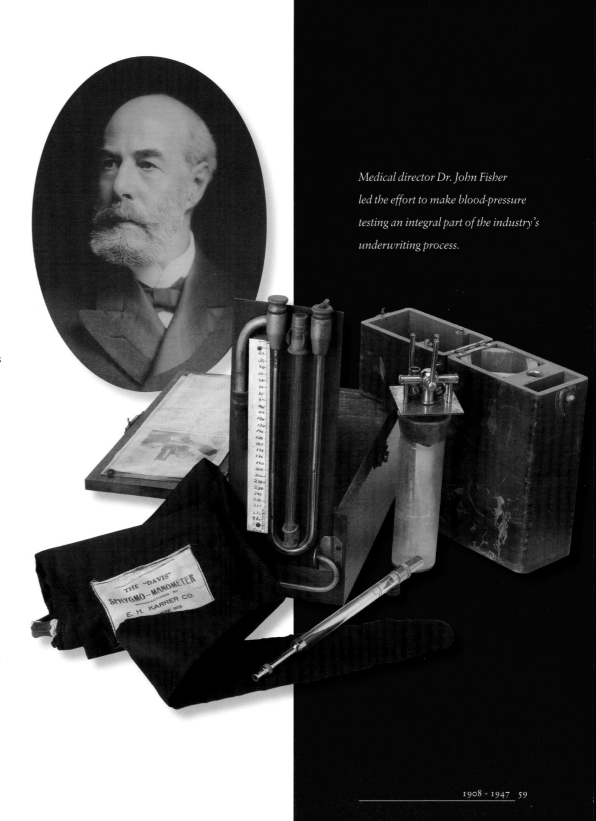

Medical director Dr. John Fisher led the effort to make blood-pressure testing an integral part of the industry's underwriting process.

The Northwestern Mutual Life Insurance Co

More liberal contracts and a new emphasis on business insurance helped Northwestern keep pace with its competitors.

Quality of risk, quality of product, and quality of operations—all rooted in a deeper commitment to trusteeship—were the hallmarks of what amounted to a Northwestern religion, and the company continued to practice it with missionary fervor. "I am glad that I am a life insurance agent," said Illinois representative H.A. Clark in 1910, "for in my opinion, there is no other profession under the sun, unless it be the ministry, that one can do so much good for humanity as in the life insurance business." George Markham himself expressed a similar sentiment in 1913: "A most beneficent calling is ours, who are devoting the best part of our lives to the end that our fellow-men may face the inevitable, knowing that their loved ones will not come to want."

But Northwestern Mutual did not live in a world apart. Market pressures forced the company to make adjustments, not all of them minor, in both its outlook and its operations. As other firms lifted restrictions on travel, residence, and occupation, Northwestern had little choice but to follow. The list of proscribed jobs and addresses shrank steadily, particularly with the introduction of a new contract series in 1910. Even then, the company was not about to let just anyone buy its insurance. The Deep South was off limits as long as malaria and typhoid outbreaks remained common, and certain occupations were still beyond the pale, including saloonkeepers,

soldiers, coal miners, policemen, ocean fishermen and—a 1913 addition—"automobile racers and their mechanicians." At the same time, Northwestern wanted to share in the expansive spirit of the times. The company began to offer a waiver-of-premium clause for total disability in 1916; any policyowner could, for an extra charge, "insure his insurance." George Markham, his vaunted conservatism notwithstanding, proposed an even more radical idea in 1910: expanding into Canada. Northwestern had sold insurance north of the border for a brief period in the 1870s, and Markham wanted to return to a country he considered "a very desirable field in which to secure business." His fellow trustees gave the idea a chilly reception. They had considerably warmer feelings for a new line: business insurance. With active support from the home office, some agents began to sell standard life and endowment contracts to partnerships and corporations rather than individuals. If a partner or key man died, the business could use its insurance settlement to buy out his stock, compensate for his lost services, or maintain its corporate credit. Broadening the line in some areas and holding it in others, George Markham and his associates were trying to find the proper balance between the dictates of tradition and the demands of their moment in history. What did the proposition of low net cost and the principle of trusteeship mean in a constantly changing competitive environment? How far do you go?

That was the key question of the 1908-1947 period, and it is the question Northwestern Mutual has been asking ever since.

The company went far enough to keep its agents prosperous and productive. There were roughly 4,500 men (and a few women) in the field by 1910, affiliated with 105 general agencies spread across 42 states. It was the agents, of course, who communicated conditions in the marketplace to the home office and, as in earlier years, they were a study in diversity. The greatest number did their prospecting far from the glare of city lights. Farmers were the largest single class of Northwestern policyowners in the early 1900s, making up more than 10 percent of the total in most years. District agents tended to serve farm districts almost exclusively, but special agents worked in the same fields, often through small-town bankers they hired as part-time sub-agents. One of the rural all-stars was Charles Weinfeld, a former clothing retailer who began to represent Northwestern in and around Wausau, Wisconsin, in 1905. Covering what he called a "pine stump district" dotted with "kerosene towns," Weinfeld sold nearly 250 policies every year, enough to make him a repeat winner of the company's award for most lives written. Other firms tried to hire away such a stellar salesman, but Charles Weinfeld was loyalty personified. "I have nailed my banner so tight to the Northwestern flagpole," he said in 1913, "that even a cyclone cannot disturb it."

Although Weinfeld and his counterparts generally traveled by train, a new technology was beginning to transform the lives of Northwestern's rural agents: the automobile.

Charles Weinfeld, who worked in a "pine stump district" of northern Wisconsin, regularly led the field in number of lives written.

The company's agents paused for a group portrait at the 1910 annual meeting.

Automobiles like this 1907 International "Auto Buggy" made it easier for agents to reach their prospects.

In 1911, F.A. Griswold, a Connecticut representative, declared it just the thing for "country" prospecting: "Many salesmen find the automobile almost indispensable. They can see so many more men, and in so much shorter a time. The impression that it makes is favorable too…." Cars were still a luxury item at the time, and guaranteed to arouse curiosity. An Iowa agent, H.L. Williams, stressed the motivational powers of the new vehicle: "You will draw inspiration from the fresh air which fills your lungs and from the exhilarating motion of your car. You will feel

keyed up to the highest pitch of efficiency and the net result will be an increase in the volume of your business with its attendant rewards."

City agents had less formidable distances to cover, of course. Charles Weinfeld once changed trains four times in two days to place $10,000 of insurance—an amount that a New York or Chicago agent could have sold on a single floor of a single building. The most successful of Northwestern's urban agents became an industry legend: Dr. Charles Albright. He was born in Tennessee in 1867, the son of a Confederate soldier who had spent most of the Civil War in a Union prison off the Ohio coast of Lake Erie. Despite the war's outcome, the younger Albright was raised in relatively genteel surroundings—his family owned plantations—and he gravitated to medicine as a career. The soft-spoken Southerner was completing an internship in Chicago when Dr. John Fisher came south in search of a third physician for Northwestern Mutual's medical staff. Albright got the job and made Milwaukee his permanent home. He also met Laura Uihlein, a Schlitz Brewing heiress, and promptly fell in love; the couple were married in 1899.

Although Albright was a thoroughly competent doctor, he soon wearied of his duties in the Medical Department. With John Fisher at the helm (he would not retire until 1936, at the age of eighty-eight), there was absolutely no room for advancement. Burning with desire "to achieve distinction in some field of action," Albright felt himself pulled in another direction entirely. Impressed by the Northwestern Mutual agents he encountered on a daily basis, the doctor discovered what he termed "some latent leanings toward salesmanship." In 1905, after an extended sojourn in Europe, Doctor Albright decided to become Agent Albright. The higher-ups in the home office, including agency head Henry Norris, gave him little chance of success, but the newcomer showed an uncanny ability to relate to his prospects—a group that included, in the early years, the business elite of Milwaukee. Writing relatively large policies on relatively few lives, he sold $936,000 of life insurance in 1907—his sophomore year in the business—to lead the entire field force. "Dr. Albright," said Henry Norris as he presented the award, "is just as persistent and just as successful in turning up applications as he used to be in turning them down." Charles Albright would remain Northwestern's volume leader for the next thirty years—a record that may stand for all time.

With the doctor leading the way, Northwestern's agents increased the company's insurance in force from $945 million in 1908 to $1.68 billion in 1918—a gain of 78 percent in a single decade. That was somewhat off the torrid industry pace of 106 percent, but still fast enough to keep the firm solidly in sixth place. "The Northwestern," George Markham told the agents in 1909, "was never in a more healthy

Dr. Charles Albright, Northwestern's volume leader for 30 consecutive years. By the time he retired, Albright had put more life insurance on the books than half the companies in America.

and prosperous condition than it is at this moment." In September 1909, the company's insurance in force passed the billion-dollar mark—a cause for general celebration.

Such rapid growth put intense pressure on the home office staff, whose ranks swelled from just over 300 in 1907 to 530 in 1910. When Northwestern moved into its new headquarters on Broadway in 1886, the company occupied a single floor. By 1910, employees filled all six stories and had taken over three floors of an adjacent building.

On January 26, 1910, after hearing George Markham's report on the critical shortage of working space, the trustees authorized him to prepare "suitable accommodations for the growing wants of the Company." By April, Northwestern had purchased an entire city block on E. Wisconsin Avenue at Van Buren Street—near the eastern end of Milwaukee's principal thoroughfare—and began to make plans for a monument.

The site, which lay all of five blocks from the Broadway home office, posed some special challenges. Although it was covered with buildings and to all appearances solid ground, the parcel had an unusually fluid history. Charles Sivyer, who grew up nearby during the city's earliest years, recalled it as Drum's Hollow, the location of "a big pond," presumably spring-fed, where there was "always good skating" in winter. The pond has come down through history with a different name: Lake Emily. Aggressive landfill activity had obliterated the lake— until Northwestern Mutual tried to build on it in 1912. Test borings revealed "a bed of quicksand" reaching 120 feet below ground level, fully ninety feet lower than the surface of Lake Michigan. No one suggested building an oversized houseboat for the new home office. Northwestern's solution was a forest of wooden pilings—3,147 in all—that were "driven to a refusal" and then capped with concrete to support a new structure. Lake Emily still lurks beneath

the surface, as a zone of saturated soil that must be kept constantly wet to prevent the original pilings from rotting away.

The building that emerged on Wisconsin Avenue was a neoclassical wonder. Marshall & Fox, a prominent Chicago architectural firm, designed a twentieth-century version of a Greek temple, complete with ten massive granite columns in the Corinthian style, Carrara marble floors and walls, and heavy brass furnishings. Their plans called for eight floors arranged in a "U" around a central courtyard. The architects also specified fourteen-foot ceilings throughout, a reflection of Northwestern's lofty aspirations as well as the rock-bottom energy costs of the period. Ground for the landmark was broken on July 17, 1912. George Markham stressed the building's permanent qualities, but he put the project in historical perspective:

Permanency is but a relative term. The growth of the Northwestern has made necessary seven different home offices. We of today think we are building permanently for the future. So thought our predecessors. We may be mistaken, as they were. But whatever of structures may be necessary for future administrative details, the great work of beneficence in which the Northwestern is engaged will endure.

The company was looking ahead, but it was also looking back to its roots: one of the items placed in the cornerstone was a biography of Henry Palmer.

Construction did not go entirely according to plan. The new building was supposed to be done in time for the agents' annual meeting in 1913, but deadlines came and went with little progress. The meeting went on as scheduled, but it was held in a half-finished auditorium with planked floors and tarpaulin-covered "walls" that did little to stop the stiff wind off Lake Michigan. Nor did the project finish on budget: the early estimates of $1.5 million ballooned to more than twice that figure when all the bills were tallied.

George Markham voiced his displeasure, but all was forgiven by the time of the building's formal dedication on October 21, 1914. Judge James Jenkins, the day's orator, declared the new home office "the most beautiful building that the City of Milwaukee has ever seen, a marvel of grace and dignity, and ... a beacon-light in the night of the commonplace." It would indeed be difficult to imagine a more potent symbol of Northwestern's character. Dignified, decorous, and yet absolutely monumental, the edifice expressed in granite the enduring quality and the rock-solid stability of the enterprise it housed. The structure's message was unmistakable: this is a company for the ages.

Rising from the remains of "Lake Emily," the new building took shape as an updated version of a Greek temple.

Auditorium

Cashier's Department

Employee "rest room"

Executive office

The interior featured the last word in functional elegance.

One of Northwestern's best-known (and most popular) fringe benefits was, and still is, a free lunch that has been served daily since 1915.

Northwestern was a company for the most modern technologies as well. The new home office featured "fresh washed air, filtered and dried," pneumatic tubes for message delivery, and electric lighting throughout. The company also invested in a wide array of labor-saving devices: typewriters, telephones and, in 1917, an Addressograph system with plates for nearly 600,000 policies. The day of hand-written premium notices faded into memory, but even the most aggressive efforts at automation couldn't keep up with Northwestern's continuing growth; the company found it necessary to increase its work force from 530 in 1910 to nearly 700 in 1916. Employees on every level found the home office an exceptional place to work. It was a haven of clean jobs in a city famous for heavy industry, and its fringe benefits were, for the time, extraordinary: a forty-four-hour work week (fifty was the norm elsewhere), one of Milwaukee's first pension plans (a 1915 innovation) and, most novel of all, a free lunch. Beginning in 1915, workers trooped up to the eighth floor at noon every day for a dinner served family-style, by department, with separate dining halls for men, women, and officers. The meal was undoubtedly good for employees, but it nourished the company as well, strengthening social ties within departments and building a strong corporate culture. When they had finished dessert, employees could retire to the eighth-floor "rest room," a spacious, high-ceilinged lounge filled with reading tables and wicker rocking chairs.

If the eighth floor was the entire company's gathering place, the fifth floor was George Markham's domain. He occupied a sumptuous wood-paneled office on the southeast corner of the building, flanked by his vice-presidents and just down the hall from the Loan and Bond Departments, the Finance Committee's meeting room, and a massive vault filled with the company's negotiable securities. The fifth floor's emphasis on financial activities was no accident, for Markham was, above all else, an investment specialist. Insurance and agency matters were left to others; the president's chief concern was growing the assets that policyowners

had entrusted to Northwestern. Those assets increased by two-thirds in the decade after Markham's 1908 election, rising from $248 million to $415 million, and they were invested in three principal areas: mortgage loans (53 percent of the total in 1915), bonds (27 percent, largely in railroads), and policy loans (16.5 percent). The company had been an aggressive mortgage lender since its earliest years, and it remained so under Markham, with a particular interest in farm loans. Northwestern, in fact, became the largest farm lender in the industry, investing $134 million in heartland real estate by 1918. The president's passion came shining through in an interview with the *Milwaukee Free Press* (January 16, 1916). George Markham, the reporter noted, had a reputation for "coldness, aloofness and inaccessibility," but when the subject turned to Northwestern and its investments, "his face lights up and that real enthusiasm manifests itself in voice, gesture and manner." Markham spoke with considerable warmth about the role his firm had played in the development of both the region and the nation:

> *It is a matter of pride with us that our company has had a very large share in the building up of the great middle west, especially, and also of other parts of the country.... It is a work of empire building—a work of bringing wealth, not only to the individual client, but to the nation itself—a work of building up not only an empire that is wealth-producing, but that means the feeding of the nation and of a large part of the civilized world.*

(bottom) Soldiers trooped past the home office during World War I.

Northwestern supported them by subscribing generously to Liberty Loan drives.

George Markham had to curb his enthusiasm for agricultural empire-building in 1917, when another investment opportunity temporarily stole the spotlight: Liberty Loans. World War I had started in Europe at the end of July 1914, just as Northwestern was putting the finishing touches on its new home office. The United States was officially neutral at first, but with the declaration of war on April 6, 1917, the nation shifted almost overnight from "preparedness" to full-scale mobilization. The federal government sold billions of dollars in bonds—Liberty Loans—to finance the effort, and American businesses found it both patriotic and politic to subscribe generously. Northwestern's

holdings of U.S. bonds swelled from practically nothing in 1915 to $12 million in 1918. The company also encouraged its employees and agents to invest as much as possible in Woodrow Wilson's campaign to make the world "safe for democracy."

Liberty Loans diverted funds from higher-paying investments, but their impact on Northwestern's operations was benign. Far more troublesome was the very real threat the "Great War" posed to the lives of policyowners in military service. Like every one of its competitors, the company had no desire to take on risks that were guaranteed to have higher-than-average mortality. An industry-wide war clause went into effect in late 1917, requiring new policyowners to pay prohibitively high premiums to keep their policies in force while they were in uniform. Without the additional payment, each company's liability was limited to the return of premiums already received. (Northwestern ultimately paid out $2.1 million for 948 war-related death claims, nearly all of them on policies purchased before the war clause went into effect.) With private insurance practically unaffordable, the federal government made public protection available in late 1917. Everyone in the military was eligible for up to $10,000 in "war risk insurance," all of it term, with premiums deducted from their paychecks. By November 1918, the War Risk Bureau had issued more than 4 million policies with a total coverage of $36.3 billion—

substantially more than all the private carriers in America combined. The federal bureau, in fact, referred to itself as "the largest life insurance company in the world." Rather than feeling threatened, Northwestern Mutual was one firm that considered government insurance an unmixed blessing. Not only did it solve a potential public relations problem for the private companies, but it amounted to a highly public and absolutely unqualified endorsement of the very idea of life insurance. The resulting publicity, said agent William Atkinson of Brooklyn, was worth "ten times the advertising appropriations of all the companies combined."

Better publicity did not translate to increased sales—not immediately, at least. Although Northwestern's new business had jumped 20 percent in 1916 alone, the company's momentum began to slow soon after the United States entered the conflict, and volume actually dropped 9 percent in 1918. The war clause was largely responsible, but military service also carried nearly 450 Northwestern agents from the insurance field to the battlefield. There were fewer people to sell insurance and, with 86 home office clerks in the armed forces as well, fewer people to service it. The company had to offer bonuses to attract qualified clerical workers, and more than one general agency faced a staffing crisis. Flavel Wright of Harrisburg, Pennsylvania, found his agency's manpower shortage "distressing" but offered a solution:

I do believe that there are hundreds of women in the United States who on account of their home knowledge, their intuition, and their quick sympathies, will be successful in the sale of what we call "fireside insurance," and when all is said and done, the maximum service rendered by a life insurance company is a fireside service.

The war ended before women could secure their place by the fireside. The armistice of November 11, 1918, sealed the Allied victory, and America's life insurance industry looked ahead to the prosperity that peacetime seemed to promise. At Northwestern Mutual, however, there would be no return to business as usual. As the war in Europe wound down, a long-brewing

Hundreds of Northwesterners went into military service, among them home office employee Henry Schwiebinger (top) and general agent Millard Mack of Cincinnati.

Henry Norris (top) and then George Copeland led a sometimes-restive field force during the Markham years.

tempest in the home office teapot rolled to its conclusion. Diplomacy had never been one of George Markham's strengths. "In whatever decisions I may have rendered," he said at the 1915 annual meeting, "I think the agents will give me credit for always having been perfectly open and frank, and there is not an agent of this Company that has, or needs to have, any doubt as to my position." Markham obviously considered his bluntness a virtue, but many of Northwestern's trustees and agents came to see their president as arbitrary and autocratic—an impression that deepened as he aged. The field force had already experienced a round of internal dissension. In about 1906, realizing that they had somewhat different interests, the special agents had formed an association separate from the general agents' caucus, and the district agents joined them two years later. (All three groups still came together in the Association of Agents, whose major activity was, and is, the annual meeting.) George Markham's tone-deaf approach to field relations aggravated the climate of fractiousness, and the situation grew even worse with the deaths of insurance vice-president James Skinner in 1912 and agency head Henry Norris in 1916. Skinner's position remained open, and it took time for George Copeland, Norris's replacement, to establish a foothold. In the meantime, reports of "restlessness" and "dissatisfaction" among the agents reached the home office with troubling frequency.

There was an emerging consensus that Northwestern Mutual was due for a change at the very top. George Markham was increasingly vulnerable, and it was an investment decision, ironically, that hastened his departure. In 1917, responding to criticism that the company had failed to make enough farm loans in northern Wisconsin and upper Michigan, Northwestern purchased a block of mortgages in that territory from a reputable Milwaukee brokerage house. The firm's principal happened to be Stuart Markham, George's oldest son and a Northwestern trustee. Allegations of nepotism began to swirl almost immediately. Wisconsin's insurance commissioner, Michael Cleary, concluded that there was nothing illegal or even improper about the transactions, but they furnished the pretext that a majority of trustees had evidently been seeking. On December 10, 1918—less than a month after Armistice Day—George Markham submitted his resignation. Seventy-five at the time, he moved to a daughter's home in Pasadena, where he died eleven years later. Although he never approached the Methuselan tenure of the man he replaced, Markham had followed Henry Palmer's principles religiously during his decade at the top. The company had suffered no loss of scale or substance; it had, in fact, grown steadily. The time had come, however, for someone who could temper his reverence for tradition with a more active regard for his fellow Northwesterners.

"Van Dyke the Younger"

Choosing George Markham's successor was an easy task. Early in his presidency, Markham had hired an executive to fill the same role he had played for Henry Palmer, as chief lieutenant, alter ego, and head of investments. The choice had fallen to William Van Dyke, a prominent Milwaukee lawyer and a member of the board since 1904. Van Dyke filled the position ably, and in 1919 he became the latest in the growing line of attorneys to serve as Northwestern Mutual's president. Sixty-two when he took office, the new chief executive was younger than Markham had been at the start of his term, but he also represented a return to Northwestern's roots. William Van Dyke's father, John, had served as president from 1869—only a decade after the move from Janesville—until 1874, when Heber Smith ousted him. "Van Dyke the younger" had practically grown up with Northwestern Mutual, and his background—Presbyterian, Republican, colonial stock—was a throwback to the patterns of the earliest years.

William Van Dyke took office with a favoring postwar wind at his back. Although the vast majority of servicemen let their government term insurance lapse soon after the armistice, enough of them purchased ordinary policies from private companies— with the prohibitive war clause removed—to ignite a sales boom. Veterans had developed the life insurance habit, and the industry received an additional boost, entirely unexpected and unwanted, from a medical catastrophe. In the waning months of the war, an influenza epidemic raged out of control around the world, reaching the United States in the autumn of 1918. More than 600,000 Americans died by the time the virus ran its course in 1919. "In the long run," noted Northwestern actuary Percy Evans, "the thing which makes men buy life insurance is some kind of fear." The influenza strain seemed to attack healthy young adults with particular force, and its sheer randomness persuaded even the fittest to seek protection. Northwestern's new business soared from $145.8 million in 1918 to $297.1 million in 1919, more than doubling in a single year. (The industry as a whole gained 62 percent.) Influenza ultimately claimed the lives of 2,177 civilian policyowners—nearly five times the number of Northwestern insureds who died in military action during World War I.

A sharp recession took the wind out of the industry's sails—and sales—soon after the influenza scourge had passed. After climbing another 19 percent in 1920, Northwestern's new business dipped 27 percent the next year, and nearly every competitor was adrift in the same doldrums. A brutal round of inflation

William Van Dyke continued a family tradition when he became Northwestern's president in 1919.

Michael Cleary left his post as Wisconsin's insurance commissioner in 1919 to become Northwestern's insurance vice-president.

made the downturn even more difficult. The Consumer Price Index rose 16 percent in 1920 alone, prompting a variety of campaigns against "H.C.L."—the high cost of living. Noting that the average Northwestern agent used two rate books every year, *Field Notes* stressed the need for conservation: "Do not mistreat them and try hard to make one last for a year at least." It was not until 1922 that the economy had cycled through its various postwar adjustments, and then, finally, the decade began to roar. As American business shifted into overdrive, American society followed, embracing new technologies, new types of entertainment, and new variations on traditional life insurance.

William Van Dyke had already recruited a talented newcomer to help him guide Northwestern into the emerging "golden age." Although he was an investment specialist in George Markham's mold, Van Dyke was much more responsive to field concerns than his predecessor. The standing critique of the home office—that it lacked "sales-mindedness"—had grown so general that some agents were openly campaigning for a field representative on the board or in the executive suites. Van Dyke quelled the controversy by hiring Michael J. Cleary as his insurance vice-president in 1919. A small-town lawyer from southwestern Wisconsin, Cleary had received his first important lessons in life insurance as a member of the 1907 state legislature. The freshman found himself on the committee

reviewing the torrent of bills that poured out of the 1906 legislative investigation. "It was all fascinating to me," he recalled, "and I heard practically everything that was said on both sides. The more I heard, the greater became my recognition and appreciation of the fundamentals of life insurance and of its great and beneficial impact on our nation." Cleary also heard enough about Northwestern Mutual to buy his first policy in 1908. He became such an expert on life insurance that in 1915 Gov. Emanuel Philipp, a fellow Republican, made him Wisconsin's insurance commissioner. Cleary had clearly found his niche, serving with such distinction that in 1918 he was elected president of the National Convention of Insurance Commissioners.

Michael J. Cleary, more familiarly known as "Mickey" or "M.J.," was only forty-two when he left the public payroll for Northwestern Mutual—twenty years younger than William Van Dyke—but his relative youth was not all that set the new executive apart. Cleary was an Irish Catholic in a stronghold of Yankee Protestants; the decision to hire him was not unlike a family of Puritans inviting the pope to dinner. His appointment was a powerful symbol that the company was transcending the narrow parochialism of its earlier years, but it was also a measure of Cleary's special gifts. Not the least of those was an instinctive optimism. Michael Cleary was a sought-after speaker for company events, often taking the podium to the strains of *When Irish Eyes Are Smiling*, and he never failed to leave his audience feeling energized. He had a special affinity for the field force. Cleary had actually sold a few Northwestern policies back home in Blanchardville, working as a part-time agent to supplement his law practice, and he developed a warm rapport with the "husky warriors of the rate book." But the new vice-president was no pushover on policy questions. After one of their first interviews, William Van Dyke described Cleary as "in full accord with the traditions and fundamental principles of the Northwestern." He would prove to be a staunch defender of the company's faith even when agents might have preferred a more tractable executive.

Although Michael Cleary soon became the public face of Northwestern Mutual, no one doubted that William Van Dyke was in charge. His dedication to the principles of the founders was instinctive and near-total. "Mutuality," he declared in 1922, "is the basic and most important factor in our organization—mutuality not only in name, but in the broadest and truest sense of the word." Six years later, Van Dyke resurrected the 1888 Executive Committee statement—"pre-eminently the policy-holders Company"— and offered a paraphrase of his own: "Strength of volume is superficial when compared with strength of character. The Northwestern's strength is its character." Van Dyke displayed a legendary work ethic in

nurturing that character. Virtually his only outside interest was tending the elaborate rose garden at his summer home in suburban Fox Point. Everything else, from morning to night, was Northwestern Mutual. This workaholic railed against the desire for "ease, comfort and luxury" that seemed to be the dominant theme of the 1920s. "In normal times," he harrumphed, "we were proud to labor ten hours or more per day but—due to indulgence born of artificial prosperity—the modern idea of *hard* work has become *softened* by luxury and is permeated with idle pleasure."

Van Dyke found less to criticize in the investment climate of the Twenties. Without reshuffling the deck, the president adjusted Northwestern's holdings to reflect the opportunities of the times. Railroad securities still anchored the bond portfolio, but there was a sharp decrease in the company's share of U.S. bonds as the war emergency passed. Utility bonds took up much of the slack, particularly after Frederick Walker was hired in 1926. A former engineer who had discovered a gift for finance, Walker joined the firm as a vice-president with responsibility for all bond investments. Percy Sanborn, his counterpart on the mortgage side, directed a gradual shift from farm to "city" loans as the nation's farmers were caught in a spiral of rising debt and falling prices. Commercial properties in major cities,

Name badges were fixtures at every annual meeting of agents.

William Van Dyke
(front row, in dark suit)
posed with Northwestern
Mutual's loan agents in 1929.

particularly Chicago, became the mortgage investments of choice. In 1924, the Finance Committee authorized the largest single loan in Northwestern's history to that date: $17 million to finance construction of the elegant Palmer House in the heart of the Loop.

Investment opportunities aside, both William Van Dyke and Michael Cleary found themselves decidedly out of sympathy with the ruling spirit of the Roaring Twenties. In the anything-goes atmosphere of the decade, contract features that had surfaced before the war became standard practice throughout the industry. Group insurance and double-indemnity clauses gained enormous popularity, and there was a growing emphasis on coverage for juveniles, women, and substandard risks. But the decade's main event was disability income

insurance. One company after another joined the parade, guaranteeing monthly payments if a policyowner was disabled by accident or disease, even if only temporarily. The idea had broad appeal, and Northwestern's agents found themselves under intense competitive pressure. Looking back from the safe distance of a later decade, Michael Cleary recalled disability insurance as the "persistent nightmare" of the 1920s. "No cost or other question," he said, "can equal in irritation and frustration what Northwestern men suffered in those years. I still marvel at the patience and fortitude that characterized the agency force of this Company in those trying years."

Despite the beating its agents were taking, Northwestern Mutual steadfastly, even defiantly, refused to follow the crowd. William Van Dyke dismissed group policies—"mass insurance," in his opinion—as the equivalent of chain-store marketing. "The Piggly-Wiggly idea will not sell life insurance," he declared in 1920. Michael Cleary leveled an even broader blast in 1924:

> *The life insurance field is today infested —and I use that term deliberately—with a conglomerate mass of contracts that are hybrids of life insurance and disability insurance, life insurance and accident insurance, life insurance and annuities, life insurance and real estate investments, and life insurance and newspaper subscriptions.*

The proliferation of products in the 1920s was inconsistent with Northwestern's deepest instinct: Keep it simple. Hybridizing the contract and loading it down with extra features was viewed as a violation of everything the firm stood for, and halfway measures were repugnant. Charles Parsons, the Toledo general agent and soon-to-be head of agencies, described his company's choices starkly in 1923:

> *Either it must enter the race for volume by adopting the multiple line principle and writing all kinds of business by offering all things to all men, or it must continue as the outstanding pure life insurance company seeking business from those who prefer a select company. In the one, the field is complicated and menaced by the fiercest of competition with the race always to the swift. In the other, we dominate the field and stand practically alone. Which shall it be? There is no middle ground. Compromise would be fatal, and would make us neither the one nor the other. Old members would soon lose their confidence and prospective members would no longer regard us with favor. We cannot be followers of others. We must be leaders—leaders in everything that makes for sound life insurance and for better service to policyholders.*

A $17 million loan helped finance construction of Chicago's elegant Palmer House Hotel.

The Northwestern Mutual Life Insurance Company

BELIEVES

That the business of life insurance is one of trusteeship, and that commercialism has no place in it;

That exact equality of obligation, benefit and service to each policyholder is consequent upon the relationship between policyholder and Company and is enjoined by the laws of most, if not all, the states;

That the same standards of selection should be applied to all applicants for life insurance, if mutuality and equality are to be preserved. To require a medical examination of part of the members and not of others, without segregation, violates this theory, and consequently the Northwestern does not, and will not, do a non-medical business;

That to include health and accident features in the policies of part of its members, without segregation and at less than self-supporting rates, results in discrimination; that the cost of these features is still unknown; that they inject uncertainty, controversy and a resulting loss of prestige into the business, and hence, the Northwestern has not adopted the Disability Annuity and Double Indemnity features;

That its first year lapse rate, averaging less than seven per cent, and its "repeat orders" from policyholders exceeding fifty per centum per annum of its new volume, result from its simple, clear and certain contracts and the intelligent, responsible, personal selling and service of its agents;

That each policyholder needs, and is entitled to, a service that can only be obtained from personal negotiations with a competent and responsible agent; that wholesale and mass selling of life insurance tend to minimize the efficiency of agents and to eliminate them altogether, thereby resulting in loss of service to policyholders and consequent dissatisfaction to them. The Northwestern, therefore, has not adopted wholesale and mass selling plans;

That it has a deep and binding obligation to the 600,000 men who are its present policyholders; that it cannot admit others, who do not comply with established standards, into an equal partnership with them, without being chargeable with bad faith; that volume, beyond enough to keep the Company healthy and serviceable, is of no important consequence. The Northwestern, therefore, will not lower its standards nor covet volume;

That if future results are to be as satisfying as past experience to its policyholders, the Company must adhere to established standards and that, if it abandons such standards, it must, of necessity, increase its costs. This the Northwestern will not do.

The Northwestern Mutual Life Insurance Company
MILWAUKEE, WISCONSIN

Published in 1926, the Northwestern Credo reaffirmed the company's commitment to trusteeship and simplicity of operations.

Although every executive preached from the same text, Michael Cleary emerged as the most passionate defender of the corporate faith. In speech after speech, he framed Northwestern's position in moral terms, restating and amplifying the principles that set the firm apart. In 1926, Cleary articulated those principles in a magazine ad that became known as "the Northwestern Credo." "The business of life insurance is one of trusteeship," the Credo began, and it went on to specify what that belief implied: "exact equality of obligation, benefit and service to each policyholder" through the medium of "simple, clear and certain contracts" made available through "the intelligent, responsible, personal selling and service of its agents." In an industry generally known for vague emotional appeals, the Credo was a refreshing change of pace. It was rooted, of course, in the Henry Palmer era. Michael Cleary, William Van Dyke, actuary Percy Evans, and agency head Charles Parsons never tired of invoking the spirit of Palmer and his colleagues. In 1920, decades before "corporate culture" entered the lexicon of American business, Cleary described the origins of Northwestern's "individuality":

The personalities of men long since dead have so impressed its succeeding officials living that they have kept the faith, producing a distinct, continuing and well recognized corporate personality, which has been our splendid heritage and which if adhered to is a sure guaranty of excellence through the years to come.

In a 1923 speech, Cleary praised the founders and then, without a hint of self-consciousness, urged the agents to "take increased devotion to that cause for which they gave the last full measure of devotion"—a line borrowed, word for word, from the Gettysburg Address. Henry Palmer was hardly a fallen Union soldier, but Cleary was trying to make a point: selling for Northwestern in the chaos of the 1920s amounted to holy war. The company became, almost by default, a specialist in "pure" life insurance, and William Van Dyke's team earned more recognition for what they *didn't* allow than for what they did. "It doesn't take courage to do the thing that everyone else is doing...," Michael Cleary declared in 1926. "It does take courage to say 'No.'"

More often than not, Northwestern was saying "No" to its own agents. There was a steady drumbeat of appeals from the field for disability income insurance, higher single-life maximums, broader age limits, and coverage for women. (When a speaker at the 1926 annual meeting suggested opening the door to females, the agents burst into applause.) The home office increased the maximum policy size from $150,000 in 1918 to $250,000 in 1928 and broadened the eligible age range slightly (from 16 down to 15 and from 60

up to 65), but that was as far as William Van Dyke was willing to go. Northwestern did not, however, leave its agents without the necessary tools to compete. One of the bright spots of the 1920s was a training program that broke new ground in the industry. In 1923, an Educational Department was established under John Davies, a former agent whose stated goal was "to give a man a broad background, to help him to be able to *think*, ... so that he would be equipped to be a truly professional counselor on life insurance matters." The first fruit of Davies' efforts was a twenty-four-lesson correspondence course, open only to representatives chosen by their general agents, that covered everything from the history of life insurance to canvassing and prospecting.

Northwestern Mutual agents soon emerged as leading practitioners of the "selling to needs" approach, or "program insurance." Michael Cleary, the prime mover behind the training program, believed that modern consumers would respond only to modern sales techniques:

We cannot any longer sell life insurance merely because it is a good thing and the other fellow ought to have some of it. We have got to know why he ought to have some of it. We have got to know what kind he ought to have, and we have got to know what amount he ought to have.

Typical ads of the 1920s reflected an increasing emphasis on "selling to needs."

Daisy Bagwell, "the Georgia Peach," was the company's leading female agent.

In the 1920s, the concept of life insurance broadened from providing for the basic needs of widows and orphans to a wide array of other purposes: liquidating mortgages, retiring business debts, paying estate taxes, funding educations, providing retirement income, and even endowing charities. The company's agents were trained to make a "scientific" analysis of each client's needs and then to suggest policies that would meet those needs as efficiently as possible. Two of the most popular fact-finding tools were developed by agents themselves. The Poindexter Kit, created by Kansas City general agent Urban Poindexter, debuted in 1922; and the Million Book, developed by the appropriately named Burr Million of Evansville, Indiana, followed in 1924. Both systems remained in use for decades. "Programming" invariably produced higher average policy sizes, higher persistency rates, and a higher likelihood that customers would return for more insurance as their needs changed. The approach also marked a new professionalism in Northwestern Mutual's field force—a status demonstrated by the company's participation in the fledgling Chartered Life Underwriter movement. Thirty-five agents from a variety of companies took the first CLU exam in 1928; only twenty-eight passed, including two from Northwestern. The company has had a disproportionately higher share of the industry's CLUs ever since.

As the field force became more professional, Northwestern's general agents were no longer player-coaches, selling as they supervised, but full-time managers, succeeding through the success of their associates. The "civil service rule" still applied—leading sellers were typically tapped to lead agencies—but general agents were not eligible to compete in Northwestern's sales contests after 1920. The awards themselves reflected the company's emphasis on quality. In 1920, William Van Dyke donated a sterling silver President's Cup that was presented annually to the agency with the highest persistency rating. The Marathon Club, established in 1916, recognized agents who wrote policies on more than 100 lives every year; membership rose from 13 in the club's first year to 53 in 1926. One of the repeat members was Daisy Bagwell, "the Georgia Peach," an Atlanta agent who was the most successful woman in the field force. "I have come to see," she said in 1923, "that a very ordinary salesman or saleswoman can sell circles around a man or woman of greater ability if they just keep doggedly at it." The champion Marathoner of the Van Dyke years was Bert Nelson of Peoria, who reached a high-water mark of 283 lives in 1923.

Volume, of course, was recognized as well, and Charles Albright had no serious challengers in the 1920s. The doctor's annual sales averaged nearly $3 million during the decade, and his cumulative production topped $50 million by 1929—more than $570 million in current dollars. Northwestern's highest volume award—the "AA" prize—came to be known as "Always Albright." "There is nothing extraordinary about me," he said in one of his typically brief acceptance speeches. Albright's "formula" for success was simplicity itself: "I know my product. I try to know my prospects. I endeavor to create in them a feeling of confidence about me and my Company. There is nothing else." His success was not quite that elementary. Expanding from his Milwaukee base, Albright spent parts of every month in New York, Chicago, and Cleveland, and the relational skills he had honed at home translated easily to a larger stage. His clients ranged from automaker Walter Chrysler to the actors who played Amos and Andy on the hit radio program. Looking back in 1946, the doctor indulged in a bit of bragging:

> *I came to know, intimately, most of the business leaders in this country, both past and present, and it has been said by more than one person that my list of policy-holders and prospects must resemble an imposing "Who's Who in America." Through my contacts with them I have been kept in touch with the pulse of America.*

Albright became such a trusted advisor that he was elected to the boards of Allis-Chalmers, First Wisconsin Bank, Schlitz

Brewing, and several other firms that sold everything from sugar to coal.

Charles Albright was Northwestern's own Babe Ruth, but he was hardly the whole team. Whether they swung for the fences like Albright or prospered as singles hitters like Daisy Bagwell and Bert Nelson, the company's 5,000-plus agents compiled an enviable batting average in the 1920s. They may have been handicapped, to some extent, by their company's insistence on "pure" life insurance, but that very specialization enabled them to offer a product whose low net cost continued to win fans. Selling policies at the rate of more than $1 million a day, the agents lifted Northwestern's insurance in force from $1.9 billion in 1919 to $3.9 billion in 1929—a ten-year increase of 105 percent. Impressive as that performance was, it lagged the industry-wide gain of 187 percent. Even before the decade was out, analysts were describing the 1920s as a "new era" and a "golden age" for financial products of all kinds. As markets rose and mortality improved, it had never been easier to sell life insurance, and the proportion of Americans with coverage surged from 13 percent in 1900 to nearly 50 percent in 1926.

From Northwestern's point of view, much of that coverage was acquired by taking too many underwriting chances and adding too many extraneous policy features. As always, the company was generally willing to forego

Northwestern had the highest proportion of agents in the industry who qualified to carry the Chartered Life Underwriter (CLU) banner.

higher volume for higher quality. "Give us the cream," said agency head Charles Parsons, "and the others can have the skimmed milk." Northwestern's commitment to "classical coverage" could verge on the sanctimonious at times. "We need the spirit of the crusader," said Parsons in 1929, "for we are battling for a principle." Samuel Sale, a St. Louis agent who left the ministry after forty-two years to answer a call to Northwestern, scaled even loftier rhetorical heights:

> *I can vouch before God that I have abated none of my former idealism, and the erstwhile sanctities to whose care and culture I had given the better part of my life have not failed me, but followed me into the new sphere as a fitting preparation and an inspiration for the service awaiting me there.*

Northwestern's halo was always conspicuous, but the company was never without a sense of humor. Every annual meeting was a high-spirited reunion of the extended Northwestern family, filled with sing-alongs, roasts, golf tournaments, dinner-dances, baseball games, and amateur skits that frequently poked fun at home office notables. A delegation of "militant suffragettes" once accosted an agent impersonating Dr. John Fisher and forced him to explain "why The Northwestern does not write women." (His response was not recorded.) Liquid refreshment was never far away; Prohibition, in force from 1919 to 1933, was enforced only selectively in Milwaukee.

The Jazz Age did not pass without notice at Northwestern, and the Automobile Age asserted its power as well. It was in the 1920s that motor vehicles crossed the threshold from rich man's toy to every

Northwestern's faithful gathered at the 1926 annual meeting, with Michael Cleary and William Van Dyke seated front and center.

ASS'N OF AGENTS NORTHWESTERN MUT. LIFE INS. CO. MILWAUKEE WIS.

family's necessity, providing corporate speech-makers with a bottomless well of new metaphors. "No business can today block the traffic of progress or park on the highway of advancement," proclaimed William Van Dyke in 1927. "Every business must at least keep up with the procession." Two years later, general agent Harry French compared the company's field force to "a Straight Eight motor" and the home office to "the chassis upon which the motor is mounted." French admonished Northwestern's executives to keep the entire vehicle humming: "We look to you to see that this chassis never becomes old-fashioned; that it never becomes inadequate to stand the throbbing impulses of the finely tuned motor; that it will always enable that Straight Eight to deliver its full power." In a more somber reflection of the times, automobile fatalities rose from 20 percent

of Northwestern's casualty deaths between 1912 and 1916 to 44 percent in 1927.

The spirit of the age was perhaps most evident in a new emphasis on growth. Despite a stubborn insistence on what Percy Evans called "certain notions and ideas of right conduct," Northwestern was acutely aware that it was losing ground in the industry. Ranked by insurance in force, the company slipped from sixth place to seventh in 1928, and its market share was eroding even faster, from 4.7 percent of the industry's ordinary sales in 1919 to 3.1 percent in 1928. Although its leaders had never made a god of volume, the firm developed an ambitious expansion program to pick up its sales pace. Launched in 1929 after two

(top) *Home office employees entertained their counterparts from the field at the 1921 annual meeting, while a team of pinstriped agents prepared to take on the clerks in a baseball game.*

Pressed for space once again, Northwestern drove the pilings for a home office addition in 1930.

(right) The finished product was far less ornate than the classical monument to which it was connected.

years of study, the program established both recruiting and volume quotas for every general agency: Northwestern wanted more agents to sell more insurance. "The aim," reported *Field Notes* (January 1929), "is a production sufficient to maintain a steady growth during the next five years." The specific target was new business averaging $400 million every year—a rather substantial advance on the $352 million sold in 1928.

Growth is always relative, and it was particularly so during the Roaring Twenties. Although Northwestern was trailing the competition, its agents were setting new sales records practically every year and, in the process, putting major pressure on the home office staff. Despite the latest labor-saving devices (including Milwaukee's first postage meter in 1922), the company was forced to increase its work force from nearly 700 employees in 1916 to at least 1,000 by 1929. The "new" home office, praised by some officials as a permanent solution to the firm's space problems back in 1914, was soon overcrowded. Discussions began as early as 1919, and in 1928 the board approved plans for an eight-story addition on the half-block immediately north—the site reserved for just such an eventuality. Although they were ultimately connected on every floor, the two structures did not constitute a seamless whole. Where the 1914 home office was exuberantly classical, the addition was characterized by "plain lines and comparative simplicity"—no columns, no capitals, and an exterior of limestone rather than granite. Its functions were different as well: the original home office was reserved for "executives and their immediate assistants," while the addition became, in company historian Henry Tyrrell's words, "a complete work-room for the mechanics of the business." Even though it was more utilitarian than the temple next door, the new structure was built like a fortress. Looking ahead to future space needs (but apparently not to changing architectural tastes), Northwestern put enough steel in the building to support an additional sixteen stories.

As the home office addition was going up, the rising expectations of the 1920s came crashing down. The stock market collapse of October 24, 1929, was the first in a chain of catastrophes that plunged the American economy into chaos for nearly a decade. Northwestern didn't lose a nickel in the market meltdown—largely because it didn't have a nickel invested—but the prevailing uncertainties had a major impact on the company's operations. As policyowners found other sources of ready cash drying up, they turned to the loan provisions in their insurance contracts, and policy loans surged from 15.6 percent of Northwestern's assets in 1928 to 24.9 percent in 1932. Frederick Walker was forced to sell railroad and utility bonds (at a profit) and replace them with more-liquid government securities to meet the demand; U.S. obligations rose from 5.1 percent of the bond portfolio at the end of 1929 to 15.5 percent in 1933.

Although the run on policy loans was an inconvenience, no one at Northwestern was unduly concerned—at least in the early stages of the downturn. Sales for 1929 were the highest in history, and work on the home office addition proceeded without interruption. *Field Notes* (December 1929) characterized the stock market crash as a tonic that had "cleared the air and restored

The arithmometer calculating machine and an early punchcard device—examples of the latest advances in office automation

*The 1914 home office with
its 1932 addition*

and confirmed grouches" who predicted disaster, Van Dyke counseled patience:

> *I believe that the worst is over, and that it never was as bad as it has been advertised. I believe in our God, who directs our destinies. I believe in our country. I believe in our people. I believe in our Northwestern, and I welcome the future with confidence and unshakeable faith.*

Such defiant optimism was harder and harder to maintain as the Depression deepened. Once-dependable investment outlets vanished into thin air, and Northwestern's clerks had to work nights to keep up with the demand for policy loans. William Van Dyke was on the job with them. The growing crisis put enormous pressure on a president who had already shown a predisposition to overwork. The home office addition, which Van Dyke once called "an expression of our faith in the Northwestern," opened in the summer of 1932, but he never got to see the building in its finished state. Worn out in body and spirit, William Van Dyke died on June 7, 1932, two months before his seventy-sixth birthday. The funeral service was held at his beloved Immanuel Presbyterian Church, where hundreds of mourners gathered around a casket covered with flowers from Van Dyke's own garden.

balance and stability." Addressing the agents in 1931, William Van Dyke went down a similar path. "This depression," he said, "appears to be the natural and to-be-expected aftermath of unusual conditions, including in our country a prolonged period of over-expansion, extravagance and speculation, with a seeming disregard of the value of thrift." Taking aim at the "professional pessimists, squawkers, calamity howlers

The Cleary New Deal

William Van Dyke had always prided himself on succession planning. He made sure that there were understudies for every officer in the company—with the exception, that is, of himself. When Van Dyke died, there was no one waiting in the wings to take charge of Northwestern Mutual. The trustees made Frederick Walker acting president, but they waited more than four months to name a permanent successor, choosing from a field that was rumored to include Calvin Coolidge and Charles Albright as well as Walker and dark horse Michael J. Cleary. On October 19, 1932, the dark horse got the nod. Cleary's Irish Catholicism had always made him an anomaly at Northwestern, and he was doubly so as president. Not since the days of Samuel Daggett had the company entrusted its fortunes to a leader whose interest and expertise were on the insurance rather than the investment side. It was probably his personal dynamism and widespread popularity—both distinct assets in a time of crisis—that won Cleary the job. "He is big, hearty, broad-shouldered, a nailer for work," reported *Time* (October 31, 1932). "Insurance people predict that under him Northwestern's shiny marble tomb will lose some of its historic chilliness." Cleary, for his part, saw no compelling reason to change a thing:

The fundamental policies upon which this Company has been built are sound. Consistent adherence to them has made it the greatest institution of its kind in America. These must be preserved. The Company has always had a personnel that has distinguished itself for loyalty and outrightness of purpose. It will be one of my major purposes to maintain that spirit in the organization.

Michael Cleary proved to be a master at maintaining spirit, but it would be hard to imagine a harder time to take over an insurance company than October 1932. The entire industry was in distress. With the American economy in free fall, Northwestern's new business plummeted from $379.9 million in 1929 to $191 million in 1933—a 50-percent drop in just four years. As lapse and surrender rates soared, the company's insurance in force dipped from $4.1 billion in 1931 to $3.7 billion in 1934, marking the first time since the 1870s—another period of financial panic—that coverage actually declined. On the investment side, demand for policy loans remained high, particularly after the federal government declared a "bank holiday" in March 1933 to keep panic-stricken depositors from emptying their accounts. With America's banks closed,

Michael Cleary, the genial Irishman who led Northwestern through some of the most challenging years in its history

The hardships of the Depression ushered in a series of changes at Northwestern known as "the Cleary New Deal."

LIBRARY OF CONGRESS

insurance companies experienced what Michael Cleary called "a literal avalanche" of policy loan requests, prompting the states to declare a national moratorium of their own. Policy loans were at least secured by the contracts behind them. Far more troublesome were the disasters in Northwestern's core investment accounts. Despite the extraordinary care taken in qualifying its borrowers, the company was forced to foreclose on nearly 6,500 farms during the Depression, and "special" real estate peaked at 14.3% of the mortgage portfolio in 1939—a total of $43.4 million. News from the Bond Department was even worse. In 1938, more than a third of Northwestern's railroad bonds were in default, and the company held more than $53 million in non-paying securities. The financial statistics only hinted at the depth of human misery caused by the Depression. The ongoing tragedy was starkly apparent in another number: suicides climbed from 3.45 percent of Northwestern's death claims in 1929 to 6.57 percent in 1932, when 404 policyowners took their own lives.

The company's response to the hard times of the 1930s was in some ways a throwback to Henry Palmer's handling of the crisis Northwestern faced in the 1870s. In both cases, the operative word was retrenchment. Beginning with a new policy series in 1932, the suicide limitation was increased from one

year to two and cash surrender values were reduced in the early years of the contract. The dividend scale came down in stages, falling 25 percent in 1933 alone. Home office salaries were cut 10 percent in the same year, despite an increased workload in several departments, and the board's Executive Committee was forced to meet almost daily as the crisis deepened. It was probably the agents who bore the brunt of the Depression. "Many of us," said Charles Axelson of Chicago, "have labored so industriously to keep old business on the books that our volume of new business has been disastrously small." Throughout the company, policies were stiffened, operations were tightened, and everyone waited anxiously for the worst of the bad times to pass.

There was, at the same time, an unmistakable feeling of vindication. Northwestern had been preaching the gospel of simplicity since the early 1900s, saying an unequivocal "No" to any and all contract features that were felt to be outside the bounds of "classical coverage." Disability insurance was the worst offender, and that hugely popular competitive "nightmare" of the 1920s became a real nightmare for Northwestern's competitors in the 1930s. With no other means of support, jobless policyowners stretched the definition of "disability" to the breaking point, flooding their providers with spurious claims and, in many cases, red ink. As the industry's lone holdout, Northwestern experienced a powerful temptation to gloat. Field leaders who had once sung the praises of disability insurance suddenly changed their tune. "The agents of the Northwestern Mutual," said Ralph Hamburger of Minneapolis, "can thank their God for having at the head of their company a man and men who have had strength of character and will power enough to say 'No' when it would have been much easier to have said 'Yes.'"

Although Northwestern still said "No" with regularity, that was hardly the whole story of Michael Cleary's presidency. It was only an accident that they were both elected in 1932, and their political ideologies were poles apart, but Michael J. Cleary and Franklin D. Roosevelt had much in common. Both men were highly personable, hands-on leaders who inspired confidence in those around them. Both were fond of the rhetorical flourish, and often to the same end. "The only thing we have to fear is fear itself," Roosevelt famously declared in his 1933 inaugural address. "The home office is not worrying," Cleary said one year later. "Worry does not prevent and worry does not cure, it only incapacitates." Both men took concrete action to get things moving again. As Roosevelt's New Deal tested the boundaries of public policy in Washington, Cleary pushed the limits of tradition at Northwestern Mutual, prompting inevitable allusions to "the Cleary New Deal."

What that meant in practice was saying "Yes" to a variety of features that had been off-limits for decades. There was more change in 1933 alone than there had been since the introduction of tontine insurance in 1881. The minimum insurable age for boys dropped from fifteen to ten. Annuities were offered for the first time since 1919. "Family Income" policies, blending whole life with term coverage, met the competitive need for lower-cost insurance. The most radical development was announced in October: after an absence dating back to 1876, Northwestern Mutual would once again enter the women's market. There were some important qualifiers—the new policies were capped at half the male limit, and the maximum was $5,000 for females who were not "financially independent"—but the decision marked a move to the mainstream. Northwestern was the last major insurance firm to open its doors to women. Company officials noted that they had reversed field only after "watching carefully the underwriting results of other companies," but a later edition of *Field Notes* (October 1942) demonstrated more candor. The policy had changed, wrote the editor, "when it was discovered that women had pocketbooks." Although Northwestern showed a new awareness of the strides women had made, the female market was still considered foreign territory. *Field Notes* (November 1933) offered some interesting advice to agents who wanted to test the waters:

In 1933, after an absence of 57 years, Northwestern finally began to insure women again, including the entire support staff of the Dayton, Ohio, general agency.

Give her plenty of time. Never hurry a woman. It may take her a long time to make up her mind. She has the pondering and shopping habit and she looks at her money before she spends it; nevertheless, she is a good customer, a shrewd buyer, and a good booster for the agent who sells her in the proper way.

By 1938, women made up 20 percent of Northwestern's new policyowners.

National advertising, some of it directed at women, was another cornerstone of the Cleary New Deal. The company had long avoided the mass media, preferring to let its agents do the talking, but once again Michael Cleary reversed course. On May 12, 1934, Northwestern Mutual's first national magazine ad appeared in the *Saturday Evening Post*, touting the "Billion Dollar Estate" created by and for the company's 600,000-plus policyowners. A total of forty-five ads ran in the next eight months, and the other magazines selected—*Cosmopolitan, Time, Nation's Business, American, Country Gentleman,* and *Successful Farming*—gave some indication of the company's chosen markets. A second campaign in 1935 highlighted America's "Wonder Spots"—scenic destinations where anyone could live well on $100 a month, provided, naturally, by Northwestern endowment contracts. The advertising program, which reached 120 million readers in its first year, was considered a resounding success. Nearly 93 percent of the agents surveyed in 1936 reported a definite jump in Northwestern's name recognition, and enough readers returned clip-off coupons from the ads to generate more than $2 million in new business.

The Cleary New Deal introduced new leadership as well. Two of the most significant additions to the president's "cabinet" were Edmund Fitzgerald and Grant Hill, both of whom would be powers in the company for the rest of their careers. Fitzgerald was thirty-eight when he arrived

Northwestern's first national advertisements appeared in the 1930s.

and Hill thirty-seven—mere youngsters by Northwestern standards—and they were promoted to the executive ranks on the same day: July 26, 1933. Fitzgerald, the scion of a prominent Milwaukee family long identified with shipping and shipbuilding, became Michael Cleary's executive vice-president, with broad responsibility for everything from investments to personnel relations. Hill succeeded Charles Parsons, who died in office, as head of agencies. A Marine Corps officer during World War I and a stand-out agent after his return, Grant Hill was production manager for the McMillen agency in New York City when Cleary called him to Milwaukee. The new recruit brought military discipline and a gung-ho attitude to his assignment. Hill terminated hundreds of what he called "aimless agents"—those who were insurance salesmen "in name only"—and focused his attention on "the honest-to-goodness, hard-working associate" who represented the organization's backbone. The number of Northwestern Mutual agents under contract dropped from 7,100 at the end of 1932 to 4,941 in 1936, but those 4,941 sold more insurance.

With Grant Hill at the helm, they had little choice. It was on his watch that Northwestern began to call itself "the career company," and the new director had an inexhaustible supply of ideas to boost his agents' careers: sales promotions, production contests, new training courses, a 4-L Club

(for agents writing at least four lives a month), mailing stuffers, and Northwestern-branded premium items ranging from celluloid calendar cards to coin banks. Hill had the enthusiastic support of Michael Cleary in his efforts to increase volume. "You do not know the kick it is to me," he told the agents in 1938, "to have one like 'M.J.' here, who is so field-minded, backing us up all the time." From Cleary's perspective, it was all one program. Every new initiative—insuring juveniles and women, selling annuities and Family Income policies, advertising nationally, recruiting a vigorous new executive—was designed with the field in mind. The whole point was to give agents, within the permeable boundaries of established principle, what they needed to thrive in a depressed economy. Cleary made his intentions clear in a 1934 address to the agents:

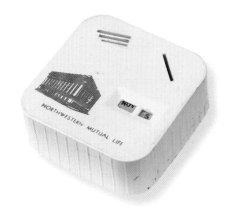

Coin banks promoted thrift— and Northwestern Mutual.

Two Cleary recruits became key figures in the company: Grant Hill (left) as head of agencies and Edmund Fitzgerald as executive vice-president.

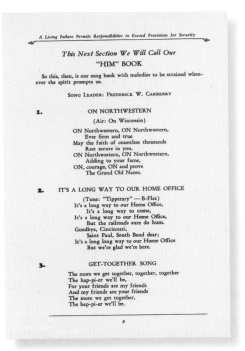

A Living Failure Permits Responsibilities to Exceed Provisions for Security

This Next Section We Will Call Our
"HIM" BOOK

So this, then, is our song book with melodies to be strained whenever the spirit prompts us.

Song Leader: Frederick W. Carberry

1.   ON NORTHWESTERN
(Air: On Wisconsin)

ON Northwestern, ON Northwestern,
    Ever firm and true
May the faith of countless thousands
    Rest secure in you.
ON Northwestern, ON Northwestern,
    Adding to your fame,
ON, courage, ON and prove
    The Grand Old Name.

2.   IT'S A LONG WAY TO OUR HOME OFFICE
(Tune: "Tipperary" — B-Flat)
It's a long way to our Home Office,
    It's a long way to come,
It's a long way to our Home Office,
    But the railroads sure do hum.
Goodbye, Cincinnati,
    Saint Paul, South Bend dear;
It's a long long way to our Home Office
    But we're glad we're here.

3.   GET-TOGETHER SONG
The more we get together, together, together
The hap-pi-er we'll be,
For your friends are my friends
And my friends are your friends
The more we get together,
The hap-pi-er we'll be.

*Group singing was a regular feature
of the agents' annual meetings.*

The 1936 group portrait

We believe at the home office that we have widened your market as greatly as you would have us widen it. We believe that we have modernized your tools and equipment as greatly as we should. We believe that there is a marvelous opportunity ahead of us, and frankly, we believe that from a producing standpoint the job is up to you.

The agents responded with as much enthusiasm as the times would allow. Attendance at the annual meeting generally topped 1,000—higher than the previous decade's, despite the Depression—and those who made the trip invariably went home ready to wage holy war for their company. The firm even had its own fight song, performed every year to the tune of *On, Wisconsin*:

> *On, Northwestern; On, Northwestern,*
> *   Ever firm and true,*
> *May the faith of countless thousands*
> *   Rest secure in you.*
> *On, Northwestern; On, Northwestern,*
> *   Adding to your fame,*
> *On, courage, on and prove*
> *   The Grand Old Name.*

The agents had spirit to spare, but there was only so much they could do to "chase away Old Man Depression"—the theme of one annual meeting skit. As sales dropped to less than half their $400 million target, the expansion campaign so hopefully launched in 1929 was quietly shelved. Even the redoubtable Charles Albright saw his production slip from a peak of nearly $4 million in 1929 to $1.5 million in 1934, and that was still good enough to lead the field. Albright, who turned sixty-five in 1932, had actually planned to retire, but he decided to stay with his company in its hour of need. In 1936, convinced that the economy had turned a corner, the doctor withdrew from competition (but not from selling) after thirty consecutive years of dominance. Albright's career production totaled $64 million by that time—more than $900 million in current dollars. "He is conceded to have sold more million-dollar policies than any man in the history of life insurance," reported *Time* (October 31, 1932). Charles Albright had, in fact, sold more insurance than nearly half the *companies* in America. His withdrawal allowed New York City agent Herman Duval to finally claim his

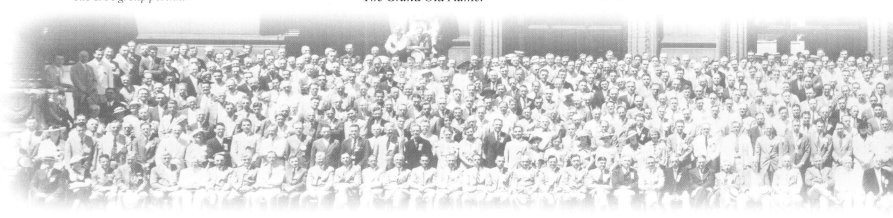

place in the sun. After twenty-two years as runner-up, Duval won the volume award in 1937, and Albright was the first to congratulate him. Northwestern's new business had been showing modest improvement up to 1937 but, despite Duval's and Albright's best efforts, the economy suffered a painful relapse. Sales fell to $195.2 million in 1939—not far off the twenty-year low of $191 million recorded in 1933.

As the agents brought new contracts and sharper techniques to a depressed marketplace, the Cleary New Deal was making its influence felt in other areas of the company. Although his expertise lay in the area of insurance rather than investments, Michael Cleary could see that the times called for a sweeping redistribution of Northwestern's assets. A steady diet of foreclosures had ruined the company's appetite for mortgage loans, particularly on farm properties. There was some interest in residential loans after 1934, but the most promising opportunities seemed to be in the securities markets. Not in railroad bonds, however: the landscape of the rail industry was still strewn with bankruptcies. After obtaining the requisite approvals from

(left) *After 22 years in Charles Albright's shadow, Herman Duval finally emerged as Northwestern's volume leader in 1937.*

Wisconsin's legislature, Northwestern rapidly increased its holdings of public utility bonds and industrial securities. Utilities, industrials, and a still-growing municipal bond account filled the gap created by mortgage loans, and the cumulative result was a sea change in Northwestern's investment mix. Between 1929 and 1939, mortgages plummeted from 44.6 percent of the company's assets to 23.5 percent, while bonds of various kinds soared from 33.5 percent to 55.4 percent. Policy loans accounted for most of the balance in both years.

A pre-electronic adding machine

There was significant change in the leadership of the investment departments as well. Seasoned hands were in charge of the major units—Frederick Walker in bonds and Howard Thomas (a former loan agent) in mortgages—but there were clear signs of the same youth movement that had brought Grant Hill and Edmund Fitzgerald to the home office. Three all-stars were hired in 1933 and 1934: Donald Slichter (utility bonds), Howard Tobin (city loans), and Philip Robinson (municipal bonds). None was over forty, and all would rise to the company's highest echelons. Slichter's aggressiveness made an especially strong impression on Michael Cleary. "Don Slichter," Cleary told the agents in 1939, "has literally traveled from Seattle to Miami and from San Diego to Quebec and Portland, Maine, seeking outlets in the utility field for Company funds." Nineteen years later, Slichter would move into Cleary's old office.

The depressed labor market of the 1930s made it easy, relatively speaking, to secure the best and brightest talent available; in Milwaukee or elsewhere, Northwestern was one of the few companies hiring. Turmoil in the capital markets, new agency initiatives, and a continuing flood of policy changes required more workers, not fewer, and the total home office payroll swelled from roughly 1,000 people in 1929 to more than 1,600 in 1939. Northwestern had become a largely female domain in the previous decade or two. Women outnumbered men by a two-to-one margin in the 1920s, but the hiring preference shifted to unemployed heads of families, most of them male, in the next decade. As a direct result, men and women were in rough equilibrium by 1933.

Not all were happy. Despite the stately surroundings and the free lunch, Northwestern began to experience labor

The investment brain trust of the Thirties: (l. to r.) Donald Slichter, Howard Tobin, and Philip Robinson

trouble in the mid-1930s, much of it self-generated. Salary ranges, job classifications, and promotion protocols varied widely from one department to the next, and a starting clerk's wages proved inadequate to the needs of whole families. Lulled into complacency by the glutted labor market, managers were painfully slow to address the problems, and their inaction fed a rising tide of workplace frustration. The restlessness that swept through the home office reflected the national mood perfectly. In 1935, after decades of trying, labor had won the right to organize and bargain collectively. The result was a wave of New Deal union activity that reached even the normally staid insurance industry. In 1937, home office workers formed the Independent Union of Northwestern Mutual Employees and presented management with a list of demands. The company's leaders, from Michael Cleary on down, viewed the looming crisis as a wake-up call. They promptly negotiated an agreement with the union and established a Personnel Department to clear up the inconsistencies and inequities that had sparked the unrest. The department's long-time director was Louise Marie Newman, who in 1951 became Northwestern Mutual's first woman officer.

The labor unrest that touched the home office was only one symptom of a much broader discontent that earned Northwestern a brief place in the national spotlight.

America's prolonged economic swoon had convinced many that the entire system was structurally flawed, that too much capital was concentrated in the hands of too few institutions and individuals. The trail of suspicion led quite naturally to the nation's life insurance companies, whose multi-billion-dollar reserves seemed to cushion them from the pressures that had flattened other businesses. In 1938, the Roosevelt administration convened the Temporary National Economic Committee to probe "the concentration of economic power" in insurance and other fields. For executives with long memories, the TNEC looked like a reincarnation of the Armstrong panel of

Louise Marie Newman joined the Personnel Department in 1937 and became the company's first woman officer in 1951.

THE INSURANCE EXAMINER

Cleary Rings the Bell
Gives Easterners Lesson in Ethics on Midwest Life Insurance
Management

Called to testify before a federal panel in 1939, Michael Cleary earned headlines for his declaration that "the policyholders are the bosses."

1905, and they feared the same results: a black eye for the industry and a wave of punitive legislation. Their worries were groundless, as it turned out, and in Northwestern Mutual's case, the probe was an unmixed blessing. Called to Washington in 1939, Michael Cleary convinced investigators that his company was a paragon of corporate virtue, careful to avoid the conflicts of interest and the self-dealing that still plagued other firms. Panel members seemed incredulous that Northwestern allowed its Policyholders' Examining Committee a completely free hand in their investigations of the company, but Cleary testified that the firm's core values demanded no less: "We are not permitted to decide that we own the Company. We are kept conscious of the fact that we are hired men up there and that the policyholders are the bosses." The quote was carried by dozens of newspapers, to general applause. The headline in the *Chicago Tribune* (February 18, 1939) was typical: "Easterners Get Lesson in Ethics from Midwest."

Cleary may have emerged as the St. Michael of the insurance industry, but the TNEC hearings would seem like the merest diversion in another year. With the German invasion of Poland on September 1, 1939, the world was plunged into war for the second time in a quarter-century. As the German and Japanese armies rolled to one quick victory after another, the United States became "the great arsenal of democracy," in Franklin Roosevelt's phrase, supplying the Allies with the munitions and supplies they needed to resist the juggernaut. The moribund American economy came roaring back to life, and it accelerated to a white-hot pace after the 1941 bombing of Pearl Harbor. Northwestern Mutual, with the rest of the nation, moved from a monetary meltdown to a military emergency without a moment's rest in between.

Although an insurance firm was hardly in the same class as a torpedo factory or a bomber plant, World War II had a direct and pervasive impact on Northwestern's operations. With gasoline and tires in short supply and all non-essential travel discouraged, the annual meeting was canceled for the duration. Some general agencies still convened each summer to hear recorded speeches from company executives, but Northwestern's annual revival was put on hold until 1946. The rationing and restrictions forced home office employees to change their habits as well.

Even diehard motorists had to ride the streetcar, and public officials mandated a system of staggered working hours to ease demand on Milwaukee's transit system. Northwestern's government-issued workday began at 8:10 A.M. and ended at 4:40 P.M. (amended to 4:10 in peacetime.) The war effort's most profound impact on the company was undoubtedly its insatiable appetite for people. By March 1944, more than a quarter of Northwestern's full-time agents had traded their rate books for rifles or radar sets, and a comparable proportion of home office men were in uniform. The company kept in touch with all of them through *The Bugle*, a mimeographed sheet that served as a sort of pre-electronic

bulletin board for Northwestern men and women who had joined the armed forces. In a 1943 posting, agent Royall Brown noted that military duty was "a little like selling insurance—you never finish your day's work."

For those on the home front, business had never been better. Wars, like epidemics and natural disasters, tend to heighten the average consumer's awareness of mortality. New business for 1941 was up 18 percent from the previous year's, in part because so many men were trying to beat the restrictive war clause that took effect at year's end; December proved to be the busiest month in Northwestern's history. Millions of GIs took advantage of government-sponsored life insurance once they were in service,

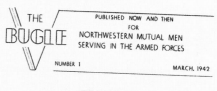

The Bugle reported on the progress of Northwesterners in the military.

Home office scrap drives yielded piles of metal for the World War II effort.

purchasing $135 billion of coverage by mid-1945. The nation's private companies turned their attention to women, children, and defense workers, both male and female, who were generally earning sizable paychecks with no hope of spending them on cars, houses, vacations, or other scarce items. "This period of enormous spendable income is the business Utopia for which we have prayed," wrote agent Tom Lauer to his peers in 1944. Even with a critical shortage of field representatives, Northwestern's new business climbed from $199.5 million in 1940 to $319.4 million in 1945—a 60-percent increase that easily outpaced the industry's 40-percent gain. Once purchased, new policies tended to stay on the books. The company had always prided itself on an exceptionally favorable first-year lapse rate; in 1944, the rate sank to a historic low of just 3 percent.

Much of Northwestern's growth came in a previously unexplored market: pension trusts. In the late 1930s, a handful of particularly enterprising agents began to sell the company's special retirement

They aren't the only ones living in trunks!

A TRUNK is their home. A time-table, their library. The present, their dream.

Today, San Antonio. Tomorrow, Maxwell Field. Next month, Dayton. Next summer, Santa Ana. Trains and furnished rooms, cinders and stars, laughter and courage.

They'll live that way till the war is won. But a lot of us at home have figuratively lived that way all our lives. And with no good reason either.

Living in a trunk is any kind of living that changes direction too frequently . . . that zigzags along without a plan that makes *sure* and *permanent* such comforting anchors as a mortgage-free home, educations, retirement years . . . *the things that matter* . . . whatever happens.

To use another figure-of-speech, we life insurance men have sent many a family and its trunk on a last trip . . . with a one-way ticket to the happiest place in the world: *independence.*

Don't forget –

that the difference between insurance companies is significant. When buying life insurance, you must well save yourself hundreds of premium dollars, if you will do these two things: (1) listen carefully to the *Northwestern Mutual agent's full story of a wonderful dividend record, and* (2) check with any of our policyholders, for they can tell you, better than we can, why no company excels Northwestern Mutual in that *happiest of all business relationships* . . . *old customers coming back for more.*

The **Northwestern Mutual** Life Insurance Company
MILWAUKEE   WISCONSIN

The company's ads reflected the patriotic tenor of the times ...

endowments to employers who used them as fringe benefits. The Social Security Act of 1935 had made American workers benefit-conscious, and there was a growing demand for private pension plans more generous than the bare-bones coverage of the government program. Northwestern's endowment contracts—all written on the lives of medically examined individuals and held in employee trusts—provided monthly retirement income as well as a death benefit. The Chrysler Corporation purchased the first major block of Northwestern pension policies in 1941, and the agent who closed the case was, to no one's surprise, Charles Albright. Although he had retired from competition, Albright could never resist the lure of one more sale, even in his seventies. The Chrysler case was so huge—nearly 2,500 policies and more than $8 million of insurance—that the doctor opened a Detroit office and hired two secretaries who worked overtime for a month just to prepare the applications. "Some dreams do come true," he told Grant Hill.

Promising enough before the war, the pension trust business swelled to enormous proportions after Pearl Harbor. With wages frozen by government decree, pension plans were one of the only ways to increase employee compensation without breaking the law, and they were tax-deductible besides. Northwestern's pension sales rocketed from 450 policies in 28 trusts at the end of 1940 to 92,500 policies in 865 trusts by mid-1948.

In 1944 alone, pension trusts accounted for 20 percent of the company's new business. The buyers ranged from giants like the Chrysler Corporation and the White Castle hamburger chain to small-town banks and machine shops. Even the smaller trusts brought in policies by the carload, but Michael Cleary emphasized that his company was not selling group insurance. "That is good Northwestern business," he said. "It is personally examined, it is personally inspected. It is not jumbo business. We don't like jumbo business." Agents who could master the intricacies of the pension market grew to like the jumbo commissions. Specialists like Alfred Ostheimer and Al Kaufmann, two East Coast all-stars, earned considerably more money than Cleary. Ostheimer actually led the field for a number of years, in lives as well as volume, but the pension business was viewed as a world of its own; the Association of Agents reserved its top "AA" award for the leading "personal" producer.

What made Northwestern's endowment contracts so attractive was the firm's ability to offer higher guarantees than its competitors, an ability that rested on the familiar trinity of mortality, expenses, and investment income. The company was invariably a leader in all three categories, but it received very little help from the investment side in the 1940s. As agents and employees went off to war, so did Northwestern's assets. America's

military effort was financed by a series of mammoth federal bond issues, and every corporation and citizen was expected to subscribe. Northwestern's U.S. bond holdings soared from $120 million in 1940 (9 percent of assets) to $594 million in 1945 (31 percent). The bonds were unquestionably safe, but their returns were something less than stellar—generally only 2.5 percent. With other outlets for private funds scarce or nonexistent, Northwestern's net return on invested assets sank to a new low of 3.33 percent in 1945. "The interest factor has ceased to be the important factor that it was in the determination of net cost," Michael Cleary lamented at the beginning of the war, and he called 1945's results "disgustingly and discouragingly low." Northwestern was ultimately forced to change some of its operating assumptions—a result of improved public health as well as flagging investment returns. In 1946, after prolonged discussion, the company adopted a new standard mortality table and dropped its reserve rate from 3 percent—where it had rested since 1899—to 2 percent. The result was higher premiums that caused a flurry of buying activity before the changes went into effect.

The "investment problem," as Edmund Fitzgerald called it, paled to insignificance in the light of America's continuing military struggle. That struggle finally ended with the

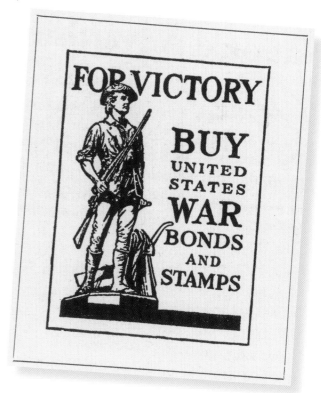

… and its investments were heavily weighted toward war bonds.

results were so promising that in 1947 the refresher courses became the Career School, a Northwestern institution that would give thousands of agents their grounding in the business. The first general postwar reunion took place in July 1946, when the agents convened for their annual meeting after a break of five long years. Nearly 2,000 people—a new record—crammed Milwaukee's Riverside Theater for the opening session. As patriotic music swelled in the background, the curtains opened to reveal a living tableau of the flag-raising on Iwo Jima. "Let us look forward," a narrator intoned. "Before us is the promise of peace. Before us is the vision of plenty. Strong of heart and earnest of mind let us dedicate ourselves to the work that lies before us." The spirit of dedication was much in evidence at the 1946 meeting, but the spirit of play, suppressed for so many years, was just as apparent. The post-session nightlife at the hotels was unusually lively, and a pair of New Jersey agents circulated a poem that was decidedly irreverent:

> *Now I lay me down to snore,*
> *Insured for several thousand more;*
> *If I should die before I wake,*
> *My wife would get her first real break.*

Michael Cleary shared in the general spirit of celebration, but he addressed a larger issue. The entire industry, Cleary said, had shown a resilience that warranted the public's enduring trust:

A jubilant crowd converged on downtown Milwaukee to celebrate victory over Japan, Aug. 14, 1945.

Allied victory over Japan on August 14, 1945. V-J Day brought fifteen years of depression and war to a close, and the entire nation reacted with a shout of joy and a sigh of relief. Northwestern Mutual wasted no time getting back to normal. In November 1944, nearly nine months *before* the Japanese surrender, the company had offered its first week-long "refresher course" for agents returning from service. Other sessions followed, and the

We can say with proper modesty that life insurance is one financial institution that has demonstrated its ability to weather the strains and stresses of peace and war, good times and bad. I know of no strain short of national collapse that it has not been subjected to in the last three decades....

And so I look to the future with sincere pride in what life insurance has done and with complete confidence in what it will continue to do for the men, women and children of America and for America itself.

Those were the last words Cleary ever spoke to a general assembly of Northwestern agents. The strains and stresses had taken their toll on his health as well as the industry's, and on February 22, 1947, the president died of a heart attack at his East Side home. Cleary had spent nearly half of his seventy years at the home office, much of it in the president's suite during a period of unprecedented volatility. From hard times through wartime, he had led Northwestern with energy, warmth, and a profound grasp of the firm's larger mission. "We believe our Company has something that we may call a soul," said agent Herman Duval in his eulogy, "and we believe also that whatever this is there will never be a more complete or a truer expression of it than was found in the person and character of Mr. Cleary." Grant Hill paid a simpler tribute to the man who had brought him to Northwestern: "Because of Mr. Cleary, ours is a more human life insurance company."

Edmund Fitzgerald addressed the agents at their first postwar meeting in 1946.

A refresher course for returning agents in 1944 quickly evolved into Northwestern's Career School.

The central themes of the Cleary years echoed through the entire 1908-1947 period: tumult, testing, and tradition triumphant. American society underwent a transformation in the first half of the twentieth century, becoming more urban, more secular, and more oriented to the concerns of the masses. Those broad social changes, overlain by two world wars and a cataclysmic depression, created pressures that washed away old expectations and raised up new ones. The general drift of the insurance industry, diverted though it may have been by depression and war, was toward more products sold in more markets to generate more volume. Northwestern absorbed the expansive spirit of the times, but never to the point of abandoning its moral core. Demonstrating "the courage to say 'No,'" the company adhered to a standard of order handed down from the nineteenth century. George Markham, William Van Dyke, and Michael Cleary repeatedly invoked the name and example of Henry L. Palmer. It was Palmer, all three said in various ways, who had infused Northwestern with its "vital personality" and its "distinct character"—its corporate culture, in more contemporary terms. That culture's underlying principles were trusteeship and mutuality, and its visible hallmarks were competitive excellence, simplicity of operations, and low net cost.

Other companies might broaden and diversify, but tradition demanded that Northwestern follow the faith of its fathers. As a result, the company became a specialist in whole life insurance sold on the lives of individuals—a specialist not so much because it chose to be, but because its competitors chose *not* to. As the gap between Northwestern Mutual and the rest of the field widened, every president of the period celebrated that growing difference and pledged to preserve it. In 1920, when he was a newly minted vice-president, Michael Cleary articulated his vision of the proper, indeed the only, path to follow:

If we, who are charged with the present conduct of the affairs of The Northwestern Mutual Life Insurance Company, and our successors in the office and the field, will remain true to the policy of these courageous men of the past there need be no fear. All will be well with the Company.

Although Northwestern set its course by a definite moral compass, principles can never be separated from performance. The company's convictions, however deeply held or eloquently expressed, were constantly tested in the hurly-burly of the marketplace. The inevitable conclusion, year in and year out, was that they gave Northwestern a competitive edge. More than one insider observed that Northwestern's commitment to excellence—a corollary of its belief in trusteeship—had produced an organism resembling a circle. Described at various times as a "virtuous circle" and a "circle of effects," it was portrayed most memorably by Elgin Fassel as a "circle of success." Fassel, who succeeded Percy Evans as head actuary in 1945, described the circle in operation:

1) The management of the Northwestern knows that superior agents write high grade policyholders.
2) Such policyholders buy their insurance in substantial amounts, giving a high average policy and reducing unit expense costs.
3) They appreciate what they buy and hold on to it, producing low lapse rates and high renewal commissions.
4) They are intelligent enough to value and preserve their health, yielding low mortality.
5) It follows that such business will show the highest profits. High dividends please the policyholder, leading to substantial repeat business, and the circle is gone around again. Pleased policyholders, pleased agency force, pleased management.

It is no accident that the Northwestern has the lowest insurance costs and at the same time is recognized as having the finest field force in the business. Our Company planned it that way.

The circle of success was forged during Henry Palmer's administration. In the forty years following his retirement, under three presidents of widely disparate gifts and outlooks, the circle remained unbroken. 🙟

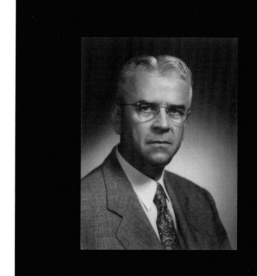

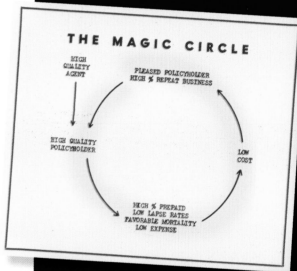

Chief actuary Elgin Fassel visualized the Northwestern Mutual system as a "magic circle" or "circle of success," with agents providing the initial energy.

"A DISTINCTIVE QUALITY OF INDEPENDENCE"

It was a brave new world that greeted Northwestern Mutual after World War II. Some highly placed pessimists predicted that the United States would slip back into depression without the artificial stimulus of war, but just the opposite occurred: peacetime released pent-up social pressures that pushed the American economy to the highest point in its history. The birth rate began to soar nine months after V-J Day—the leading edge of a baby boom that sparked a succession of other booms, including an explosion in the demand for life insurance. New families, new homes, and new cars meant that Americans had more to protect than ever before; full employment and higher incomes gave them more money to pay for that protection. The nation's insurance in force increased 150 percent in the first postwar decade, rising from $155.7 billion in 1945 to $389.1 billion in 1955. But some old patterns persisted in this new environment. Market shifts first apparent in the early 1900s became prevailing trends at mid-century, and the most obvious was diversification. Postwar prosperity encouraged the development of more companies selling more products through a greater variety of channels than ever before.

Northwestern Mutual rose on the same tide that lifted every other insurance firm but, true to form, the company declined to follow the fleet. Three presidents—Edmund Fitzgerald, Donald Slichter, and Robert Dineen—took the wheel during one of the most expansive twenty-year periods in American history. They presided over some revolutionary changes, but all three had the same central concern: holding a steady course through the shifting currents of postwar America.

The Industry's Aristocrat

If Michael Cleary's 1932 election was a surprise, his successor's was not. After fourteen years at Cleary's right hand, Edmund Fitzgerald was the obvious choice for president, and the board made it official on April 23, 1947. Fitzgerald was in some ways a throwback to the executives of the nineteenth century: patrician, Presbyterian, and a pillar of Milwaukee society. His grandfather and all six great-uncles had captained ships that sailed the Great Lakes, and a drydock firm owned by his grandfather and then his father had lifted his family into the local elite. A 1916 Phi Beta Kappa graduate of Yale, Fitzgerald was working as a banker when Cleary recruited him. Despite his silk-stocking background, the new president continued the informal tone set by his predecessor. A man of great style, Fitzgerald combined Ivy League poise with

a deft common touch. He had the requisite social graces to put everyone around him at ease, whether they were fellow executives or elevator operators. "I do try for a measure of relaxation and detachment," Fitzgerald said. "A laugh here and there, an occasional wisecrack or a bad pun can help a lot."

Edmund Fitzgerald was only fifty-three at the time of his election, making him the youngest man to head the company since John Van Dyke took office in 1869. Like kings or popes, Northwestern's presidents had typically served for life, or nearly so. Henry Palmer retired at eighty-eight, George Markham stepped down at seventy-five, William Van Dyke died in office at seventy-six, and Michael Cleary at seventy. That all changed when the board made one of the simplest but most sweeping decisions in its history: effective November 1, 1947, retirement was mandatory for all executive officers at age sixty-five. The move, which followed a national trend, ensured vigorous leadership and fresh viewpoints in the booming postwar economy: Northwestern Mutual would never again be a company governed by old men.

As the first president who knew when he would be leaving, Fitzgerald was freed to focus on the task at hand: directing Northwestern's response to the sweeping changes in the insurance industry. The return of prosperity fueled an astonishing proliferation of competitors. Between 1945 and 1957, the number of life companies in the United States soared from 473 to 1,273,

Edmund Fitzgerald, the polished patrician who led Northwestern Mutual during the post-World War II period

nearly all of them stock firms seeking to emulate the success of established giants like Northwestern. The industry diversified as fast as it grew. Life companies branched out into the health and accident fields, while property and casualty firms acquired life affiliates. A 1958 article in *Best's Review*, a leading trade journal, asked, "Will everybody be multiple-line?" Even the companies that still concentrated on life insurance broadened their offerings dramatically. Disability income policies came roaring back into favor, and accidental death clauses were enormously popular. Hundreds of firms offered "special" contracts with premium discounts for size, "classified" insurance on substandard risks, and "combination" plans that blended term and whole life coverage. But the greatest growth was in the field of group insurance. Fringe benefits were as much a part of the workplace as coffee breaks and mimeograph machines after World War II, and group term insurance was a standard component of the benefit package. In 1945, one-fourth of the nation's non-farm workers had group life coverage, and group sales accounted for 8 percent of the industry's new business. In 1957, half the labor force was covered, and group plans made up 22 percent of new sales.

The growth of group insurance had a dramatic impact on one of Northwestern's more recent specialties: pension trusts, those large bundles of individual endowment policies that employers used as fringe benefits.

Company officials from Fitzgerald on down had never been entirely comfortable with the business. It was too concentrated, too difficult to service individually, and too close to group coverage. Hoping to slow down the train, Northwestern raised its underwriting standards and limited the number of lives it would insure in new trusts. At the same time, the company faced an onslaught of competition from group specialists, who offered greater flexibility, lower costs, and dramatically lower agent commissions. As Northwestern stepped back and other firms stepped forward, the pension field's contribution to new premium dollars dropped from 30 percent in 1951 to 15 percent in 1958. Even the new sales were counterbalanced by surrenders of old policies, a trend that began soon after World War II and accelerated steadily. The biggest blow came in 1962, when the Chrysler Corporation, whose trust had swelled to 21,000 policies, decided to surrender every one of them; Northwestern's payout totaled $39,695,502. Agents continued to sell to new trusts, primarily in small firms, but the company straddled a rather uncomfortable middle ground, neither in nor out of the pension field.

A change-making machine used in the company's credit union

In speech after speech, Edmund Fitzgerald honed an image of Northwestern Mutual as the aristocrat of the life insurance industry.

The growth of group insurance and the proliferation of other products posed a direct threat to Northwestern's competitive position, but the company was not about to join the crowd. "In all our actions," Fitzgerald reminded the agents in 1947, "we have sought to maintain and have maintained a distinctive quality of independence." That independence, he continued, gave the firm its identity in the marketplace: "In our emphasis upon medically qualified ordinary business, we have made ourselves specialists in that field." Such was the Northwestern tradition, and so it remained under Edmund Fitzgerald. The president's stance was rooted in a combination of money and morals. Nothing was more important to Fitzgerald than the low net cost of his company's insurance. That was Northwestern's "all time number one consideration," he said, and it became practically an obsession after World War II. With investment returns sinking to their historic low of 3.01 percent in 1947, the company couldn't count on bond and mortgage yields to sustain the

dividend rate that made it a net-cost leader. Fitzgerald looked instead to expenses, and departmental budgets and staffing requests came under unprecedented scrutiny. Managers explored every possible way to do their work faster, better, and cheaper—a search that led Northwestern directly into the computer age. Even executive compensation was affected. As salaries elsewhere soared in the postwar boom, Fitzgerald held the line. Independently wealthy, he never earned more than $60,000 himself, creating a logjam at the top of the company. In such a cost-conscious environment, expensive growth initiatives received a cool response, whether they involved new products, new territories, or new agents. Looking back in 1957, Fitzgerald said, "We believed seriously that the present policyholder who was the victim of controlled and lower interest rates ... should not at the same time be assessed the cost of an expansion of sales activity."

Although Northwestern's refusal to follow the pack was at root a financial decision, Edmund Fitzgerald gave it a powerful moral dimension as well. In speech after speech, interview after interview, he worked and reworked the image of Northwestern as the industry's aristocrat: well-bred, dignified, classically simple, devoted to quality without thought of compromise. The company, in his view, offered "a specialized service superlatively well," attracting "discerning persons" who wanted the "prestige" of a "rather unique enterprise." The aristocratic image reflected his own background as well as the company's, and Fitzgerald saw it as an antidote to the mass-produced sameness that threatened to engulf postwar American society. Addressing the agents in 1957, he restated the theme of individualism:

> *To me that sentiment understates the response which you will continue to receive when you make that person aware that you bring not a bag of samples, not a suit of clothes on the rack, not a row of prefabricated houses, but a perception of things he is seeking in his own life . . . something of value.*

Larger companies with more complex product lines generally trumpeted their size and variety, in effect making a virtue of necessity. Fitzgerald, by contrast, made a necessity of virtue: never on his watch would Northwestern abandon the specialist's faith. But the president's impassioned defense of his company's narrow role did not imply a return to the nineteenth century. Like Michael Cleary before him, Fitzgerald endorsed a number of changes that reflected competitive realities. In 1956, the maximum policy size was raised to $600,000 and the minimum insurable age was lowered to one month. Premium rates were pegged to policy size in the same year. Since administrative costs were generally the same regardless of size, Northwestern

decided that it was only mutual to lower rates on policies that contributed more to surplus. It was no accident that the new system helped agents meet the competitive threat of "special" contracts.

Perhaps the most radical departure from past practice involved substandard risks. Ever since its birth on the Wisconsin frontier, Northwestern had considered itself a company of the elite: healthy individuals whose superior mortality generated healthy dividends. Applicants who couldn't meet the firm's strict underwriting standards were forced to go elsewhere. There was no sound actuarial reason to deny them coverage—higher premiums could compensate for higher mortality— and the prevailing policy meant the loss of millions in new business every year. In 1956, Northwestern became the very last of the top 100 firms to insure substandard risks, and they quickly accounted for 9 percent of new business. The company was also among the last to insure residents of the Deep South. The region began to truly rise again after World War II, and dramatic improvements in public health persuaded Northwestern to re-enter Alabama in 1950, South Carolina in 1952, and Florida and Texas in 1957—all after an absence of at least fifty years.

Covering the baby boom: Northwestern lowered its minimum insurable age to one month in 1956.

NORTHWESTERN MUTUAL LIFE INSURANCE CO.

The company's Career School became an industry legend under the ever-vigilant leadership of Harold "The Colonel" Gardiner.

Every liberalization and modernization of the Fitzgerald years came in response to the persistent prodding of the agents. Their numbers actually declined after the war, falling from 4,054 in 1947 to 3,883 in 1957, both full- and part-time. Although their ranks were thinner—the result of Grant Hill's high standards and Edmund Fitzgerald's reluctance to invest in expansion—the ratio of full-time agents in the field force rose from 50 to 63 percent during the same years, and they were perhaps the best-trained in the industry. In the first decade after World War II, an agent could move from the compulsory short course through the thirteen-week reporting program, then "graduate" to Career School and a variety of intermediate and advanced courses. The training effort developed under the watchful eye of Harold Gardiner, Northwestern's director of education for more than twenty years. Known as "the Colonel" for his wartime Army rank, Gardiner ran the programs with military precision and a scrupulous sense of decorum. If agents attending the Career School told off-color jokes or used profane language in his presence, the Colonel was known to send them home.

Extensive training produced an exemplary field force. By 1956, 15 percent of Northwestern's full-time agents were CLUs, compared with 3 percent for the industry as a whole; and nearly a third had earned the Quality Award (which recognized superior persistency rates), compared with fewer than 6 percent of the nation's career agents. Northwestern continued to have more life members of the Million Dollar Round Table (agents selling at least $1 million of insurance for three consecutive years) than any of its competitors. The growing professionalism of the field force had a profound impact on the company's policyowner base. It has often been observed that agents "write to their level." In the early years of the century, farmers had been the largest class of Northwestern insureds, but the long-term trend was toward occupations associated with higher incomes and college degrees. In 1951, 55 percent of Northwestern's policyowners were professionals, managers, or self-employed persons (the U.S. average was 18 percent); 55 percent earned at least $5,000 a year (vs. 17 percent); and 56 percent were insured for at least $10,000 (vs. 18 percent).

A new advertising campaign reflected and reinforced the upscale trends. Beginning in 1948, the *Saturday Evening Post, Time, Newsweek*, and other national magazines ran full-page ads featuring photographs of prominent Northwestern clients by the renowned Yousuf Karsh of Ottawa, Ontario. Practically every subject was an executive or a professional, and each portrait appeared alongside a testimonial to the central importance of life insurance. The campaign had a powerful appeal to the upwardly mobile prospects who were swelling the ranks of the middle class.

Northwestern's agents were well-positioned to catch the rising stars of postwar American society, and the result, despite their reduced numbers, was a dramatic increase in sales per agent. Even though the field force shrank 4 percent between 1947 and 1957, the company's new business increased 60 percent, rising from $466.2 million to $748 million. With the death of Dr. Charles Albright in 1946, Northwestern would never again have a sales leader who towered over all the rest, but there were certainly standouts. Alfred Ostheimer of Philadelphia led the field for five consecutive years after the war. Between 1941, his first year

Portraits of policyowners by celebrity photographer Yousuf Karsh were the mainstay of Northwestern's advertising campaign from 1948 to 1969. Karsh's subjects included Catherine Cleary (far left), an attorney, banker, and company trustee who was also Michael Cleary's daughter.

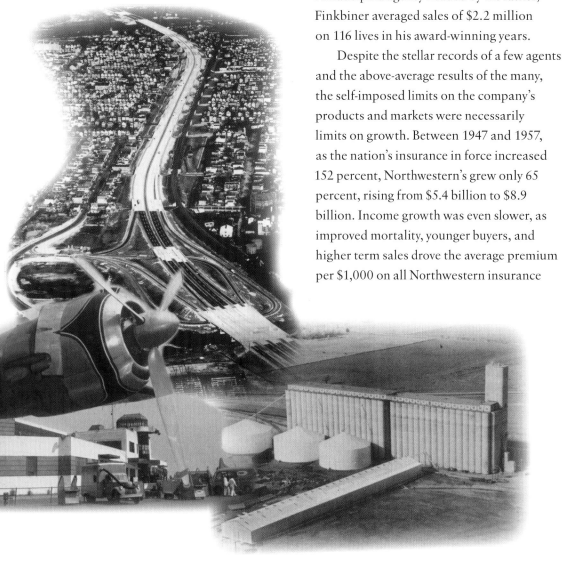

with Northwestern, and 1952, Ostheimer averaged sales of $3.9 million on 1,393 lives annually. His cumulative volume was nearly twice that of the second-ranked agent, but Ostheimer was a pension trust specialist. Far more typical was Aaron Finkbiner, Jr., the volume leader (pension business excluded) in 1954 and 1956. Working out of the Philadelphia agency headed by his father, Finkbiner averaged sales of $2.2 million on 116 lives in his award-winning years.

Despite the stellar records of a few agents and the above-average results of the many, the self-imposed limits on the company's products and markets were necessarily limits on growth. Between 1947 and 1957, as the nation's insurance in force increased 152 percent, Northwestern's grew only 65 percent, rising from $5.4 billion to $8.9 billion. Income growth was even slower, as improved mortality, younger buyers, and higher term sales drove the average premium per $1,000 on all Northwestern insurance

policies from $40.36 in 1947 to $26.52 in 1957. The industry-wide trend required agents to sell more insurance simply to stay even. Almost inevitably, the company slipped a notch in the rankings, falling from eighth place by insurance in force in 1947 to ninth in 1957. Edmund Fitzgerald was not unduly concerned. The salient phrase from the Executive Committee statement of 1888— "less to be large than to be safe"—continued to ring in the ears of every Northwestern executive, and growth was by no means their primary consideration. "Ours is a business of service to and for others," Fitzgerald reminded the agents, "with the interests of the policyholders always controlling."

Growth on the investment side was another matter entirely. Northwestern had traditionally counted on solid returns to maintain its net-cost superiority, and Fitzgerald's tenure began in a trough. Not only did yields dip to 3.01 percent in 1947, but scores of corporate borrowers were paying off their old bonds and issuing new debt at the rock-bottom interest rates prevailing. In 1957, Edmund Fitzgerald recalled his exasperation at the events of the Forties: "A lot of fine investments with good rates were called and refunded and paid out, and all we could do was to loan the Government the money at 2.5 percent." It would be an understatement to say that things improved in the first postwar decade. By 1953, even though other companies were growing even faster, Northwestern's agents were bringing in $1 million in new premium revenue every day. The company's assets rose from $2.16 billion in 1947 to $3.73 billion in 1957—an increase of 73 percent—and the soaring economy provided a wealth of investment opportunities. The result was a complete restructuring of Northwestern's investment portfolio. Bonds dropped from 82.6 percent of the company's assets in 1947 to 56.6 percent in 1957, while mortgages rose from 8.9 percent to 32.9 percent.

The most dramatic changes took place within the firm's bond account. As the war emergency became a memory, U.S. government obligations plunged from 36.2 percent of Northwestern's assets to a mere 4.7 percent in the decade after 1947. Industrial and utility bonds took up nearly all the slack. Policyowner dollars financed cement plants and college dormitories, toll roads and airplanes, grain elevators and nuclear power plants, but Northwestern purchased relatively few bonds on the open market. Don Slichter, who became vice-president of the Bond Department in 1949, negotiated directly with borrowers—a practice he had pioneered in the 1930s. Direct placement offered higher returns, stiffer prepayment penalties, and the right to purchase stock in the borrowing enterprise. By 1957, direct placements accounted for 64 percent of Northwestern's utility bonds and 91 percent of its industrial securities.

On the mortgage side, residential loans became the centerpiece of the portfolio, a place once held by farm lending. Howard Tobin, the high-spirited Chicago Irishman who took over the Mortgage Department in 1945, followed the American people to the suburbs. Between 1945 and 1960, Northwestern financed the construction of 120,030 single-family homes and 840 apartment buildings—enough to house all the residents of a major city. Residential loans jumped from roughly 1 percent of the company's assets to 18 percent during the same period. To complement the houses, city loan managers financed suburban amenities like shopping centers and medical clinics.

Under Tobin and Slichter, Northwestern's investment side was a good deal more aggressive than its insurance side. The results were modest by contemporary standards— Edmund Fitzgerald found a 4.13-percent industrial loan worth bragging about in 1952—but any upward movement was like manna from heaven after the depressed

... to supermarkets and shopping centers throughout the country.

Help at the top: Edmund Fitzgerald welcomed Robert Dineen as his insurance vice-president in 1950.

returns of the 1930s and '40s. Northwestern's net rate of return rose from 3.01 percent in 1947 to 3.9 percent in 1957—one of the highest yields in the industry. In 1953, for the first time since 1925, Northwestern raised its dividend rate, a regular occurrence for the next thirty years.

Edmund Fitzgerald gave Tobin, Slichter, and the rest of his executive staff a good deal of latitude—an approach somewhat different from Michael Cleary's. Fitzgerald believed in Northwestern's labyrinthine committee system as a way to build long-term perspective into every corporate policy. "The ultimate results of many of our present decisions," he said in 1948, "will not, cannot be observed until long after many of us here present are gone." But the president also chafed at the system's enormous time requirements. "At times I wonder," he groused to the eastern agents in 1953, "if some of us in Milwaukee have time for anything but committee meetings." The result was a concerted effort to push authority farther down the organizational pyramid. Michael Cleary had thirteen executives reporting to him at the time of his death. By 1953, Fitzgerald had only five. Four of them were, like the president himself, recruits of

the Cleary era: Grant Hill (agencies), Donald Slichter (bonds), Howard Tobin (mortgages), and Philip Robinson (operations). The fifth was a newcomer: Robert Dineen. During a lengthy convalescence after surgery for a detached retina in 1949, Fitzgerald realized that he needed help at the top. A careful search led to Dineen, New York State's insurance superintendent at the time. The head of the New York department has traditionally been first among equals in the nation: recruiting Robert Dineen was a mark of Northwestern's stature in the industry. The New Yorker moved west in 1950 as the company's insurance vice-president, and Edmund Fitzgerald's workload was soon significantly lighter.

Hiring executive talent was in some ways easier than finding clerical help. The "baby bust" of the 1930s was apparent in the shrunken labor market of the 1950s, and Northwestern was growing far too rapidly to get by with the workers on hand. "Like all employers," said Edmund Fitzgerald in 1952, "we are shorthanded and could use about 10 percent more people." Despite Fitzgerald's continuing emphasis on economy, the number of home office employees rose from 1,369 in 1947 to 1,659 in 1957—a 21-percent increase that was still well behind the firm's 65-percent gain in insurance in force. New employees found themselves in a somewhat paradoxical workplace. On the one hand, Northwestern Mutual was a highly regimented institution with well-developed protocols and procedures. Supervisors still passed the peas and pork chops to their charges every lunch hour—"like first sergeants eating with their troops," as one officer put it. Coffee and tobacco were strictly forbidden, and there was a thriving black market in everything from candy bars to smoked fish. But Northwestern also shared fully in the wave of "togetherness" that swept the nation after World War II. Home office employees established a recreation committee in 1946, the Sportsman's Club in 1948, the Women's Association in 1952 (inexplicably renamed the "Girls' Club" two years later), a stamp club in 1954, and a toastmaster's club in 1956. There were fashion shows, chorus concerts, athletic contests, and art exhibits. The postwar issues of *Pillar*, a home office magazine introduced in 1941, featured photographs of babies, weddings, family Christmas celebrations, and summer vacations. In 1952, Northwestern even established the Dunworkin Den, a first-floor lounge for retired employees. There was an earnest innocence afoot, and it helped make the "home office family" more than a figure of speech.

Employees and agents alike paused to mark a major milestone in 1957: the centennial of Northwestern's incorporation. Events ranged from an open house that drew nearly 7,000 people (including—a sign of the times—more than 600 children) to

America's postwar penchant for "togetherness" was reflected in home office activities that ranged from "Girls' Clubs" to employee choruses.

The Northwestern Mutual
presents
"Shadow of a Giant"
...aukee
...torium
...y
...-22

MON. EVE. **9:00 p.m.**
July 22, 1957

Milwaukee Auditorium

July 22, 19...

Milwaukee Auditorium

Northwestern paused in 1957 to celebrate its centennial with an elaborate stage show,
Shadow of a Giant, *that spotlighted home-office talent.*

Shadow of a Giant, a musical extravaganza that allowed more than 150 home office employees to display their acting, singing, and dancing skills. The show never made it to Broadway, but audiences left the Milwaukee Auditorium humming songs like *The Happy Widow with $5,000 (Bless the Insurance Man)*. Throughout the year, Northwestern's hidebound commitment to tradition surfaced in ways both large and small. When the Centennial Committee suggested steam-cleaning the home office exterior to wash away more than forty years of grime, the Executive Committee vetoed the idea, explaining that its members "preferred the present patina."

The centennial was a major event, but 1957 was significant for another reason: Edmund Fitzgerald announced his decision to step down, effective in April 1958, to make way for new leadership. In his eleven years at the helm, Fitzgerald rebuilt extensively, expanded selectively and, through it all, maintained the utmost fidelity to tradition. In a climate of rapid growth and general change, he continued his company's progress against the current, and Northwestern Mutual remained the industry's aristocrat. At the eastern agents' meeting in January 1958, Fitzgerald ended his last major speech as president on a familiar note:

> *We are not going to dilute The North-western's effort by trying to be all things to all men. We are going to continue to be THE company—if it means being the only one of its kind—where skillful and well-informed agents provide sound and serviceable life insurance at low cost to individuals who will need and under-stand that kind of relationship, that kind of economy and that kind of service. The others will diversify as they wish. But when ordinary life insurance is thought of Northwestern will be THE competition. What we need to do is not more things, but more of the things we are doing.*

The Scholar and the Lawyer

When Edmund Fitzgerald stepped down from the presidency in 1958, he actually stepped up to a newly created position: chairman of the board. Two of his lieutenants—a scholar and a lawyer—succeeded him in the company's top job: Donald Slichter from 1958 until 1965, and Robert Dineen from 1965 to 1968. Both men had dual titles—president and chief executive officer—and both stayed until mandatory retirement at sixty-five. Fitzgerald remained a frequent visitor to the home office, serving as board chairman until 1960 and a trustee until 1969, but he was in no sense a power behind the throne. He scrupulously avoided interfering with either Slichter or Dineen and rarely gave unsolicited advice. Like every good role model, Fitzgerald led by example rather than explicit instruction.

Donald Slichter's election marked a return to an old Northwestern tradition: picking a president from the investment side of the company. He had served with distinction as head of the Bond Department, but Slichter clearly had the intellectual capacity to handle even larger responsibilities. He was practically raised on the University of Wisconsin campus, the son of a mathematics professor who

First Donald Slichter (right) *and then Robert Dineen continued Northwestern's modest momentum between 1958 and 1968.*

Donald Slichter was a scholarly figure who rose to prominence on the investment side of the company ...

became dean of the graduate school in Madison. "His whole character is touched by the atmosphere of the university," said Edmund Fitzgerald. Although he was trained as a chemical engineer, Slichter is best remembered as a scholar: thoughtful, temperate, a careful researcher, a man with catholic curiosities and an interest in long-range issues. He described himself as "not much of a joiner" and "that great twentieth-century oddity—a non-golfer," but Slichter was by no means an ascetic intellectual. Although he was not an extrovert in the Cleary or Fitzgerald molds, the new president had an instinctive human touch that won him a wide circle of friends.

That touch reached its fullest development during his years as CEO. No one was surprised to hear Slichter, the veteran investor, praise life insurance time and again as "the best all-around savings medium there is," but some insiders were shocked by the intensity of his interest in the field force. Slichter and his wife, Dickie, put on tens of thousands of miles each year, attending every regional meeting and hopscotching from one general agency to the next. A good listener, Slichter saw himself as "a safety valve" for disaffected agents, but many veterans welcomed his visits as a tangible expression of management concern. "It was my particular obligation," Slichter said in retirement, "to see that there was very high morale in the field, and that would . . . assist and almost assure morale in the home office."

There was an Eisenhower quality to Slichter's administration. Although he didn't play golf, this scholarly figure managed Northwestern with a benign competence that reminded some observers of the late general. He was certainly capable of making decisions, but Slichter's approach was calm, even-handed, more deliberate than dynamic. The tone changed significantly when Robert Dineen took charge in 1965. Dineen was much closer to Harry Truman than Dwight Eisenhower in personal style. Plain-spoken, hard-working, and never one to walk away from a good fight, he soon became the most controversial Northwestern president since George Markham. Dineen was, by both instinct and training, a lawyer. The son of a Syracuse building contractor, he practiced insurance law in upstate New York until Gov. Thomas Dewey called him to Albany as insurance superintendent in 1943. Dineen's lawyerly instincts survived the move to Northwestern in 1950, but his courtroom became the company's committee system. Regardless of the issue, Dineen expected closely reasoned arguments from all sides, and he encouraged active, even heated, debate. When he reached a decision, he fought for his viewpoint as tenaciously as if he were representing a client. The president's approach was entirely natural, but it required some adjustments on the part of his associates, particularly Northwestern's agents. Whatever feelings he aroused, Dineen's style had one beneficial effect, in Edmund Fitzgerald's opinion: "He stirred us up."

Despite major differences in the backgrounds and temperaments of the three postwar presidents, the transitions from Fitzgerald to Slichter and Slichter to Dineen were virtually seamless. The broad economic conditions were the same for all: runaway prosperity, mild inflation, and a burgeoning middle class. The competitive environment was the same as well: more companies, more insurance, and continued diversification. The industry's annual sales crossed the $100 billion threshold in 1964, and its insurance in force exceeded $1 trillion in 1967—more than double the 1958 figure. Group coverage remained the fastest-growing segment of the industry, rising from 29 percent of the nation's insurance in force in 1958 to 36 percent in 1967. But the greatest similarity among the presidents was the perspective they shared. Like the leaders who preceded him, Edmund Fitzgerald had made fiscal conservatism and simplicity of operation Northwestern's cardinal rules. Neither Slichter nor Dineen felt the slightest need to tamper with those rules, and neither had the time in office or the inclination to erect monuments to himself. (Dineen's tenure was the shortest since 1869, when Lester Sexton died after two months at the helm.) Their central goal was to keep Northwestern on an even keel, and the result was the same blend of stable growth and selective change that had characterized Northwestern Mutual since the days of Henry Palmer.

The 1958-1967 years may have been "a period of relative calm," as Don Slichter put it, but there was still plenty of room for change. The period's biggest event, in fact, was nothing short of revolutionary: the coming of the computer. In one decade, Northwestern went through two presidents and three generations of computers. Few industries were better positioned to take advantage of the new machines than life insurance; every major company generated an enormous volume of nearly identical files that required frequent revision—work better handled electronically than manually. Northwestern had long been quick to embrace the latest labor-saving technologies, from Addressograph machines in 1917 to a home-grown microfilm system (designed by actuary Elgin Fassel) in 1939, but computers represented a different order of magnitude. Northwestern got in on the ground floor and grew with the industry. The company was not the first to computerize but, in the breadth and depth of its operations, Northwestern Mutual was a genuine pioneer.

Computers entered the business world in January 1954, when General Electric installed a UNIVAC I in its Louisville appliance factory. Just two months later, a pair of Northwestern actuaries, Charles Groeschell and William McCarter, attended a one-week "executive course" put on by UNIVAC's chief rival, IBM, at the company's Poughkeepsie headquarters. Both men came back aglow with enthusiasm for the new machines, and

… while Robert Dineen was a lawyer who relished the give and take of well-reasoned argument.

The Electronics Committee worked diligently to bring Northwestern into the Computer Age. Its members included Lew Nagel (left) and Will Reimer.

they found a receptive audience in Edmund Fitzgerald. Still obsessed with maintaining net-cost superiority, Fitzgerald was quick to see that computers had enormous potential to cut operating expenses. Within a week, he had appointed an Electronics Committee and instructed its members to bring Northwestern into the Computer Age with all due speed.

A handful of insurance companies had installed the machines, but they were generally little more than glorified calculators, handling computations for individual departments. Northwestern's working group gravitated quickly to an integrated approach. They designed a system that cut across departmental lines and acted as a backbone for the entire company's operations.

At the heart of their approach was the daily cycle. Most companies planned to process their premium bills, dividend payments, and other transactions on a monthly basis, with separate runs for each type of data. In the daily cycle, the computer passed through the entire file of policies every day, extracting those that required attention. In effect, a new master file was created every twenty-four hours. The daily cycle provided faster turnaround times and greater flexibility than any system in use or on the drawing board. What made it possible was the simplicity that had been a Northwestern hallmark since the days of Henry Palmer. With relatively few products and relatively few special cases, a job that would have been a nightmare in

The future arrived on Dec. 26, 1957, when the company took delivery of an IBM 705 computer—the first purchased by any business in America.

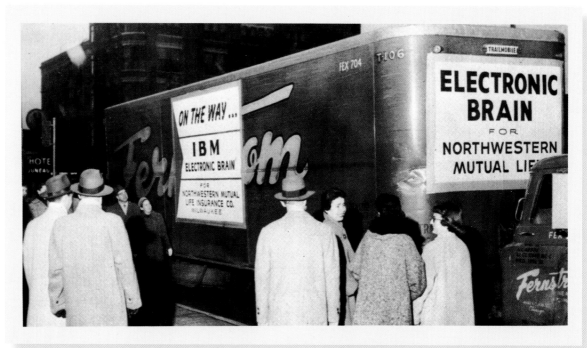

other companies could be accomplished with relative ease. Once again, fidelity to tradition gave Northwestern a competitive edge.

The next task was the selection of equipment. After months of study, the company settled on an IBM 705, and on December 26, 1957—almost in time for Christmas—a semi-trailer pulled up to the home office with "Electronic Brain" signs identifying its cargo. The computer had arrived ahead of schedule, and it took until spring for work crews to prepare its new home on the northeast corner of the second floor. Northwestern had decided to buy rather than lease, thus becoming the first business in the country to own a mainframe IBM. Foreshadowing later developments, the price of the machine dropped from $1.9 million to $1.6 million between the date it was ordered and the date it arrived. Donald Slichter became Northwestern's CEO just after the computer was installed, and one of his first acts was to sign the check. With a single purchase, he spent more on office equipment than Edmund Fitzgerald had during his entire presidency.

Northwestern took pains to ease both its employees and its agents into the new era as gently as possible. Even before they had ordered the computer, company officials appeared before home-office assemblies and agent gatherings to explain how "electronic data processing"—the original term for information systems—fit into the company's

future. Two pledges were made: no one would lose a job to automation, and nearly all hiring for new jobs would be done from within. More than 300 employees took an aptitude test for the first programming class in 1957, and the computer managers chose twenty. For those who didn't know a binary digit from a bin of oats, Northwestern made further efforts to humanize the machine. Company publicists dropped the intimidating "giant brain" imagery in favor of nicknames like "Eddie EDP" or "Ed Process." Policyowners received a brochure with a cartoon that showed a smiling console reading a policy while its four arms wrote, typed, and filed. When the 705 was delivered, the IBM salesman presented Northwestern with an abacus "just in case."

Then the real work began: conversion of the company's routine operations from a manual basis to computers. It was an arduous process, involving millions of file cards and miles of magnetic tape. Most of 1958 was absorbed in writing programs, training programmers, and preparing the systems for the task ahead. The Marquette, Michigan, general agency was chosen as the pilot because of its small size (9,000 policies). Conversion

A scale model of the IBM 705

The new machine and its operators took up residence in a reconfigured section of the second floor.

of its records was completed in June 1959. Ninety-five general agencies remained, but Northwestern's data processing managers were confident that they could convert one agency every week. As complications developed, the pace came much closer to one per month.

Equipment failure was the most aggravating complication. The 705's vacuum tubes generated enormous amounts of heat and, with prolonged use, their filaments grew brittle and burned out. By April 1960, "down time" accounted for 10 percent of the computer center's working hours. The problem wasn't solved until early 1962, when an IBM 7080 was purchased. The 7080 was a second-generation machine, built on a platform of transistors rather than tubes. The new computer was smaller than the 705, more reliable, and four times faster.

There was a gradual evolution in administrative structure as well as hardware. For the first seven years of its existence, Northwestern's data processing project had been managed by committees. Since virtually every department was affected, Fitzgerald and then Slichter had wanted to ensure the broadest possible input and the closest possible coordination. As conversion progressed, however, the computer center assumed a life of its own. In March 1961, Data Processing became a separate department under the direction of Wil Kraegel, an actuary who had been a member of the first working group in 1954.

Kraegel and his staff reached another milestone in 1962. On September 21, conversion of the ninety-sixth general agency was completed. After breathing a collective sigh of relief, the department added up its efforts. In a process that took more than three years, the Data Processing staff had placed 1.7 million policies on 15 miles of magnetic tape. Nearly 5.5 million punch cards had been used to translate the data, and the machines that punched the holes had generated 47 bushels of confetti.

Edmund Fitzgerald had envisioned the computer as a cost-cutting tool. Before conversion was complete, however, Northwestern began to explore the possibilities for improved service as well as reduced costs. With the artificial restrictions on data lifted, the computer experts constantly generated new ideas, almost like children experimenting with a marvelously complex toy. A phrase commonly heard in the Data Processing Department was, "If we can…, why don't we?" Premium collection was one of the first functions to be entrusted to the IBM, and computer-generated proposals followed. Each could be tailored to the age and financial needs of the prospect, saving agents a considerable amount of time. Electronic policy issue began in 1964, with the face sheet of each new policy prepared by machine. Five steps in the issue process were condensed to one, providing the client with a one-glance summary of his or her policy. Electronic pre-underwriting was launched as a

The IBM 7080, installed in 1962, was a second-generation computer that relied on transistors rather than vacuum tubes.

pilot project in 1966. The computer was given "authority" to screen applications and begin approval of the simplest ones, shortening the delays many agents typically experienced.

The most important demonstration of Northwestern's computer power was the Insurance Service Account (ISA), introduced in 1962. Monthly payments for everything from cars to telephone service were becoming the norm in America, but nearly two-thirds of Northwestern's clients still paid for their insurance on an annual basis. The company's procedure was less flexible than its competitors', and it was especially cumbersome for owners of multiple policies. Every policy was billed individually, requiring payments of different amounts at different times of the year. The Insurance Service Account solved both the competitive and the administrative problems. Every policy owned by a family or business was placed in a single account. Northwestern calculated the combined annual premium, and the owner added money to his or her account (usually on a monthly basis) to pay off the total amount. Robert Templin, who became head of the Agency Department in 1959, was soon hailing ISA as "the greatest selling tool ever invented," and executives of other insurance firms were openly envious. ISA was convenient, it was flexible, and it gave a feeling of psychological unity to a policyowner's insurance coverage. Above all, it enabled agents to use the "pennies a month" appeal. By adding a small amount to the monthly payment, or even by using dividends, a client could effortlessly add to his or her coverage. By 1964, 40 percent of Northwestern's new business was billed on Insurance Service Accounts.

A more subtle sign of the computer's influence was apparent in the company's language. Bits and bytes, mainframes and databases took their place alongside the mortality tables and reserve rates of tradition. Words like "dump" and "massage" took on entirely new meanings, and there was a steady increase in the use of acronyms. EDP was the first home office function identified by its initials, but by no means the last. Northwestern, like many other institutions, seemed to be in danger of drowning in alphabet soup. In 1964, at the request of bewildered agents, the company published an official *Glossary of Abbreviations*. Its ten pages and 250 listings provided relief for those who couldn't tell a BRAP from a HOLUA, and it enabled readers to speak in a kind of code. EDP, for instance, enabled NML's SAs to use ISA in their quest for the MDRT—all, of course, with the blessing of the CEO.

By the mid-1960s, data processing was an accepted fact of life at Northwestern, acronyms and all, and its influence continued to expand. Like a vigorous plant outgrowing its container, the company's computer operations had to be continually "re-potted." The effort had begun in 1957 with barely twenty employees. By 1966, there were more than 200, many of them newcomers to the company. In that year Northwestern accepted delivery of an IBM 360, a third-generation computer featuring silicon chips rather than transistors. Although new people and new systems caused some adjustment problems, it was clear that data processing had achieved the goal Edmund Fitzgerald set for it: cost control. Between 1958 and 1967, Northwestern's insurance in force rose from $9.3 billion to $15.5 billion, an increase of 67 percent. During the same period, thanks to the computer, the total number of home office employees rose from 1,661 to 1,775, an increase of only 7 percent.

But the computer was much more than a labor-saving device. It brought a new dimension to Northwestern's operations, enabling the company to do more things and to do them better, whether the goal was selling more insurance or planning for the future. Electronic data processing represented, in some ways, a clean break with the past, but it owed something to the leaders of the 1800s. The simplicity that had long been Northwestern's signature enabled the company to emerge from the conversion process with perhaps the most comprehensive and flexible system in the industry. The firm's willingness to "bite the bullet," to commit itself to a system that touched every corner of its operations, was clear evidence that Northwestern wanted to preserve its uncluttered tradition. The computer was, above all, a complex way to stay simple.

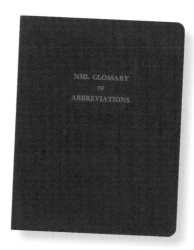

Acronyms multiplied so rapidly that Northwestern felt compelled to publish its own Glossary of Abbreviations *in 1964.*

Entering the digital age was the boldest development of the Slichter-Dineen years, but the company departed from tradition in other particulars. Perhaps the most radical innovation was the accidental death benefit, generally known as double indemnity. Despite constant pressure from the field, every president since William Van Dyke had refused to even discuss double indemnity, rejecting it as a gimmicky form of accident insurance. Victor Henningsen, who became chief actuary in 1953, wanted to take a fresh look at the question. Northwestern, he concluded, could easily charge more than enough to compensate for its increased exposure, particularly since claims were likely to be quite modest. (Accidents accounted for only 4.6 percent of all policyowner deaths in 1955.) Edmund Fitzgerald allowed Henningsen to explore the issue, but the president preferred that any change come after his departure. Northwestern's version of double indemnity debuted in 1959, and it was considerably more liberal than the competition's, with lower premiums and fewer exclusions. Before the year was out, nearly half of the company's new policyowners were choosing the accidental death benefit.

Another popular feature indicated Northwestern's interest in the nation's young adults, a group whose incomes were rising with the American economy. In 1963, the company offered a new rider that guaranteed a client's right to purchase additional $10,000

policies at six option dates (ages 25, 28, 31, 34, 37, and 40) and at marriage or the birth of a child. The additional purchase benefit was designed to meet the "guaranteed insurability option" offered by other companies. A final liberalization broadened Northwestern's geographic reach. The company re-entered Mississippi in 1959 (after an absence of eighty-seven years) and obtained its first Louisiana license in 1965, giving the firm a presence in all forty-eight contiguous states. (Hawaii was added in 1970, Alaska in 1979.)

Some of the product and policy developments of the 1958-1967 period symbolized at least a modest retreat from the company's devotion to select-risk, level-premium whole life insurance. At heart, however, Northwestern remained an aristocrat. Speaking to the eastern agents in 1965, Donald Slichter sounded like the Edmund Fitzgerald of a decade earlier: "While other companies have multiplied, expanded, and diversified, we have increasingly emphasized that we are a specialty company, serving the individual as an individual and not as a mere number in a large group entity." At the same meeting a year later, Robert Dineen gave a speech entitled "Progress with Principles," a ringing endorsement of Northwestern's traditions.

The company's attitude toward its marketplace might be described as cautious accommodation. Northwestern changed enough to avoid becoming a corporate antique but never went so far as to jeopardize its underlying culture. That go-slow attitude virtually guaranteed that there would be no breakthrough developments on the agency side of the business. The company's representatives continued to demonstrate a high level of professionalism, qualifying for the CLU designation and the Million Dollar Round Table in record numbers, but they did not demonstrate significant growth. Between 1958 and 1967, the number of full-time agents increased from 2,384 to 2,481—a gain of only 4 percent, despite a nonstop recruiting effort. Even though Northwestern retained twice as many of its new agents as the average firm, the rate of attrition in the industry was so high that the company's general agents had to recruit at least 500 people every year just to stay even. What did change was

the productivity of the average agent. The company's new business more than doubled between 1958 and 1967, and new premium income increased 70 percent—without a corresponding gain in the field force. As in the previous decade, the same number of agents were selling much more insurance.

Two agents virtually monopolized the period's production awards: John Todd and Hugh Thompson. Todd was a Chicago powerhouse who had joined Northwestern in 1931, served as a general agent during World War II, and then returned to the field with a vengeance in 1951. Working in the upper echelons of the Chicago area's business world, he led the field for four years with average sales of $6.4 million on 129 lives. Thompson represented the next generation. He joined the company in 1949 as a college student

John Todd (left) *and Hugh Thompson were the company's leading agents in the 1950s and '60s.*

Robert Templin guided Northwestern's agency system with skill and energy during the Slichter-Dineen years.

A college agent program was formally launched in 1967, giving the company a foothold in the rapidly growing baby-boomer market.

and developed rapidly under the tutelage of Deal Tompkins, a legendary district agent based in Charleston, West Virginia. Working in the Charleston area, Hugh Thompson was Northwestern's leading agent for four years between 1958 and 1967, averaging sales of $5.9 million on 169 lives. He and Todd were both enthusiastic teachers whose presentations and publications helped make thousands of agents better salespersons.

The person ultimately responsible for field performance was Robert Templin. A Marine during World War II and then a Northwestern agent in Fort Wayne, Indiana, he came to the home office in 1948 as an agency assistant and soon became Grant Hill's protégé. When Hill retired in 1959, after twenty-six years on the job, Templin was named his successor. A gifted organizer and an astute politician, he became one of the most influential field executives in the company's history. Bob Templin was not, however, an agent of dramatic change. He established new general agencies in the fastest-growing areas of the country, including Long Island and southern California, and reached out to the baby-boom generation with Northwestern's first formal college agent program in 1967, but the watchword of the Slichter-Dineen years was "steady as she goes." The company's growth rate was as regular as a heartbeat: its annual ratio of new business to existing coverage averaged 8.5 percent between 1958 and 1967, never straying more than a percentage point from that figure. The sale of new products counterbalanced the decline of old ones so effectively that ten-year projections made in the late 1950s proved uncannily accurate.

Beneath the apparent stability, change was brewing. The life insurance industry was beginning to experience a series of structural shifts that would ultimately affect every firm in the field. One of the earliest was a move away from exclusive agents. Seeking to minimize costs and maximize sales, even established firms started to sell their policies through brokers and independent agents. Some veteran field representatives found themselves competing with their own products, and there was growing speculation that career agents were a dying breed. Another threat arose, ironically, from the same economic prosperity that was lifting insurance sales to record heights. The life insurance market had long been a largely intramural affair, with every company selling more or less the same family of products. Postwar affluence gave the industry its first push into the big leagues of "financial services." The soaring stock market attracted legions of new investors, and mutual funds—their typical point of entry—multiplied like rabbits; the combined assets of the nation's mutual funds soared from $9.2 billion in 1958 to $53 billion in 1970. Life insurance agents found it hard to sell long-term protection to prospects focused on short-term gains, and dozens of insurance companies, hedging their bets, launched mutual funds of their own.

The shifting investment climate had a direct impact on Northwestern's product mix. "Buy term and invest the difference," urged a vocal cadre of investment gurus, and term sales rose from 24.5 percent of the company's new business in 1958 to 31.2 percent in 1967. Agents were disturbed because they considered term commissions a vow of poverty. An upward spike in policy loans caused even greater consternation in the home office. The 5-percent interest rate attached to most policies proved irresistible as bank rates climbed even higher. Some policyowners borrowed against their cash values to lower their effective premiums—a practice known as "minimum deposit" buying—while others put the money in alternative investments. In either case, policy loans climbed from 4.3 percent of the company's assets in 1958 to 9.3 percent in 1967. Northwestern had been there before. In 1910, when policy loans approached 15 percent of assets, William Van Dyke lamented that many policyowners were using their cash reserves "to procure funds for stock speculations and the purchase of automobiles and other luxuries." Don Slichter sounded an identical theme nearly five decades later, criticizing those who borrowed "to pay for rainbows in other investment skies."

The Monroe mechanical calculator entered service in 1961.

A pair of uncommonly canny investors led Northwestern in new directions after World War II: Peter Langmuir in securities ...

Northwestern was pursuing some rainbows of its own in the investment skies. Slow but steady growth increased the company's assets from $3.9 billion to $5.5 billion between 1958 and 1967—a gain of 41 percent—and money managers had little trouble finding outlets for the funds. There were no radical shifts in the broad investment categories: bonds dropped from 55 to 41.5 percent of assets during the period, but mortgages held steady at about 35 percent. The real change was in Northwestern's attitude. Life insurance companies had traditionally sought long-term, fixed-return investments to match the long-term, fixed-dollar policies they sold. They may have held anything from railroad cars to cow pastures as security for a loan, but they were inherently reluctant to own, manage, or share the risk of loss on any investment they made. The economic boom following World War II convinced many to abandon the safe haven of tradition. Bond managers turned to incentive financing, requiring "equity kickers" in loans they made: stock rights, production payments, and partial ownerships. Mortgage lenders made their companies partners in large projects and sometimes even launched real estate developments of their own. The risks were greater in the equity field, but so were the potential returns. Long known as one of the industry's more conservative investors, Northwestern turned that reputation around in the 1950s

and '60s. Caution and conservatism may have prevailed on the insurance side, but the company's investment managers were known for their aggressive interest in equities.

The shift was partly a response to the times and partly a reflection of the people in charge: Peter Langmuir in securities, and Howard Tobin and Francis Ferguson in mortgage loans. Langmuir, a Yale graduate in economics, had come to Northwestern in 1947 as an industrial bond specialist, and within three years he was manager of his division. A savvy, single-minded investor, he was the obvious choice to head the Securities Department when Don Slichter moved up to the presidency in 1958. Under Langmuir's direction, Northwestern developed a reputation as "kicker-oriented." Premium dollars went out to meat-packing plants and marble quarries, greeting card factories and whiskey distilleries, and virtually every loan was a direct placement. Although each carried a fixed rate of interest, Langmuir generally pushed for some extra incentive. In 1960, for instance, Northwestern loaned $8.5 million to a Texas firm with an option on an oilfield, taking 25 percent of the company's stock as part of the deal. The stock alone was eventually worth $7.5 million—above and beyond the interest payments on the loan. By 1967, industrial securities, many with equity kickers, accounted for 23.5 percent of Northwestern's assets—an all-time high. Pete Langmuir also led his company into the stock market. Although Wisconsin had lifted the restrictions on stock ownership years earlier, Northwestern was slower than most firms to chase the bulls of Wall Street. The market's continuing climb made it difficult to resist. The company had developed a modest position in preferred stocks during the 1950s, and Langmuir shifted its emphasis to common stocks. By 1965, the combined stock portfolio held 7.8 percent of Northwestern's assets, up from 1.8 percent in 1958.

There was similar ferment in Howard Tobin's Mortgage Department. Commercial loans helped developers create office buildings, shopping centers, supermarkets, filling stations, and hospitals, most of them on conventional terms, but Northwestern was among the first in the industry to participate in sale-lease agreements. The company typically bought the land and buildings in a new shopping center, for instance, and then leased it back to the developer on a basis that amortized the debt and paid interest. The borrower had a fund of extra capital, and Northwestern had an above-average rate of return. Sale-lease agreements were the counterparts of the equity kickers sought by the Securities Department.

These "city loans" were accompanied by new activity on the agricultural front. Northwestern had been the industry's leading farm lender in the 1920s, and the massive foreclosures of the 1930s had made it the leading farm owner. The company was

understandably reluctant to re-enter the agricultural market, even after World War II: new loans were limited to small family farms in the Midwest and rarely exceeded $100 per acre. All of that changed with the arrival of Francis Ferguson. Raised on a dairy farm in upstate New York, Ferguson came to Northwestern in 1951 as a farm loan specialist. By 1956, he was running the farm mortgage division, and before long he had rewritten the rules that had governed the operation for thirty years. Ferguson took Northwestern from the family farm to agribusiness. He shifted the focus from the Midwest to the South and Southwest. Large irrigated operations became the investment of choice, and millions of dollars went out to finance the expensive dams, pumps, wells, and canals necessary to grow crops on arid land. The average farm loan climbed from $10,000 in 1951 to $63,000 in 1960, and some financed the development of farms as large as 100,000 acres. Ferguson was on the lookout for entrepreneurs wherever he could find them. He once loaned money to a farmer who had installed heating elements in his asparagus beds, producing an early harvest that sold for ten times the normal price. Under Ferguson, farm loans of all kinds rose from 3 percent of assets in 1958 to nearly 8 percent in 1967—their highest point in fifty years.

Ferguson's performance made him the brightest star in the Mortgage Department, and Howard Tobin took an active interest in the young man's future. In 1963, after

… and Francis Ferguson, the firm's future president, in mortgage loans.

The ore carrier Edmund Fitzgerald, *shown below with its namesake, was perhaps the most famous investment in the history of life insurance, first as the largest ship on the Great Lakes and then as a tragic victim of "the gales of November."*

Tobin had moved literally across the street to become president of the Wisconsin Gas Company, Ferguson succeeded him as the department's vice-president. He was barely forty-two at the time. With responsibility for the entire operation, Ferguson soon found another new investment outlet: student housing. By 1965, college dormitories made up nearly 20 percent of Northwestern's new mortgage investments—some built on university land and leased back to their schools, others constructed off-campus and operated by full-time managers. Roomier and more attractive than the typical college dorm, the units seldom had vacancies. In 1967, Northwestern Mutual developments housed 21,000 students—more people than all the Hilton hotels in the country.

Peter Langmuir and Francis Ferguson were young, shrewd, and aggressive. They helped raise Northwestern's pretax investment yield from 4.01 percent in 1958 to 5.04 percent in 1967—well above the industry's 4.8 percent average and the first time since 1929 that the yield had exceeded 5 percent. The company's willingness to experiment was paying dividends, and not just financially. Oilfields and asparagus farms were definite departures from Northwestern tradition, but the firm's newfound interest in equities produced perhaps the most famous investment in the history of life insurance: the ore carrier *Edmund Fitzgerald*. Lake shipping was

a logical outlet for the company's funds. The booming postwar economy had created an enormous demand for iron ore from the Lake Superior region, but the Great Lakes fleet was more than thirty years old on average. The need for new ships reached a critical point after 1954, when the United States finally agreed to join Canada in the St. Lawrence Seaway project. Led by a president with a lifelong interest in the Great Lakes, Northwestern Mutual responded. By 1956, the company's investment in bulk carriers totaled $31 million—the largest on the lakes.

In keeping with its emphasis on equities, Northwestern's focus soon shifted from financing to building. In 1956, the firm reached an agreement with Oglebay-Norton, a mining and shipping giant based in Cleveland, to create the largest ship ever to sail the Great Lakes—a ship built and owned by Northwestern but leased to Oglebay-Norton under a "bareboat charter" for twenty-five years. The sale-lease agreement was identical to those already in place on a number of shopping center projects. Construction of Hull 301 began at the River Rouge shipyards near Detroit in August 1957. Northwestern's trustees gave the ship a proper name eight months later, christening it the *Edmund Fitzgerald* in honor of the man who was about

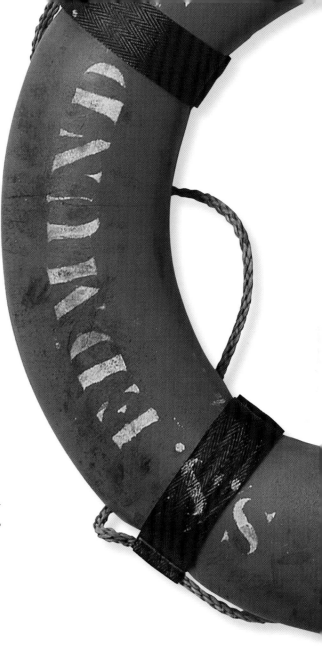

A life preserver from the ill-fated Fitzgerald

to step down after eleven years at the helm. The craft was launched with much fanfare on June 7, 1958. It was the largest object ever to hit fresh water, with a capacity of 25,891 tons and an overall length of 729 feet—one foot less than the longest lock at Sault Ste. Marie.

Shuttling between the ore docks of northern Minnesota and the steel mills of Ohio and Indiana, the *Edmund Fitzgerald* set a new volume record during its first full season in 1960 and repeated the feat four times in the next six years. Even after a new generation of carriers, some more than 1,000 feet in length, had captured the volume title, the *Fitzgerald* was known in maritime circles as a "glamour ship," with first-class crew quarters and guest accommodations that featured walnut furniture, deep pile carpeting, and a wet bar. Edmund Fitzgerald was a frequent passenger in his retirement, and he knew many of the crew by name.

The *Edmund Fitzgerald* began its last trip from Lake Superior's western shore on November 9, 1975. The lake is notoriously rough in late autumn, and Captain Ernest McSorley soon found himself in a gale, with sixty-mile-an-hour winds and thirty-foot waves. As the journey continued, McSorley radioed the *Arthur Anderson*, another ore carrier following close behind, that he had developed a slight list but was in no apparent danger. "I am holding my own," he reported. Then, at 7:10 P.M. on November 10, the *Fitzgerald* disappeared from the

Anderson's radar screen. The vessel and its crew of twenty-nine had gone down without even time to send a distress signal, much less lower the lifeboats. The precise cause of the tragedy may never be known, but it's possible that the *Fitzgerald* struck bottom on a shoal off Caribou Island. With its hull torn open, the ship may have taken on so much water that it nosed under a large wave and never came up. Investigators later found the *Fitzgerald* broken in half nearly 530 feet underwater, its stern section upside-down and both halves 28 feet deep in mud.

As the first fatal shipwreck on the Great Lakes since 1958, the incident was front-page news for a time, but it might have receded to a quiet place among the legends of the inland seas. Then, in 1976, Canadian singer-songwriter Gordon Lightfoot released *The Wreck of the Edmund Fitzgerald*. It was a memorable combination of two venerable musical forms: an old-fashioned disaster song with the rhythm of a sea chantey. *The Wreck of the Edmund Fitzgerald* was on the Top 100 charts for five months, taking its place among offerings like *Disco Duck* and *You Sexy Thing*. Radios and jukeboxes all over the globe repeated the story of death in "the gales of November." The song also conferred an unusual status on Edmund Fitzgerald: it made him the only life insurance executive in world history whose name became a household word.

The two decades between 1947 and 1967 were a paradoxical blend of rebuilding, retrenchment, and experiment at Northwestern Mutual. Edmund Fitzgerald took charge of a company just emerging from fifteen years of depression and war, and he selectively updated its policies and procedures to meet the challenges of a rapidly shifting market. Like Michael Cleary before him, Fitzgerald also became a passionate defender of the Northwestern faith, combining a determination to remain the industry's aristocrat with an unwavering insistence on economy. Donald Slichter and Robert Dineen together had less time in the president's office than Fitzgerald. In a long-term business like life insurance, neither could have been expected to lead the company in bold new directions. Perhaps the greatest contribution of both presidents was their willingness to let the modest momentum of the Fitzgerald years continue.

Northwestern paid a competitive price for its postwar conservatism. Between 1947 and 1967, as the industry's insurance in force multiplied by a factor of six, Northwestern's failed to even triple, increasing by 188 percent. The company was generally content to stay in the slow lane: getting there safely was much more important than risking a wreck. As competitors whizzed past in shinier cars with more glamorous features, Northwestern dropped from eighth place by insurance in force to twelfth.

Its leaders may have moved deliberately, but anyone who dismissed Northwestern as a company of buggy whips and coach lamps failed to see the enterprise in its full dimensions. On the operating side, the firm embraced computers with a zeal that was truly groundbreaking. On the investment side, Northwestern was at the forefront of the industry's move to equities. In both cases, the company's leaders sought maximum efficiency and maximum returns as means of maintaining their net-cost superiority. Northwestern demonstrated that it could be both nimble and non-traditional in the pursuit of its larger goals. Those qualities would prove indispensable in the next period. For American society as a whole, the river was narrowing, the current was accelerating, and there was the unmistakable sound of rough water ahead. 🐚

Calendars featuring the work of famed wildlife artist John James Audubon were first published in 1946—a practice that continues to the present day.

"A HEIGHTENED SENSE OF DESTINY"

"The sleeping giant," some pundits called Northwestern Mutual. The company was respected, even revered, by its peers in the insurance business, but no one ever mistook its leaders for daredevils. Northwestern was viewed as the most stubbornly traditional of the nation's largest firms, a company so quiet that few people outside the industry knew how good it was. The image was not entirely accurate but, compared with the tumbleweed behavior of some competitors, Northwestern had changed with all the speed of a glacier.

Both the image and the behavior underwent a transformation after 1967. The sleeping giant was very much awake, and it displayed a dynamism and aggressiveness that some observers found totally out of character. The shift in perspective was in some ways a response to the times. America's long postwar joyride came to an end in the late 1960s. Protests and confrontations roiled the previously placid waters of American society, and the Vietnam War became one of the most divisive conflicts in the nation's history. On the political front, the Watergate scandal brought Richard Nixon's presidency to an inglorious end and shook the republic to its foundations. On the economic side, America experienced its most severe bout of inflation since the World War I era. Year by year, the status quo came slowly unraveled, and even the normally staid life insurance industry shared in the general tumult.

At Northwestern Mutual, the mood was heightened by the rise of a new leader, Francis Ferguson, who presided over changes that would have seemed unthinkable a generation earlier. With substantial help, he harnessed the firm's latent energy and brought Northwestern into the late twentieth century. The company did not abandon tradition—Ferguson, in fact, emerged as a staunch defender of the Northwestern way—but its method of pursuing traditional goals changed dramatically.

"Fergie" Takes the Wheel

Francis Ferguson was a throwback to Michael Cleary in some respects: a farm boy who was raised in modest circumstances and never lost his native informality; nearly everyone knew him as "Fergie." But Ferguson was shaped by harsher realities than Cleary had ever faced. On his fifth mission as a B-17 bomber pilot during World War II, he was shot down behind German lines and forced to endure nineteen months in a prisoner-of-war camp. Only twenty-four years old when Germany surrendered, Ferguson emerged from the war with a rock-hard belief in self-reliance and an equally strong will to succeed. The farmer's son earned a degree in agricultural economics from Michigan State University in 1947 and joined Northwestern Mutual four years later, beginning the career that would culminate in his election to the presidency on May 1, 1967.

The new leader served a high-level apprenticeship before adding "chief executive officer" to his title—a practice that has since become a Northwestern tradition. For sixteen months, while Robert Dineen continued to preside as chairman and CEO, Ferguson visited virtually every general agency in the country and immersed himself in the study of company operations. "As far as I was concerned," Dineen said later, "he was going to school." On September 1, 1968, Ferguson finally took the wheel as head of the company. Even during the transitional period, it was apparent that his style was a significant departure from the Northwestern norm. Francis Ferguson was a man who inspired meekness in those with a capacity for it. Physically imposing, personally exacting, he took a visceral joy in the exercise of power as chief executive. He was plain-spoken, periodically profane, and so candid that he sometimes alarmed his public relations staff. But Ferguson was also a paradoxical figure: gruff and sentimental by turns, personally ambitious but dedicated to Northwestern principles, a careful listener but an autocratic decision-maker. To some company veterans, those qualities made him a painful break with the genteel Northwestern tradition. To others, he was a breath of fresh air—or, more accurately, a whirlwind.

Francis Ferguson, the plain-spoken dynamo who infused Northwestern Mutual with his own entrepreneurial spirit

Although he had a surplus of energy, Ferguson did not apply it randomly. Deliberate as well as dynamic, he asked fundamental questions and looked for rational answers, with a minimum of bias or preconceptions. One of his first steps, accordingly, was to make strategic planning a top priority. The 1966 Policyowners' Examining Committee prompted the decision. Its members asked an eminently reasonable question: if life insurance really is a long-term business, why is so little attention being paid to long-range planning? Why not indeed?, responded the company's top executives, and six of them, including Dineen and Ferguson, flew to an Arkansas resort for a few days of corporate introspection in 1967—the first executive planning rally in a series that has continued ever since. The questions raised there were so compelling that Ferguson formally launched the Department of Corporate Planning and Development in 1968. He described its mission in the broadest possible terms—"the creation of an atmosphere of healthy inquiry about why and how at all levels of our company"—and confidently predicted that it would be "one of the most significant steps this company has ever taken."

The executive Ferguson chose to lead the planning effort was Laflin "Bob" Jones, a singular figure in the company's long history. Raised in a Northwestern family (his father, Evan, was corporate secretary), Jones came to the home office in 1929, fresh out of Dartmouth College. Although writing was his first ambition, he spent his entire career at Northwestern, rising from Agency Department clerk to vice-president for all insurance operations. Jones still found time to write. He authored a well-received short history of the company in 1957, but he is best remembered for the plays he wrote, skillful presentations of the human dramas related to life insurance—most of them staged at annual meetings to hearty applause. A man of gracious reserve, broad views, and interests ranging from classical piano to philosophy, Bob Jones added a distinctive flavor to Northwestern Mutual. When he retired in 1972, Edmund Fitzgerald called him "the most practical intellectual I ever met."

In his new role as chief planner, Jones took an ecological approach. He saw Northwestern, its market, and the society around them as organisms, living things that were interactive, mutually dependent, moving in a kind of dance. The purpose of planning was to decide the tune and the tempo Northwestern would dance to in its particular role. Jones did not choose the music on his own. In 1969, Northwestern hired McKinsey and Company, a management consulting firm, to take an in-depth look at its operations and outline the issues affecting its future. McKinsey's

Ferguson posed with his mentor, Robert Dineen, beneath a portrait of Henry Palmer.

Laflin "Bob" Jones, the part-time playwright and full-time intellectual who crafted Northwestern's first strategic plan

researchers found much to praise—a top-flight field force, the industry's lowest net-cost standing, excellent penetration of the lucrative business and professional markets—but they also found a company rapidly falling behind its peers. Growth rates in every category were well below the industry averages, and recruitment of new agents had actually slipped backward. After more than a century, the company was still a Midwestern institution, with nearly a third of its sales concentrated in five states of the Old Northwest. In the home office, the McKinsey team found widespread complacency, an excessive reliance on the committee system, and a culture of conservatism that had made some people allergic to change. There was, at the same time, a clear awareness that change was coming, and both confusion and excitement about its potential impacts. The McKinsey study found a company in transition, a giant stirring in its sleep but unable to stop dreaming of the past.

Northwestern, it was clear, had only two choices: to grow, relatively, or to shrink. Focusing his attention on net cost, Edmund Fitzgerald had chosen the latter course, and his go-slow approach still had adherents among the firm's senior managers. Other executives, particularly the younger set, had no interest in working for a high-quality also-ran; they argued that faster growth would bring economies of scale into play, producing lower unit costs and a greater sense of challenge and engagement.

With Francis Ferguson moderating the debate, there was little question about its outcome. Addressing the agents' annual meeting in 1968—the year *before* McKinsey was hired—he stated his views with characteristic boldness: "We must seek the kind of growth that can provide opportunity. Growth brings excitement and a heightened sense of destiny in home office and agency operations alike.... Planned growth will enhance a sense of accomplishment and purpose." Ferguson had no desire to change Northwestern's basic course, but he was determined to use some of the fuel stored by his predecessors in pursuit of that "heightened sense of destiny." He focused and enlarged the company's desire *not* to be an also-ran. Under Ferguson's leadership, Northwestern crossed over to the fast track.

The task of developing the roadmap fell to Bob Jones. Even as the McKinsey survey was under way, twenty-two management study groups grappled with questions that had been, to say the least, sensitive, including group insurance, selling through brokers, mutual funds, and the pension market. Bob Jones digested the various reports and then, during a two-week "vacation" in Wisconsin's Door County, drafted Northwestern's strategic plan. Its first sentence gave traditionalists little cause for concern: "The purpose of NML is to continue to be the leading American company providing family and business security by specializing in life insurance and related services for the individual." Accomplishing that goal was the thornier question. The plan was based on the implicit assumption that, in order to maintain Northwestern's position as "the leading American company" in individual life insurance, growth was absolutely necessary. Of all the goals set in the strategic plan—and there were many—one stood out: $100 million in annual new premium by 1978. The 1968 figure was only $43 million, making it clear to all that Northwestern had a decade of hard work ahead.

The focus quickly shifted to the field force. Every new premium dollar was generated by an agent, and the company's relative sales stagnation since World War II reflected the relative stagnation of its recruiting efforts. The company counted 2,481 full-time representatives in 1967—only 2 percent more than in 1960 and 11 percent more than in 1947. With the $100 million goal firmly in mind, Northwestern set the most ambitious agency-building goals in its history: three new general agencies a year and, in existing agencies, an increase in the total number of full-time recruits from 500 to 600 a year by 1973. In addition, all agents were expected to increase their premiums by at least 6 percent per year.

Good will and impassioned rhetoric are no substitute for money when it comes to stimulating sales growth. Northwestern completely revamped its compensation system between 1968 and 1970, developing a variety of incentives that rewarded recruitment,

encouraged youth, and still recognized quality business. It took a year or two, but the incentives worked. By 1975, Northwestern's full-time field force had reached a new peak: 3,532 agents, 37 percent more than in 1969 and just over the Depression-era high point of 3,479. Acquiring them was not cheap. It cost thousands of dollars to finance the development of each new agent, and expenses became a concern as the company began to experience other pressures. Northwestern still wanted to grow, but its emphasis shifted from the horizontal to the vertical in the mid-1970s: from the creation of new agencies to more intensive development of existing fields. The vertical approach proved just as effective,

The growth of the field force was reflected in attendance at the 1977 annual meeting.

Dennis Tamcsin (inset) guided Northwestern's agency system for more than 20 years with a winning combination of discipline and constant encouragement. From college agents (top) to seasoned veterans attending Career Forum (bottom), everyone in the field felt Tamcsin's influence.

swelling the roster of full-time agents to 4,749 in 1982—nearly double the number on the job when Francis Ferguson took office. Even with the customarily high rate of attrition, Northwestern showed a net gain of 168 agents per year in the 1969-1982 period—almost eight times the growth rate of the previous decade.

As the field force filled out, the company developed a corresponding "farm team." Acutely aware that its best prospects for the future were baby-boomers currently in college, Northwestern expanded its presence on the nation's campuses. By 1972, nearly half of the firm's 108 general agencies housed college units, each doing its part to build "a field force within the field force." The number of college agents (all part-time) jumped from 71 in 1966 to 464 in 1980, and a significant proportion graduated to careers with Northwestern. By 1976, 10 percent of the company's full-time representatives were former college agents, many of them serving clients they had first met on campus.

No business could double its sales force without experiencing at least some cultural stress. Northwestern took in thousands of newcomers after 1969, many of them young adults with no knowledge of the company's history and absolutely no grounding in its culture. Every general agency relied on seasoned veterans to serve as mentors for its recruits, but the home office developed more formal efforts to assimilate and educate them. Career Schools were expanded from two to five a year. The Advanced Planning School, a week-long clinic for career agents, began in 1968. Career Forum, a continuing education program for top producers with at least ten years of experience, was introduced in 1977. There were also new attempts to keep agents in the Northwestern loop. *FieldNews* debuted in 1971 to provide the latest information on company affairs, and there was even a short-lived magazine (*Very Important People*) for agents' spouses.

Every program related to expansion was the province of the Agency Department, whose size and functions kept pace with growth in the field. In 1968, Robert Templin was promoted from agency executive to vice-president for all sales activities, and three years later he was named to the Board of Trustees, the first agency head to be so honored since Henry Norris in 1912. Templin's rise opened up a new executive position on the level just below him: superintendent of agencies. Dennis Tamcsin, a former Cleveland agent who had shown a distinct flair for management, assumed the post in 1973, becoming, at thirty-five, the youngest executive officer in the company. Tamcsin was, like Bob Templin and Grant Hill before him, both a Midwesterner and a former Marine, and he brought the same articulate enthusiasm to the office that his predecessors had displayed. He stayed until 1999, ending his career as one of the longest-serving and most influential agency heads in Northwestern's history.

The field force showed continuous improvement in quality even as it increased in quantity—a tribute to the leadership skills of Templin, Tamcsin, and the entire corps of general agents. In 1974, when Northwestern's expansion program had been under way for five years, 25 percent of the company's eligible full-time agents were members of the Million Dollar Round Table and 40 percent were National Quality Award winners. Both figures were significant improvements over the previous period, and both placed Northwestern first among America's twenty largest insurance firms. Professional standards continued to rise as well. The number of Chartered Life Underwriters in the company passed the 1,000 mark in 1973, and their proportion increased from 27 percent of full-time agents in 1967 to 34 percent in 1982. As in earlier years, quality agents attracted quality buyers, reinforcing the time-honored circle of success. In comparison with other insurance customers, Northwestern clients tended to purchase larger policies that stayed on the books longer, and they were inclined to come back for more; roughly half of all new sales were made to existing policyowners.

Growth and change on the agency side were matched by continuous ferment on the insurance side. Without new products to sell, Northwestern's field force might have been, in a sense, all dressed up with no place to

The Programmed Individual Presentation (PIP) machine, an audio-visual device used for agent training in the 1970s

go, but the company launched a wide range of new policies after 1967, some of them distinct departures from past practice. By far the most important was Extra Ordinary Life (EOL). Introduced in 1968, EOL was a hybrid contract, combining whole life and term insurance in a self-contained whole. Dividends were automatically used to turn a portion of the term insurance into paid-up whole life insurance each year, and in time the entire term element was converted. The new contract was an especially creative response to an industry-wide trend toward lower premiums. Consumers wanted more protection for less money—a desire usually satisfied with term insurance—but EOL offered them permanent, level-premium coverage at very attractive rates. It was the first contract of its kind in the United States; no one else had both the computer power and the dividend scale to make the hybrid design work. Company officials had high hopes for the new product, but even the optimists were amazed by its success. Extra Ordinary Life replaced whole life as Northwestern's most popular policy within a year, bringing in 34 percent of all new premium dollars in 1970, 44 percent in 1974, and nearly half

in 1978. Agents who feared that a lower-premium policy would mean lower earnings for them were surprised to find the first-year commissions of EOL sellers rising at triple the rate of those who abstained. Teamed with the Insurance Service Account, EOL was probably Northwestern's most powerful marketing innovation of the twentieth century.

Although it was certainly the centerpiece, EOL was by no means the only new product developed during the Ferguson years. The most radical departure from tradition was disability income insurance. Company officials had been railing against "DI" since the days of George Markham, blasting it as a form of accident insurance. Time has a way of softening even the most determined resistance. In the 1960s, Northwestern began to see the "living benefits" of DI as an attractive complement to the death benefits of its other insurance contracts—particularly since its own agents were already selling competitors' disability products in great volume. Francis Ferguson announced a shift in thinking at the 1969 annual meeting: "The actuarial figures and dollar signs are more plentiful, well tested, and the line is now ready to take its place in a quality mutual company." Northwestern's version of disability insurance debuted on August 1, 1969, but its high premiums and numerous exclusions attracted few takers. As the company grew more comfortable with its new addition, the contract was steadily liberalized and its premium rates were steadily reduced. By 1982, to the surprise

Extra Ordinary Life (EOL) was a ground-breaking hybrid policy that became Northwestern's best-seller almost overnight.

THE NORTHWESTERN MUTUAL LIFE
INSURANCE COMPANY • MILWAUKEE NML

NML
has
NEWS for the '70

Your Northwestern Mutual Life agent enters the 1970s with newly developed services designed to fit your insurance program to your specific needs with even greater flexibility than NML has offered in its 113 years of individual coverage.

An extraordinary example which is accounting for more than one-third of NML's new sales is
EOL

NML's new Extra Ordinary Life policy (EOL) meets the needs both of the young man just starting to build family protection, and of the businessman who wants to protect the human values so important in his enterprise.

Significant to both is EOL's delivery of maximum protection in combination with relatively large cash values in relation to premiums.

A man 30 years of age, for example, can start with instantaneous total coverage

EXTRA ORDINARY LIFE

EOL

LIFE
INSURANCE
THAT LASTS A
LIFETIME

NORTHWESTERN MUTUAL LIFE

of many insiders, Northwestern Mutual was the nation's fourth-largest disability insurer, with more than $52 million of premiums in force.

Two additions to the term line enjoyed faster starts. Northwestern had always been ambivalent about its term contracts, considering them pale substitutes for permanent insurance, but the demand for low-premium coverage in the postwar decades was undeniable. Following a national trend, the company's term sales rose from 17 percent of face amount in 1947 to 31 percent in 1967. Extra Ordinary Life proved remarkably effective in reversing the trend, cutting term sales to 12 percent of new business in 1972, but there remained a definite demand for low-cost, short-duration coverage. Northwestern introduced a decreasing term product in 1971, targeted to clients in their child-raising, home-buying years. Yearly renewable term (YRT)

insurance followed in 1972—a liberalization of the five- and ten-year term contracts Northwestern had been selling for decades. Within a year, YRT policies accounted for 17 percent of the company's new business, second only to EOL. Decreasing term and yearly renewable insurance met real needs, but they had an important secondary goal: recapturing some of the business Northwestern agents were placing in other companies.

Three chief actuaries guided product development during the Ferguson years: Victor Henningsen from 1953 to 1968, Russell Jensen from 1968 to 1973, and Dale Gustafson from 1973 to 1983. They differed widely in temperament, but all three were Scandinavian Midwesterners trained at the University of Iowa. The trio tinkered constantly with the product line, generally in the direction of liberalization. Dollar limits

Three chief actuaries, all Scandinavian Midwesterners, guided product development during the Ferguson years: (l. to r.) Victor Henningsen, Russell Jensen, and Dale Gustafson.

were raised, exclusions were pared, and recent offerings were steadily upgraded. There were corresponding changes in price structure. The reserve rate was raised from 3 percent in 1968 to 4 percent in 1978, the highest it had been since 1869. Because the company guaranteed higher interest on investments over a contract's lifetime, it could charge less for insurance. That revision, coupled with lower mortality and new products like EOL and YRT, exerted a downward pressure on premium rates. For all Northwestern insurance policies sold, the premium per $1,000 fell from $22.15 in 1967 to $13.73 in 1979.

There was comparable tinkering on the pension side of the business, but it tended to generate more noise than progress. Northwestern could never decide whether it was in or out of the employee benefits field. Unwilling to follow its competitors into the group arena but just as unwilling to abandon a potentially lucrative market, the company struggled to find a satisfactory middle ground. In the 1960s and '70s, the firm unleashed a minor blizzard of retirement annuities—variable, flexible, tax-deferred, single-premium, individual, and others— and changed them regularly in response to market patterns, agent pressures, and federal regulations. The old pension trust area became by far the most complicated (and least profitable) segment of Northwestern's operations. As products less specialized and more competitive received a greater share of the field force's attention, tax-qualified sales slipped from 18 percent of new premium revenue in 1967 to less than 9 percent in 1979. The company had better luck in the next decade, particularly after a 1981 tax law allowed every working American

Samuel C. Johnson (far right) *and fellow members of the 1970 Policyowners' Examining Committee prodded Northwestern to step up its advertising efforts.*

to deduct up to $2,000 for an individual retirement account. Individual accounts were Northwestern's specialty, and the firm's IRA premiums soared 1,146 percent in 1982 alone.

Most of the new products of the Ferguson years—EOL, DI, YRT, IRAs, and several others known primarily by their acronyms—represented a tangible shift away from the narrow specialist role of earlier years. Their success was dramatic: in 1979, products introduced during the previous twelve years accounted for 60 percent of Northwestern's sales. That success was certainly the work of a revitalized field force, but it also reflected a new approach to sales promotion. The company had long been one of the most conservative advertisers in the business, relying on a single medium since 1934—national magazines—and a single campaign since 1948—Yousuf Karsh's portraits of prominent policyowners. That campaign eventually ran its course. Photographs of graying executives, however artfully composed, began to seem curiously antique in an age of tie-dyed T-shirts and psychedelic posters; Yousuf Karsh received his last commission in 1968.

Richard Haggman, Northwestern's advertising director since 1956, had ample reason for concern. A 1970 Gallup poll showed that only 10 percent of the nation's adult males had ever heard of his company; Northwestern was America's twelfth-largest insurance firm but ranked only thirty-fourth in name recognition. The 1970 Policyowners'

Examining Committee added fuel to the fire. Its members included Samuel C. Johnson, whose Johnson Wax Company owned some of the best-known brand names in the world. Johnson took one look at Northwestern's advertising budget and declared that it was, to paraphrase slightly, "like spitting in Lake Michigan." The time was ripe for a new medium and a new message.

The obvious medium was television, and Northwestern, entirely by coincidence, started at the very top. The Summer Olympics were scheduled for Munich in 1972, and an ABC team flew to Milwaukee early in the year to visit Schlitz Brewing, already a major sponsor. The network staff paid a courtesy call on Northwestern while they were in town, informing Haggman that a one-sixteenth sponsorship was still available. The cost was $1.4 million—nearly twice the company's entire 1971 advertising budget. To the surprise of many, Northwestern agreed to participate. The next step was crafting a message strong enough to fill thirty minutes of airtime. Haggman's staff, working with the J. Walter Thompson Agency of Chicago, decided to emphasize simplicity. The final commercials, filmed during June in the Chicago area, featured one actor describing Northwestern's low-pressure agents, high

NORTHWESTERN MUTUAL LIFE INSURANCE COMPANY
1972 SUMMER OLYMPICS
"Size Seven"--One of Ten Commercials Produced for the Olympics

The company's response was a major "media buy"—the 1972 Summer Olympics—and a series of low-key but extraordinarily effective commercials.

The Quiet

In 1972, Northwestern's new slogan "introduced" a company that had been insuring policyowners since 1857.

dividends, imposing size, and century-old traditions. The one-on-one approach was intended to parallel the individual relationship between agent and client.

One more element was needed: a simple, memorable tag line that viewers could take with them. The Thompson agency proposed "The Best-kept Secret," "The Great Unknown," and a laundry list of other options. Returning from Chicago by train one evening, Dick Haggman scribbled "The Quiet Company" on a pad of paper. He did not feel that lightning had struck; Haggman kept the slogan as a tentative choice until his staff or the agency could come up with something better. The phrase, it turned out, wore exceedingly well. Later research showed that it called up an image of stability, responsiveness, diligence, lack of pretense, thrift, and a host of other positive qualities. "The Quiet Company" was also, in 1972, a perfectly understated way to "introduce" a firm that had been around since 1857.

With its package ready, Northwestern Mutual made one of the most successful advertising debuts in television history. The Olympic Games have always been "must watch" viewing during the late-summer rerun season, and public interest soared with the terrorist attack on the Israeli delegation—a stroke of "luck" the company would gladly have done without. By the time the Olympic torch was extinguished, Northwestern's commercials had been seen in 90 percent of the nation's television homes, well above projections. Their low-key approach was in marked contrast to the brass bands and fireworks of other advertisers; surveys showed that viewers remembered them twice as readily as other insurance commercials. Practically overnight, Northwestern soared from thirty-fourth place in public awareness to third, and clients began to write checks to "The Quiet Company." J. Walter Thompson concluded that Northwestern had gained more exposure for less money than any client in the agency's history.

Company

New agents, new products, and new advertising produced a single outcome: new sales records. When Francis Ferguson announced Northwestern's $100 million premium goal in 1969, some insiders were openly skeptical. Aided by nonstop recruiting, productivity gains, and inflation, the company's agents made steady progress. In 1976, Ferguson issued a "Bicentennial Challenge," urging them to reach the goal in the upcoming year. The agents made it with room to spare, bringing in $108 million of new premium in 1977—one year ahead of schedule. Some brought in more than others, of course, and the repeating sales leaders of the Ferguson years were a study in contrasts. John Todd of Chicago secured his place as an industry legend. Todd qualified for the Million Dollar Round Table for the first time in 1936 and kept qualifying for the next sixty-two years—an MDRT record. David Hast, a Pittsburgh agent who joined Northwestern in 1949, called himself "a tortoise," plodding along methodically and making a multitude of contacts. He placed first in 1975 with sales of $12.2 million on 285 lives. Lyle Blessman, by contrast, won a year earlier with a volume of $18.4 million on just 29 lives, most of them cattle ranchers and beet farmers in northeastern Colorado.

The performance of the field force as a whole was impressive, and comparative figures for the industry gave Northwestern even more reason to celebrate. The company's new business soared from $1.4 billion in 1967 to $14.2 billion in 1982, a 914-percent increase in fifteen years, while ordinary insurance sales for all companies rose only 547 percent. Competing against firms with much broader product lines, Northwestern moved from twelfth place to tenth in insurance in force during the period, and from twentieth to ninth in volume of new business. The sleeping giant was very much awake, and it was giving the other giants reason to worry.

The Rational Workplace

The triple-digit growth of the 1967-1982 period put significant stress on Northwestern Mutual's home office: its employees, its computer operations, and even the buildings themselves. As the pressures mounted, internal systems crafted by earlier generations began to seem worn-out and anachronistic, and the same fresh spirit of inquiry that underpinned Northwestern's external growth campaign sparked some pervasive internal changes. Under Francis Ferguson, the company launched perhaps the most sweeping reorganization in its history, creating a workplace that was more transparent, more efficient, and more rational than ever before.

A sweeping home office reorganization created several new departments, including New Business in 1981.

Northwestern entered the post-1967 period with an internal structure that had not changed appreciably since the nineteenth century. The major departments were still organized by subject area and clerical skills rather than function. The Treasurer's Department, easily the largest, kept Northwestern's books, whether the matter at hand was premium payments or general agency audits. The Secretarial Department, second-largest, handled all transactions related to ownership and benefits, from beneficiary changes to death payments. The Actuarial Department also worked on policies, making all of the calculations affecting values. Northwestern, in short, was organized vertically. The departments were as separate and parallel as a row of elevator shafts. The people at the top had access to every elevator and every floor, but other employees had to take the stairs.

In 1968, after a two-year study led by actuary Frank Rice, Northwestern turned the home office operation on its axis, shifting its orientation from the vertical to the horizontal, from the skills of those performing the task to the needs of those being served. Pieces of several old departments were reassembled into two new ones that functioned, in effect, as the company's "in" and "out" boxes. Policyowner Services handled all work coming in *from* customers, whether they were paying premiums or updating their addresses, while

Policy Benefits managed everything going out *to* customers, from policy loans to benefit payments. The compelling simplicity of the move produced significant gains in efficiency. The ratio of policyowner letters answered within five days soared from 11 percent in 1969 to 80 percent in 1970, and the number of days required to open an Insurance Service Account fell from six to one.

The approach was effective, but it became obvious, over time, that functionalism could be overdone. Work units in the operating departments became so specialized that an insurance application or service request might have passed through a dozen pairs of hands before a case was closed. In 1981, after another in-depth study, the Underwriting and Policy Issue Departments were combined in a new department known simply as New Business. The country was divided into four regions, and home office teams were given complete responsibility for everything from pre-underwriting to post-approval processing in each of them. Policyowner Services was regionalized at the same time. Specialists became generalists, as sixty-three job descriptions were compressed into six, working in teams assigned to specific general agencies. The new systems promoted greater efficiency as well as greater accountability. In Policyowner Services, for instance, the number of pending cases dropped from 46,555 in fall of 1979 to 7,860 in spring of 1981.

As the various departments were unbundled and then rebundled, there was a dramatic rise in the number of executives with group responsibilities. Northwestern's leaders had been multi-tasking since the days of Henry Palmer, but the trend became more pronounced as the company grew larger and more complex. By 1974, nearly all the departments were grouped in clusters under four senior vice-presidents. Robert Barrows, who had joined Northwestern as a mortgage specialist in 1948, managed all aspects of the investment operation. Russell Jensen moved up from chief actuary to head of the entire insurance side. Robert Templin had charge of Communications—a department established in 1973—as well as Agency. Donald Mundt, a lawyer born and educated in Nebraska, handled the administrative side of the business. Mundt was a central figure in the executive shifts of the period. Adding duties by the year, he became Northwestern's executive vice-president in 1977, with ultimate responsibility for eleven of the company's eighteen departments. Easygoing, sensitive, and yet firmly grounded in Northwestern's principles, Mundt earned a reputation as one of the most astute managers of people in the company's postwar history.

The Data Processing Department, one of Don Mundt's charges, evolved even faster than the rest of the company after 1967. The IBM 360, a third-generation computer installed in 1966, was "upward-compatible": it could

Robert Barrows (top) *headed the entire investment operation—the same role Donald Mundt played on the administrative side of the company.*

use magnetic hard disks as well as magnetic tape. The difference between the two was fundamental. In the tape system, trained operators used punchcards to input data that was stored at specific points on a given reel; they might have had to spin through an entire tape to reach a particular "address." In the disk system, volumes of data were collected in a common digital pool, where information could be instantly accessed by anyone with rudimentary keypad skills. Hard disks represented a quantum leap forward in speed, flexibility, and power, and Northwestern committed itself to the new technology in 1967. The tape-to-disk conversion project was named DALIS—Direct Access Life Insurance System. It was a gargantuan effort, involving scores of employees working with millions of documents over a period of several years. File by laborious file, manual records covering policy title, settlement

options, policy loans, dividend histories, and a host of other variables were transformed from paper to billions of magnetic impressions on platter-sized metal disks. As each step was completed, terminals were installed in the appropriate departments; the number of home office terminals soared from 19 in 1970 to 640 in 1982.

One beauty of the new system was its flexibility: previously separate files could be combined and cross-referenced in any way imaginable. In 1975, for instance, two subsets of the policy base were combined to yield, for the first time, a comprehensive master file of all policies arranged by owner. Data-processing managers sometimes described the conversion project as "going to database," and the number of discrete bases soon topped a dozen. Another advantage of random-access computing was its portability. Terminals extended the system's reach from one closely

Faster, more powerful mainframes increased Northwestern's operating efficiency ...

guarded center to any location in the home office and, via telephone lines, to any location in the country. The most important locations outside the home office were, of course, the general agencies. In 1974, Northwestern began to develop a terminal system linking home office and field—a system named, appropriately, LINK, or Life Information Network. Operational in 1977, LINK functioned as a sales assistant, secretary, file clerk, and bookkeeper rolled into one. Agents could enter detailed financial data for their prospects and receive, overnight, customized proposals. When a sale was made, they could submit basic underwriting information by computer instead of mail and then check on the status of pending applications without calling the home office. For existing clients, agents could activate Insurance Service Accounts and provide up-to-date information on individual policies. LINK was the most

sophisticated agency computer system in the entire industry and, like all computer breakthroughs, it moved in two directions at once, extending the human reach while reducing the need for human effort.

Decentralization was the dominant trend, but it took place within definite limits. The early terminals were simply remote units of the home office mainframe, as intimately connected to it as an octopus is to its tentacles. The advent of the personal computer changed the ground rules completely. The new units were more like independent offspring than tentacles; they were not so much decentralized as detached. Facing a two- to three-year backlog of requests, the Data Processing Department actively promoted do-it-yourself computing at Northwestern. The first small machines appeared in the Law Department in 1982, and they spread quickly through both home office and field.

… while the advent of personal computers put more power in the hands of end users.

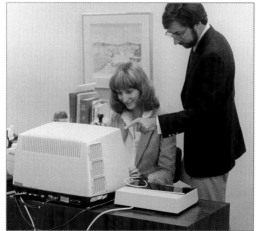

The minicomputers that powered LINK I had been literally slaves of the home office mainframe. LINK II, launched as a pilot project in 1981, gave the agents not only access but independence. Personal computers enabled them to program their own proposals, create and maintain client files, and process any type of written material. LINK II equipment was installed in every general agency by the end of 1982, and it marked a significant turning point. When Northwestern's first computer arrived in 1957, there had been foreboding as well as excitement. Some feared that the machine would cause a loss of human control, and that it would concentrate too much power in the hands of technicians. With the rise of small computers in the 1980s, just the opposite occurred. Individual agents and individual managers had a powerful tool they could use at their own speeds, for their own purposes. The computer had come full circle.

Northwestern was determined to keep its place near the head of the technological parade, and the Data Processing Department grew accordingly. Its staff more than doubled between 1967 and 1982, rising from 132 full-time employees to 297. Even more striking was a related shift in the makeup of the home office work force. The computer practically eliminated Northwestern's lower-level clerical positions, and it promoted an increasingly dense concentration of skills. Supervisors, officers, and specialists grew from 14 percent of the home office staff in 1958 to 28 percent in 1979, and there was comparable growth on the upper clerical levels, creating a bulge in the middle of the company's hierarchy. The computer changed Northwestern's internal structure from a pyramid to a diamond.

Computers, of course, were the quintessential tool of the rational workplace. The whole point of data processing was to enable Northwestern to do more things, and to do them faster, better, and cheaper than it could manually. Forcing change in some areas, facilitating change in others, the new machines played a central role in virtually every phase of the company's operations, from designing products to selling them, from approving applications to collecting premiums. But the cost-saving aspects of the computer were just as obvious. The rapid growth of the Data Processing staff was more than counterbalanced by a relative decrease in the size of other departments. The total number of full-time home office employees grew from 1,656 in 1967 to 1,999 in 1982—a gain of only 21 percent during a period when Northwestern's insurance in force increased 508 percent.

For all its powers, the computer could only postpone expansion, not prevent it. Even moderate staff growth taxed the capacity of the 1914 home office and its 1932 addition. Despite continuing efforts to consolidate and streamline operations, shrinking space became a growing problem.

Frank Rice, chief architect of the 1968 reorganization, tackled a different project in 1973: a detailed study of the company's office needs. Rice concluded that the camel's back was nearly broken. Few departments were intact by 1973. Data Processing, for instance, had spilled over from its original home on the second floor north to locations on five floors (including the basement) in both buildings. There was little room for new activities, and Northwestern was in danger of losing the efficiency it had so carefully fostered. The company could, in Rice's words, "survive to '75," but major adjustments would be necessary beyond that point.

A committee chaired by Don Mundt spent the next three years hatching ideas, making charts, and studying plans. Its members considered proposals that were definitely outside the box: building a sixty-one-story skyscraper (with twenty floors of penthouse apartments), demolishing the 1914 structure and erecting a new headquarters, moving to Arizona (an idea that probably surfaced in mid-winter), decentralizing to offices around the country, and perching a glass-and-steel tower atop the dull granite of the 1932 addition—an idea that in execution might have resembled tail fins on a Model T. Clearer thinking ultimately prevailed. The committee's final recommendations were based on deep affection for the 1914 landmark, concerns about the efficiency of its 1932 addition, and a realization that Northwestern would

eventually need more space than both buildings combined. In July 1976, the company decided to renovate the first, demolish the second, and erect a large general office building to the east. The original home office, its 1914 elegance renewed, would become a front door, a flagship, a symbol of Northwestern's heritage. It would house the top executives, public-contact departments like Communications and Personnel, and specialized groups like lawyers and actuaries. The new East Building, set back to preserve the lake view, would be the operations center, housing the bulk of the clerical force. The two structures would be joined by an all-weather "connecting module" containing a variety of common-use facilities. The remaining open space would become a green plaza, setting Northwestern off from its surroundings in a genuine "campus" arrangement.

Ground for Northwestern Mutual Place—the campus's official name—was broken in December 1976, beginning a six-year siege of dust, noise, and general inconvenience. A 732-car parking structure went up first, filling most of the block just north of the home office. The East Building took shape next as a sixteen-story glass-and-granite box with 500,000 square feet of floor space, nearly a third more than the 1914 and 1932 buildings combined. Each floor was a massive rectangle of

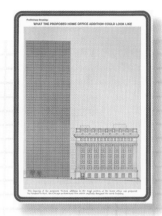

Pressed for space, Northwestern considered adding a glass-and-granite tower (above) *to its 1932 home office addition. The company decided instead to tear it down* (below) *and build from scratch.*

open space, broken only by a central elevator core and rows of offices along the perimeter. The design, or lack of it, enabled Northwestern to arrange its space in modular fashion. A top-to-bottom renovation of the original home office was third on the list, and it proved to be the most expensive and time-consuming part of the entire project. Virtually every square inch of the landmark was altered in some way; work crews gutted whole floors for new facilities like a cafeteria and a learning center, and smaller projects ranged from refinishing the board room woodwork to installing antique water fountains. Demolition crews, in the meantime, were hard at work on the 1932 addition. Built to support twenty-four stories, it did not go down without a fight, but the site was finally cleared. The "connecting module" that rose in its place became an atrium—a gigantic window box with hanging lights, fig trees, flowers, and an oval reflecting pool. The entire project was plagued with delays, design changes, and cost overruns, but Northwestern Mutual Place was finally dedicated on July 16, 1982. Home office employees trooped outside to raise glasses of champagne in celebration. "I have nothing against workmen," said Francis Ferguson, "but thank God they're gone." Northwestern Mutual Place was the most ambitious building project in the company's history, and it became the perfect embodiment of the rational workplace.

Ready for occupancy in 1978, the East Building gave Northwestern 500,000 square feet of new office space.

Learning center

Board room

Guest dining room

Lobby

The original 1914 home office was renovated from top to bottom, with a soaring glass-enclosed atrium as its centerpiece.

*Known as Northwestern Mutual Place, the entire ensemble was a
striking addition to Milwaukee's downtown.*

The Outside World Intrudes

The changes of the Ferguson years amounted to a modest revolution. A new strategic plan, new agents, new products, new advertising, and a new campus all carried Northwestern a considerable distance from the safe haven of its heritage. But the various steps had one thing in common: they were, within limits, under the Northwestern's control. All resulted from internal decisions that were made to ensure The Quiet Company's survival and prosperity in a noisy marketplace. The innovations and alterations would have been news enough in the 1967-1982 period, but the fact is that Northwestern was, in some important respects, no longer the master of its own destiny, however heightened that destiny may have seemed to Francis Ferguson. A juggernaut of forces—social, political, and above all economic—forced the company into a reactive posture. The entire insurance industry was marked by a progressive sense of embattlement after 1967; more and more effort was spent adjusting to conditions imposed from outside.

Inflation was the most potent of the forces facing Northwestern and its competitors. The cost of living had been impressively stable since World War II, rising at an average annual rate of just 1.7 percent from 1949 to 1967. Then Lyndon Johnson tried to finance his Great Society social programs and the Vietnam War at the same time, contributing to a dramatic rise in the price of both guns and butter. Inflation crossed the 5-percent threshold in 1969, reached the double-digit level at 11 percent in 1974, and rose to a peak of 13.5 percent in 1980. That long upward climb produced any number of ironies: by 1979, an agent had to sell $1.5 million of insurance to qualify for the Million Dollar Round Table.

Few businesses are as allergic to inflation as life insurance. Perhaps its most insidious effect was to compromise the contract at its very core. Life insurance is a dollar business, and its financial mainstay has always been a lifetime guarantee of fixed death benefits in return for fixed premium payments. As inflation galloped ahead, $10,000 of whole life coverage acquired in 1949 had the purchasing power of $3,300 in 1979. The American economy had created a new product—decreasing permanent insurance. Consumers were dismayed to find their policies "wearing out," and many voted with their feet. Whole life sales dropped from 42 percent of the nation's new business in 1960 to 31 percent in 1979.

As a self-proclaimed specialist in whole life insurance, Northwestern was particularly vulnerable, but Northwestern, fortunately, had Extra Ordinary Life. It is difficult to exaggerate the new product's importance. EOL was introduced in 1968—at the very beginning of the inflationary cycle—and it offered a high level of permanent coverage for a low

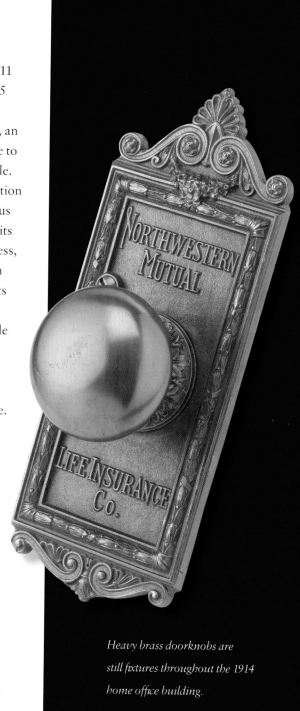

Heavy brass doorknobs are still fixtures throughout the 1914 home office building.

The demand for policy loans kept hundreds of Northwestern employees working overtime.

level premium. As the rest of the industry stampeded to term, permanent insurance rose from 69 percent of Northwestern's new business in 1967 to 88 percent in 1972—the highest point in nearly fifty years.

Timely product change enabled the company to dodge one bullet, but another was on the way—the demand for policy loans. The industry's standard 5-percent interest rate had once seemed positively usurious, but those days ended in the late 1960s. As the price of hamburger and houses soared, so did the price of money. The prime rate reached 6 percent in 1966, 10 percent in 1973, and 15 percent in 1979—on its way to a peak of 21.5 percent in 1980. Five-percent policy loans began to seem like free money. During the Depression, life insurance cash values had been a last resort; policyowners borrowed to save their homes and put food on the table. In the inflationary climate of the 1970s, cash values were a first resort, and a growing number of policyowners used their loans as investment capital. The process was called "disintermediation," a grandiose term for a simple concept: eliminating the middleman. Instead of trusting their funds to insurance investment managers, policyowners did it themselves, earning considerably more than 5 percent on even the safest investments. The trend was aggravated by the growth of minimum-deposit selling. Buyers systematically borrowed against cash values to pay their

premiums, drastically reducing their outlays for insurance and gaining a tax deduction for interest payments in the process.

Northwestern Mutual had some of the most sophisticated policyowners in the industry and, thanks to the company's generous dividends, some of the highest cash values as well. Whenever the prime rate rose, so did the pressure on those reserves. During a 1969 credit crunch, Northwestern's clerical staff put in sixty-five-hour weeks to keep up with the flood of loan applications, and still there was a two-week backlog. Nearly two-thirds of the year's new income went back out the door as loans—the highest ratio in the industry. Although loan demand rose and fell, its effects were, like the inflation rate's, cumulative. Northwestern's policy loan account climbed from $512 million in 1967 to $1.6 billion in 1975 and $2.5 billion in 1979. Loans were the company's largest single "investment" in 1970, at 16 percent of total assets, and they kept growing to 20.2 percent in 1975 and 30.6 percent in 1982—more than three times the industry average.

Despite suggestions to the contrary, there is nothing intrinsically evil about policy loans. Because the company, in effect, holds the policies as collateral, they are extraordinarily safe investments. In the 1970s, however, the volume of loans was viewed as nothing less than disastrous. With new investments earning 10 percent, sending funds out the door at half that rate seemed like putting money in a sock. The company objected, in part, on moral grounds; it was basically "unmutual," Francis Ferguson declared, for the minority who borrowed against their reserves to depress the investment yields and therefore the dividends of the majority who didn't. Depressed yields were also a clear and present danger to Northwestern's bottom line. "Excessive policy loans," Ferguson told the agents in 1973, "are the greatest single threat to this company's position of cost leadership." They were a threat to its persistency as well. Although Northwestern's customers remained the most loyal in the business, the rising number of highly leveraged policies pushed the firm's overall lapse rate from 2 percent in 1967 to 3 percent in 1979.

With so much at stake, Northwestern moved with unusual aggressiveness to blunt the impact of policy loans, first by raising the interest rate on its new policies to 6 percent—the highest rate allowed in most states—and then by leading a national campaign to raise the ceiling to 8 percent. In 1975, long before the proposal had cleared every state legislature, Northwestern became the first firm in the industry to adopt the 8-percent rate on new business wherever it was permitted. The company stood virtually alone at 8 percent for two years—a situation that caused considerable consternation in the field force—but home office executives defended the move as absolutely necessary.

The next step was direct recognition of borrowing activity in the allocation of dividends. In 1982, after years of legal research and internal discussion, Northwestern moved to direct recognition on new business; borrowers, because they contributed less to the enterprise, received a proportionately smaller share of investment earnings than non-borrowers. One year later, the company launched Update '83—a campaign to convince existing policyowners to accept direct recognition. The most powerful incentive was a record dividend allocation of $701 million, 18 percent higher than 1982's. Under direct recognition, most non-borrowers were offered a 9.75-percent rate of return, against 6.9 percent for clients who had stripped their policies of cash values. With short-term interest rates in modest retreat, a tax-sheltered 9.75-percent return had definite appeal. Update '83 was a resounding success, and there was a corresponding drop in new loan requests. After years of turmoil, Northwestern had finally found a solution to the policy loan problem that was both equitable and effective.

The impact of inflation on policy loans was fairly predictable; when market rates exceeded policy rates, people borrowed. As the cost of living spiraled ever higher, insurance companies faced a problem that no one had anticipated: skyrocketing federal taxes. The government taxed investment income on the basis of a 1959 formula—

The problem was solved, or at least minimized, by Update '83, which recognized loan activity in the allocation of dividends.

Update '80 offered a lower reserve rate and higher insurance coverage at no additional premium.

unique to the insurance industry—that worked relatively well under normal economic conditions. As the inflationary spiral rose, however, it pulled interest rates up behind it, creating enormous gains in the taxable portion of investment earnings and enormous pressure on the dividends they supported. The cumulative effects were staggering. In 1959, mutual insurance companies could deduct 90 percent of their dividend payments from federal taxes; in 1979, the ratio dropped to 50 percent. Real investment yields suffered accordingly. At Northwestern Mutual, the gap between pre- and post-tax yields was 0.29 percent in 1957, 0.71 percent in 1967, and 1.33 percent in 1979, when taxes reduced the net return from 7.41 percent to 6.08 percent. No one denied that the law was disproportionately harsh on life insurers. Between 1959 and 1978, after-tax income for all American corporations rose 350 percent while income taxes grew only 200 percent. The life insurance industry's position was reversed: a 300-percent gain in income and a 500-percent increase in taxes.

Legislative remedies would come eventually, but Northwestern wanted relief *now*. The most obvious solution lay in its reserve rate. Because the 1959 formula taxed companies on the difference between their assumed interest earnings (the reserve rate) and the interest they actually earned, it made sense to reduce the spread between the two. Northwestern raised its reserve rate on new policies from 2.25 percent to 3 percent in 1968 and then 4 percent in 1978. The decisions were not made lightly. A higher reserve rate meant lower taxes, but it also meant a narrower margin of safety and substantially lower insurance premiums—a matter of grave concern to the company's agents. Close tracking of the 4-percent policies demonstrated that lower premiums resulted in larger average policies and more policies sold per agent. Their fears of lower commissions were quieted for the moment, but many agents wondered how long they would have to live on a diet of increased productivity.

A move that stimulated sales and reduced taxes at the same time had obvious benefits, and Northwestern began to explore the possibility of making the 4-percent reserve rate retroactive to existing policies. The result was Update '80. The program offered pre-1978 policyowners a chance to raise their reserve rates and share in the resulting tax savings, which translated to a 14-percent average increase in the face amount of each policy—at no extra premium. Nearly 1.5 million policyowners were eligible for a total of $4.5 billion in additional coverage. Update '80 was an industry first. No other company had both the desire and the computer power to make such a costly, time-consuming program work. It began as a basic application of a venerable Northwestern tradition—treating all policyowners alike—and quickly became the focal point of the most intense marketing effort in the company's history. "Just watch our smoke," Francis Ferguson promised the western region's agents in late 1979. The amendment campaign was christened "Get More Out of Life," and Northwestern was identified as "The *Usually* Quiet Company"—a message that the Super Bowl and other television buys brought to over 80 percent of the national viewing audience.

By autumn, the home office staff was mailing 8,000 offers, processing 5,000 acceptances, and answering 900 toll-free phone calls every working day. The Update year closed with a 67-percent rate of acceptance and a 16-percent increase in new premium, but Northwestern also reaped an abundant harvest of good will. In an era of rampant inflation, Update '80 provided substantially increased protection at no additional cost. In a period of rising lapse and surrender rates, it gave existing policyowners a powerful incentive to stay with the company. At a time when America's business establishment was under fire, it made Northwestern a highly visible champion of fair play and concern for the customer. Francis Ferguson called Update '80 a "most magnificent manifestation of mutuality." Its success proved that, in Ferguson's words, "Big business and good business are not mutually exclusive."

Inflation was the gremlin behind the glaring tax inequities of the 1970s. Inflation was also the force that fueled the dramatic rise in policy loans during the same years.

Update '83 and Update '80—direct recognition and the reserve rate amendment—solved those problems, or at least rendered them more tolerable, in ways that were both highly creative and still entirely in keeping with Northwestern's principles. The problems facing the investment departments between 1967 and 1982 were not so easily remedied. The company's investors grappled with not only inflation but also bouts of recession, a stagnant stock market, and new limits on their freedom of action. Policy loans were the most serious brake on investment activity. As the company's largest single holding—exceeding 30 percent of assets at their peak—policy loans dried up investable capital and forced Northwestern into short-term, liquid instruments simply to meet the next spike in demand. Investment planning became a contradiction in terms, and long-term borrowers learned not to count on Northwestern for help with new ventures.

The liquidity account—Treasury bills, money market funds, preferred stocks, and other easily negotiable instruments—was one leg of the investment triangle that took shape during the Ferguson years. In an earlier period, surplus cash and temporary holdings had been signs of inefficiency. After 1967, as interest rates continued to climb, the liquidity account's yields were the most impressive in the portfolio. By the end of 1982, short-term investments totaled nearly 13 percent of Northwestern's assets. The remaining legs of the triangle—long-term instruments

The Update campaign enabled policyowners to "Get More Out of Life"—a message Francis Ferguson and his team wore on their chests.

San Diego

Chicago

Dallas

Determined to stay ahead of inflation, Northwestern took an equity interest in real estate developments from coast to coast.

and equities—involved significantly more planning and higher levels of risk. Long-term bonds and mortgages formed the necessary base of the portfolio, providing a steady, predictable flow of cash to meet death claims and ongoing expenses. Northwestern still bought the bonds of companies specializing in everything from aircraft to zinc, and it still loaned mortgage money to the developers of shopping malls and office towers. The investments seemed traditional, but their terms were not: maturities were shorter, dollar amounts were larger (the mortgage loan minimum climbed to $250,000 in the early 1970s), and nearly every investment included some type of incentive financing. Bonds and mortgages made up 51 percent of the portfolio in 1981—down from 77 percent in 1967, but still a majority of assets.

It was in the field of equities—the third leg—that Northwestern separated itself from the pack. The variety and volatility of the equity portfolio would have shocked Henry Palmer, but Ferguson and his executives were determined to find investments that would ride upward with the cost of living. Northwestern, in effect, tried to protect itself by taking risks; within carefully defined limits, the company removed the floor as well as the ceiling on its potential returns. The stock market was perhaps the easiest point of entry into equities, and common stocks rose from 4.6 percent of the firm's assets in 1968 to 7.4 percent in 1974. Like many insurers, Northwestern joined the parade just in time to see it end. After a 390-percent increase between 1949 and 1967, the Dow Jones Industrial Average flattened, rising a scant 1 percent in the next decade. In 1974, a particularly hard year for stockbrokers, Northwestern's stock portfolio suffered real and paper losses of $138 million, nearly a third of their value in the previous year. Common stocks dropped to 1.9 percent of the company's assets in 1981, their lowest point in more than twenty years.

Northwestern's real estate developments—both joint ventures and independent projects—were somewhat less volatile and certainly more colorful equity investments. Policyowner dollars went out to luxury second-home resorts in Hawaii and on Hilton Head Island; sprawling agricultural developments in Arizona and coastal North Carolina; and commercial centers in San Francisco, Houston, and Milwaukee. Not all were equally successful. A real estate recession in the mid-1970s dampened the demand for expensive second homes, and the same downturn crippled a Northwestern real estate investment trust launched in 1971. On the positive side of the ledger, Ghirardelli Square, a San Francisco chocolate factory converted to shops and restaurants, gave Northwestern an iconic (and modestly profitable) presence on the West Coast. Closer to home, the Grand Avenue Mall, a multi-level retail center built around an elegantly refurbished 1916

Milwaukee

Milwaukee

Ghirardelli

San Francisco

Northwestern's oil and gas investments took the company into uncharted waters—with some gratifying results.

arcade, became a catalyst for the ongoing revitalization of Milwaukee's downtown.

Of all Northwestern's equity ventures, energy exploration was both the most radical and initially the most rewarding. Years before the Arab oil embargo made energy a national obsession, Francis Ferguson had concluded that petroleum was an undervalued resource. In 1972, to the immense surprise of executives in both the oil and the insurance fields, Ferguson led his company into a partnership with four energy firms that had won offshore drilling leases in the Gulf of Mexico. Northwestern's stake in the project, originally $44 million, swelled to $137 million in 1979, making the offshore platforms the largest single investment in Northwestern's history. Business journalists were quick to see the ironies in a staid old life insurance company "wildcatting" in the coastal oilfields, and Ferguson took his share of ribbing at industry meetings. The last laugh was not long in coming. Although the initial finds were disappointing, a tract off Texas was far richer than anyone had expected. The payoff began in 1977 and increased annually, providing Northwestern with a return well in excess of 20 percent.

From Gulf oil to golf resorts, equity investments strengthened Northwestern's bottom line, but they were never lucrative enough to counterbalance the massive weight of the policy loan account. Almost inevitably, the company lost ground to

its competitors. In 1967, before the loan epidemic began in earnest, Northwestern's pre-tax investment yield was 5.04 percent, well above the industry's 4.82-percent average. In 1982, the company's net rate of return rose to 7.8 percent, but the industry average climbed significantly higher, reaching 8.91 percent. Northwestern's investors may have been frustrated at times, but they learned to accept change and challenge as the only constants in the post-1967 financial markets. They also developed a taste for the risks and rewards inherent in new ventures. Although the company never lost sight of its long-term obligations to policyowners, innovation and risk-taking emerged as the clear paths to superior returns.

Francis Ferguson remained a hands-on investor, particularly in the energy arena, but he relied on a staff of seasoned field generals. Their leader was Robert Barrows, another native of upstate New York and another World War II pilot. In 1973, after a stint as head of the Mortgage Department, Barrows had been named senior vice-president for investments. In a time of tight money and general volatility, the board wanted an executive whose sole job was to coordinate the activities of all the investment departments. Only three years later, Bob Barrows received one more promotion, taking a position as Ferguson's assistant and heir apparent. Triumph was followed by tragedy. Only a few weeks after joining Ferguson,

Barrows discovered that he had cancer. Despite last-ditch attempts to stem the disease, he died on May 20, 1977, at the age of 54.

Barrows' successor as head of the investment operation was another company veteran: Donald Schuenke. A product of Milwaukee's blue-collar South Side, Schuenke (*shenk'-ee*) had joined Northwestern in 1963 as a young investment lawyer. He developed an impressive ability to improve the firm's position in last-minute contract negotiations, and his skills earned him promotions to general counsel in 1974 and investment chief in 1976. Schuenke's staff featured some rising stars, including another South Sider who had joined the company in 1969 as a stock trader: Edward Zore. Don Schuenke had only four years to make his mark on the investment departments. On August 1, 1980, at the age of fifty-one, he became Northwestern's fourteenth president and a member of the board. Ferguson retained the chief executive officer position and moved up to the board chairmanship.

The volatile economy was certainly the major external force affecting Northwestern, but change and challenge were just as prevalent on the social front. A new mood of skepticism and dissent swept through American society after 1967, touching even the usually placid insurance industry. One expression of that skepticism was a vibrant consumer movement that materialized in the early 1970s. Hoping to do for life insurance what Ralph Nader had done for—or to—the automotive industry, a vocal cadre of critics blasted what they viewed as overpriced products, misleading advertising, and unscrupulous agents. Calls for a foolproof method of cost comparison between insurance companies were especially loud. Northwestern, in truth, had little to fear from the reformers: the company ranked at or near the top of the industry regardless of which yardstick was used. In 1972, Francis Ferguson called the consumer movement "one of the most positive and exciting things ever," adding, "It can only help NML."

Northwestern felt the era's social ferment more directly in its own home office. The company had long been a bastion of white male managers and white female clerical workers. The first woman was promoted to a managerial post in 1938 and the first African American on any level was hired in 1951, but Northwestern was something less than a trailblazer on the road to cultural diversity. That changed in the 1970s, partly in response to federal directives and partly out of a desire to look more like the rest of American society. The ratio of women in official, managerial, and professional jobs (federal categories) climbed from 15 to 43 percent of the total between 1970 and 1979, and their share of Northwestern's technical jobs nearly doubled, rising to 68 percent. African Americans, Latinos, Native Americans, and other minorities became a more familiar sight

The company's work force looked more and more like the rest of American society in the 1970s. Attorney Peter Bruce (back row, left) would retire in 2007 as Northwestern's chief insurance officer.

Francis Ferguson was an agent of changes both large and small. In 1979, he lifted the decades-old ban on coffee—a move that personnel director Milford "Jake" Jacobson (bottom) heartily endorsed.

in the halls of the home office. In the official/manager/professional categories, their ratio increased from 0 to 5 percent between 1970 and 1979; in the technician class, from 3 to 7 percent. Neither group was well-represented in the highest levels of the company, but the days when women were expected to type and minorities were expected to work elsewhere had vanished forever.

Whatever their backgrounds or positions, Northwestern employees experienced a sharp cultural shift after 1967. "Mother Mutual" had always behaved like a Victorian parent: supportive but stern, enforcing traditional rules long after they had fallen into disuse elsewhere. The company steadily retreated from that posture under Francis Ferguson. In 1971, after decades of tar-stained washroom walls, employees were allowed to smoke at their desks—a practice that ended just as abruptly in 1986. Northwestern was perhaps the industry's last employer that prohibited not only coffee breaks but coffee itself, a ban that Ferguson lifted in 1979. Employees pooled their resources to buy percolators, and furtive trips to neighborhood coffee shops came to a sudden end. A more sweeping change occurred in 1973, when the company introduced flexible hours, a system that allowed most workers to choose any starting time between 7 and 9 A.M. Supervisors who had feared that their employees would lie in bed as long as possible were surprised to find half the work force arriving before 7:30.

The various liberalizations reflected the desire of Northwestern's employees to be treated like responsible adults—a desire communicated most clearly by the company's labor union. Organized as an independent in 1937, the union became a local of the Associated Unions of America shortly after World War II and then affiliated with the Office and Professional Employees International Union (AFL-CIO) in 1972. Some of the period's internal reforms arose from negotiations with the OPEIU and others developed independently, but all were well-timed. The generation that showed up for work after 1967 had little appetite for corporate parenting. As Northwestern became a more progressive, more responsive employer, workers gave tangible evidence of their approval: the number of days lost per employee fell steadily every year, and turnover in non-management positions dropped to its lowest point since World War II.

In September 1982, after more than fourteen years on the job, Northwestern's highest-ranking employee announced that he was stepping down, effective the following March. When Francis Ferguson took the wheel in 1968, he had said that no CEO should stay until mandatory retirement at sixty-five. A decade, perhaps, was sufficient. Beyond that point, he insisted, the fresh trails of the early years became ruts, and all you could do was "re-massage your old prejudices." True to his word, or nearly so, Ferguson was sixty-one when he made the announcement.

The Ferguson years were, in retrospect, a time of major initiatives on multiple fronts. After two decades of relative somnolence, Northwestern Mutual had decided to grow, and the results were striking. Between 1967 and 1982, the company's field force nearly doubled and its sales volume increased tenfold. Northwestern offered one of the most innovative products on the market. Its planning programs and computer systems were the envy of the industry. The firm had become a presence, however quiet, on national television. Its home office was a distinctive blend of old and new, and its investments, particularly those in energy, broke new ground for the life insurance business. Even the intrusions of the outside world were met creatively. The Update programs—direct recognition and the reserve-rate amendment—were pioneering solutions to industry-wide problems.

Northwestern found the "heightened sense of destiny" that Francis Ferguson had been seeking for it, but never at the expense of tradition. Although it became a livelier company, doing more things and doing them better, on the whole, than in previous years, the firm retained a deep fidelity to the principles of its founders. Ferguson looked both backward and ahead in 1979:

New conditions, new ideas, and new problems will always be part of our environment. But I believe that we will continue to find that the best results are still accomplished in the old way. We'll be guided by the principles of mutuality, trusteeship, and economy of operation, as we have in the past.

It was Francis Ferguson, an agent of significant change, who decided to highlight the Executive Committee statement of 1888—that ringing declaration of Northwestern's resolve to be "the policyowner's company"—in bold brass letters at the entrance to the new East Building.

Tradition was still served, but the challenges were far from over. Trends that surfaced during the Ferguson years continued after his departure, pushing Northwestern Mutual in directions that even he might have found surprising. Step by step, the company moved farther from the practices of its past. Year by year, Northwestern was emerging in all the wondrous complexity of its modern form. 🌱

Even as his company changed, Ferguson always felt the sustaining power of Northwestern's principles behind him.

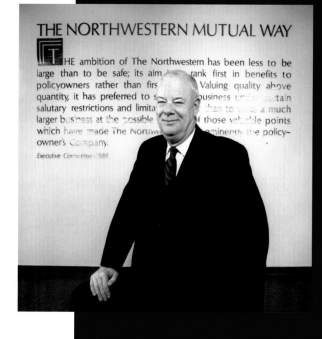

THE NORTHWESTERN MUTUAL WAY

THE ambition of The Northwestern has been less to be large than to be safe; its aim is to rank first in benefits to policyowners rather than first ... Valuing quality above quantity, it has preferred to ... business under certain salutary restrictions and limita... than to ... a much larger business at the possible ... f those valuable points which have made The Northw... eminently the policyowner's Company.

Executive Committee 1888

FORTUNE

AMERICA'S
MOST ADMIRED
CORPORATIONS

FORTUNE's Annual Survey

chapter 6
1982 - 1993

"KEEP THE FAITH"

Every business enterprise moves to a rhythm all its own. Each follows a distinctive tempo—fast and slow in alternating sequence—through the highs and lows of the economic cycle and its chosen market. At Northwestern Mutual, those changes in pace have coincided, more often than not, with presidential terms. The company has had what appears to be remarkable luck in choosing the right leader for the right time: a principled autocrat like Henry Palmer in an ethically challenged era, a charismatic optimist like Michael Cleary during the Depression and World War II, and an entrepreneurial dynamo like Francis Ferguson in a period of economic volatility. After the fireworks of the Ferguson years, it was time for another change of pace. Northwestern was ready for a calming influence, a leader who could help the company consolidate the gains of its previous fifteen years and chart a sound course for the future.

For more than ten years, that role was filled with remarkable steadiness by Donald Schuenke. Patient, methodical, and so slow to anger that he was considered unflappable, Schuenke was to all appearances a quiet leader for The Quiet Company. There was, however, no lack of drama during his decade at the

Donald Schuenke was a patient, deeply principled leader during a challenging period in Northwestern's history.

helm. It was on Schuenke's watch that Northwestern faced one of the most formidable competitive threats in its history, and it was during his tenure that the company took its first definitive steps toward the broad product platform of the present. Through it all, Schuenke maintained a passionate devotion to Northwestern's core principles. He had no desire to turn back the clock—"We are steeped in tradition without being stuck in it," he once declared—but the values of the company's founders were, in his view, nothing less than a faith to keep. During his turn as chief executive, Don Schuenke was determined to keep it.

The Challenge of Universal Life

Schuenke spent his first year as president on the customary tour of Northwestern's general agencies, meeting the troops, courting the media, and broadening his view of the company. He reminded the agents that he had once sold life insurance himself, representing National Life of Vermont as a young lawyer fresh out of Marquette University. Schuenke freely admitted that he was no threat to National Life's volume leaders, but the experience made him the first Northwestern president since Michael Cleary who had ever met a prospect or closed

a sale. What his audiences noticed about their new leader was the distinctive style he brought to the office. Schuenke was neither flamboyant nor physically imposing. He was, given his position, a remarkably unassuming man—even-handed, approachable, the kind of person you might as easily encounter on a suburban parish finance committee as on a major symphony board. A machinist's son with roots in Poland and Germany, Schuenke displayed some classic immigrant traits: thriftiness, self-reliance, and a sturdy work ethic. He was also a devout Catholic who held both himself and his company to the highest ethical standards. In September 1982, when Francis Ferguson announced his decision to step down, Don Schuenke was ready to put those values to work at the highest level. On March 1, 1983, he finally took the reins as Northwestern Mutual's chief executive officer.

Schuenke looked out on a somewhat altered landscape when he moved to the southeast corner of the fifth floor. After years in the stratosphere, investment yields and the cost of living were both returning to more normal levels. The inflation rate dropped from its peak of 13.5 percent in 1980 to 3.2 percent in 1983—Schuenke's first year as CEO—and would average only 3.1 percent for the next two decades. Thirty-year Treasury bills, in the meantime, after topping out at 14.68 percent in 1981, dropped into the single digits at the end of

1985 and have stayed there ever since. After such a dramatic run-up, however, no one in the insurance business could quite believe the corresponding downturn, and most insurers marketed their wares accordingly. The darling of the era was universal life, a product introduced in 1979 as the best of all possible worlds. Within broad limits, policyowners paid premiums in any amount they wished at any time they wished, and their cash values rose, theoretically, with their underlying investment results. Universal life offered complete flexibility and the chance, it was promised, to protect your loved ones and earn record-high returns at the same time. Because it was a new product based on new money rates, universal life's illustrations were irresistible; no traditional policy could hope to compete.

Consumers couldn't get enough of it. Nonexistent three years earlier, universal life came out of nowhere to capture 9 percent of the industry's new premium dollars in 1982 and an astonishing 38 percent in 1985. Traditional buyers began to doubt the wisdom of their purchases, triggering an epidemic of replacement activity. Policyowners by the tens of thousands traded in their old Chevrolets for the Porsche that universal life was claimed to be, and the nation's lapse rate nearly doubled between 1978 and 1985, climbing from 6.6 percent of all insurance policies to 12.3 percent. (Northwestern, normally a model of persistency, saw its own rate rise from 3.0

percent to 5.8 percent during the same years.) As the churning continued, universal life came to be known in some circles as "cannibal life."

Northwestern Mutual suddenly faced a threat every bit as daunting as the specter of disability insurance had been in the 1920s; the "competitive nightmare" of Michael Cleary's era seemed to have returned in even more virulent form. Anyone with even the most rudimentary grasp of finance understood that the prospect of double-digit investment results lasting for the entire life of a policy was about as likely as 365 straight days of sunshine in Seattle, but that didn't stop many insurers from illustrating 13-percent returns. Northwestern's response, true to form, was framed in unmistakably

The company's executive officers in 1980—the year Schuenke became president.

The introduction of CompLife in 1986 was a breakthrough event in the company's modern history.

INTRODUCING...
CompLife

It's what you've been waiting for!
Flexibility and adjustability as only the Northwestern Mutual can deliver!
It'll make you want to SHOUT!

moral terms. Chief actuary Dale Gustafson blasted universal life's marketing techniques as "a cynical exploitation of a temporary circumstance"—high interest rates—and the entire corps of home office executives, led by Don Schuenke himself, took every opportunity to preach the gospel of long-term values to the field. Stay the course, they advised the agents. What goes up has to come down. The portfolio will be king again.

Not every agent agreed. The veterans were inclined to patience, but even they had a clear message for the home office: we're getting killed out here. "I wear a fireman's hat all day long," complained an Iowa agent. Northwestern at least considered offering a universal life product of its own—the company even bought a universal software platform "just in case"—but the real need was for a product that could meet the competitive threat without compromising the firm's core commitment to mutuality; paying one class of policyowners higher returns than another was anathema. Variable Life, introduced in 1984, was the first response. It featured a level premium and a minimum death benefit, but cash values and coverage fluctuated with changes in an investment portfolio chosen by the policyowner: stocks, bonds, money market funds, or a blend of all three. The money-market option gave consumers access to the high short-term rates illustrated by the universal specialists, but Variable Life was not for everyone. Because the policyowner assumed the risk, it was a sharp departure from Northwestern tradition, and because it was an investment product, agents were subject to strict registration and reporting requirements. The new product found its market, but agents typically sold Variable Life as an addition to traditional coverage rather than an alternative.

The actuarial team, led by James Murphy from 1983 to 1988 and by William Koenig thereafter, continued to work on a policy with a more familiar structure and a more dependable floor. It finally went to market on January 1, 1986, when Northwestern unveiled its Comprehensive Life series—CompLife for short. The company had launched Extra Ordinary Life as the industry's first hybrid contract in 1968, the first to combine whole life and term in a seamless single policy. CompLife was EOL on steroids—a direct descendant of the original series but more flexible and more powerful. The contract had some conventional features—a level premium, guaranteed cash values and death benefits—but policyowners could combine the term and whole life elements in any ratio they chose, from "skinny" (nearly all low-premium term) to rich (nearly all high-premium whole life). Dividends were automatically applied to convert the term portion to permanent insurance, and additional contributions could be made at any time to accelerate the conversion process and build cash value. The

endless range of options prompted some agents to refer to CompLife as "Complicated Life," but it met an obvious need. At a time when consumers wanted flexibility and choice, CompLife let them build whatever type of insurance vehicle they wanted, from a Ford Escort to a Cadillac Fleetwood.

The new series became the focal point of the most extensive product launch in Northwestern's history. Home-office specialists led training sessions in every general agency and—a sign of the times— computer tutorials allowed agents to absorb the new product's finer points at their own speed. A barrage of print ads proclaimed CompLife a "revolutionary plan" designed to "keep the cost of family life insurance from getting out of hand." Addressing the agents at their 1986 annual meeting, Don Schuenke hailed the contract as "a new generation of life insurance" that offered "something for everyone." "But it's not universal life," he insisted. "It's better." CompLife's single most powerful selling point may have been the dividends behind it. Any portfolio of assets managed for the long term will lag both the highs and the lows of short-term investments. When CompLife debuted, short-term rates were in decline and portfolio rates were on the rise. The company adopted a dividend scale of 11.25 percent on unborrowed policies at a time when money-market funds were paying less than 8 percent, and Northwestern's returns were tax-deferred as well.

CompLife offered an unbeatable blend of flexibility and permanence that helped Northwestern's agents meet the challenge of universal life.

FRESH START

The Fresh Start program enabled owners of heavily borrowed policies to convert to CompLife.

The new product had great potential, but even the most optimistic insiders were surprised by its success. CompLife was instantly Northwestern's best-selling policy, and in 1987 it accounted for a resounding 40 percent of all new premium dollars. Not since EOL's introduction nearly twenty years earlier had one contract made such a splash. Led by CompLife, Northwestern's new business rose from $18.8 billion of coverage in 1983 to $41.8 billion in 1992—a 122-percent gain during a period when the industry as a whole could muster only 78 percent. Some agents, of course, sold more insurance than others. The lives leader for all ten of Don Schuenke's years in office (and the volume leader for six) was Daniel Brunette of Indianapolis. Brunette averaged 1,027 lives a year for the decade, and he made many of his sales the old-fashioned way: over the kitchen table. Another luminary of the 1980s and '90s was David Sprinkle, a Greensboro, North Carolina, agent who worked primarily in the corporate market. In 1990, Sprinkle became the first Northwestern agent to break the $100 million barrier, and he did it convincingly, selling $179.8 million of insurance on 325 lives. Just ten years earlier, $50 million had been enough to win the volume title.

CompLife had a salutary impact on sales, but it was notable for another reason. As agents were getting used to the new product in 1986, Congress passed a tax reform law with one provision of particular interest to the life insurance industry: interest on policy loans was no longer deductible. Northwestern promptly launched a program called "Fresh Start" that allowed the owners of heavily borrowed policies to retire their loans and increase their death benefits by converting to CompLife. As a direct result, loan repayments exceeded disbursements in 1987 for the first time in anyone's memory, and the account, as a percentage of assets, kept shrinking. From 30.6 percent of the total in 1982—their all-time high—policy loans dropped to 21.2 percent of Northwestern's assets in 1987 and 13.3 percent in 1993. There were smiles all around. Old policyowners had new coverage, the investment team had more money to put to productive use, and Northwestern finally had substantial relief from the burden of excessive policy loans.

Another nemesis faded from view at the same time. As Northwestern Mutual grew stronger in the 1980s, the purveyors of universal life grew weaker. The continuing drop in short-term interest rates dimmed the product's luster, and investment departments scrambled to make up the difference between the figures illustrated and actual returns. Some companies took ill-advised plunges into the murkier depths of the junk bond market, with results that were frequently enough disastrous. Executive Life, once the largest insurer in California, was the leading example. In 1991, the firm was declared insolvent and seized by the state insurance department. There was nothing intrinsically wrong with the product, but universal life in its 1980s form turned out to be a manipulative response to a short-lived condition.

Don Schuenke's sense of vindication could not have been sweeter. Like Michael Cleary in the 1920s, he had taken a difficult stand and lived to see its correctness confirmed. As other companies struggled to get back to the basics of life insurance, they found Northwestern waiting for them. "We never left the basics," Schuenke told the agents. "We did the right thing when we avoided universal life and offered our clients flexible coverage through CompLife instead." Looking back in retirement, he described the decision to sidestep universal life as a conspicuous highlight of his presidency. "One of my jobs," Schuenke said in 1999, "was to convince the agents to stay the course, and it worked pretty well. Of course," he added dryly, "it worked a lot better when those companies collapsed."

Northwestern Mutual's unswerving commitment to its mission—its steady performance in an unsteady world—did not go unnoticed. As other companies tinkered endlessly with their product lines, their distribution systems, and their investment portfolios, Northwestern became a much-praised model of corporate constancy. In 1983, the editors of *Fortune* launched an annual survey of executives, analysts, and outside directors in a wide range of industries to determine which firms they admired most. Agents and employees were delighted to learn that Northwestern was the most-admired life insurance company in America; they were even more thrilled to finish first in every *Fortune* survey that followed. The plaudits kept on coming. In 1984, the authors of *The 100 Best Companies to Work for in America* placed Northwestern Mutual in their top ten. Three years later, *Sales and Marketing Management* Magazine surveyed the life insurance field and pronounced Northwestern's agents the best in the business—an honor they took home repeatedly in the years that followed. The credit belonged in part to Dennis Tamcsin, the system-builder who appointed more than 90 percent of the general agents who were on the job during Schuenke's tenure.

Northwestern earned a full set of accolades in the 1980s, including "first in Fortune*" and "best in* Best's*."*

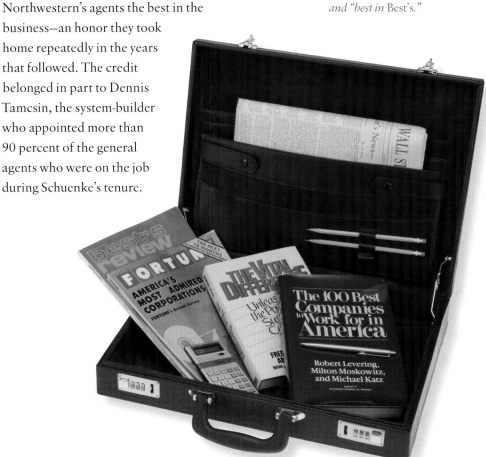

Wiring the future: computer cables became the arteries of the enterprise, whether in home office mainframes or (lower) *the nationwide LINK network.*

purchasing policies that were twice the size of the industry average and holding them twice as long. Northwestern, in turn, gave them the best value in the business—a fact confirmed by the twenty-year dividend histories published in *Best's Review* each year. No firm in the industry ranked first in *Fortune* or best in *Best's* with such impressive regularity. The ultimate source of Northwestern's success was no secret: the coherent vision rooted in values passed down from Henry Palmer's era and expressed most eloquently in the 1888 Executive Committee statement. At the annual meeting in 1988—the midpoint of his tenure—Don Schuenke paused to observe the centennial of that credo and to rededicate the company to its principles. Henry Palmer himself, in the person of a costumed actor, returned from the shadows to intone those familiar words: "less to be large than to be safe," "quality above quantity," "pre-eminently the policyowners' company." Schuenke engaged Palmer in dialogue and closed with a pledge of continued allegiance. "You gave us a faith to keep," he said, "and I promise that we will keep that faith fresh." As the session ended, every agent in attendance received an engraved copy of the 1888 statement to take home.

Northwestern Mutual was riding the crest of a wave in the 1980s: thriving in its chosen markets, respected by its peers, sure of its direction, and in touch with its past. But the company could hardly rest

Another key figure on the agency side was Richard Wright, who started the Field Financial Services Department in 1968 and went on to become one of the most influential figures in the company.

The accolades of the Eighties were certainly welcome—particularly those from inside the industry—but Northwestern was far more interested in the endorsement of its own policyowners. They had formed, through their agents, a durable bond with the company, on its laurels. As in earlier years, steady growth strained the capacity of the home office staff and, as in earlier years, the firm turned to technology for help. It was in the 1980s that computers moved from the black magic of high-security data centers to the open domain of everyone's desktop, and the shifts in technology, including communications technology, occurred with a speed that's all too easy to forget. In 1983, an 800 number (CALL-NML) was considered a breakthrough important enough to announce at the annual meeting. In 1987, as LINK II minicomputers became standard equipment in the general agencies, Don Schuenke felt moved to remind the dwindling band of holdouts that their world had changed. "To compete in the future," he advised, "agents will have to use the computer"—a statement that would have seemed self-evident to the next generation. LINK III debuted only three years later, featuring third-wave computers that were faster, more powerful, and loaded with applications. At the home office, in the meantime, a third mainframe joined the pair already in place, handling everything from annuity payments to oil investments. A fixture since the Fifties, computers grew ever more indispensable to the company, prompting an overdue name change. In 1985, the department organized as Data Processing was rechristened Information Systems, reflecting its evolution from an essentially clerical function to a place at the operational heart of the company.

Computers continued to help Northwestern do more work with fewer people. In 1957, the company employed 17.7 full-time workers for every $100 million of insurance in force. By 1982, the ratio had dropped to 2.4 employees per $100 million— the best showing in the industry—and it kept falling to 1.4 in 1988 and 0.8 in 1995. Such gains could not continue to the vanishing point. The computing needs of the business were growing faster than the physical dimensions of the computers were shrinking, and the proliferation of desktop units meant that every work station required 20 percent more floor space. There were more workers as well. The number of full-time employees grew from 2,097 in 1983 to 2,493 in 1988—a modest rise given the growth in business—but Northwestern's two-building campus seemed to be getting smaller by the day. In 1984, a hardy band of computer specialists trooped across Wisconsin Avenue to "temporary" quarters in the building immediately southwest of the home office. (Its primary tenant, ironically, had been the local office of IBM.) By the end of 1986, Information Systems

IBM CORPORATION

Introduced in 1961, the IBM Selectric typewriter was a standard office machine well into the 1990s.

The 611 Building, literally across the street from the home office, offered a temporary solution to Northwestern's space problems.

had practically taken over the seven-story structure, and work crews were rapidly bringing it up to Northwestern Mutual standards, complete with cafeteria.

The West, or 611, Building, as it was known, provided little more than a short-term answer to a long-term space problem. In January 1988, after four years of study and design work, the company broke ground for a $70 million solution: a home office addition that ultimately filled most of the square block north of the East Building. It was actually two structures in one, both clad in gray granite and glass. The first was a bi-level data center that housed Northwestern's three central processing units, their supporting equipment, and twelve miles of subfloor cable—all concealed beneath a multi-tiered cafeteria. The second was an eighteen-story office tower with 560,000 square feet of floor space—60,000 more than the East Building. Following established precedent, the 1888 Executive Committee statement was chiseled in granite at the entrance to the office tower. After a refreshingly trouble-free construction period, the North Office Building was ready for occupancy in October 1990, and it quickly absorbed nearly 1,000 people. Some worked in the investment departments, others in Communications or Corporate Services, but the greatest number were Information Systems employees. After a "temporary" sojourn that had lasted for six years, the computer team vacated the West Building, which became rental property—temporarily. Within a decade, the company would turn west again to relieve its space headaches. With completion of the North Office Building, Northwestern Mutual Place comprised a trio of structures, known internally by a rather inelegant set of acronyms: SOB, NOB, and EOB. The three were framed by meticulously tended seasonal plantings and linked by glass-enclosed skywalks affectionately known as "gerbil tubes." The entire ensemble gave Northwestern Mutual a commanding presence at the eastern end of Milwaukee's downtown.

The new building triggered a series of moves that ultimately affected 90 percent of the home office staff. Daily routines were inevitably disrupted, and the presence of two cafeterias added a new layer of complexity

The North Building, completed in 1990, provided a more permanent answer, with room for a state-of-the art data center and nearly 1,000 employees.

Madonna Hostetter

Deborah Beck

Barbara Piehler

Martha Valerio

The glass ceiling at
Northwestern shattered
in the 1980s, as women filled
more executive officer positions ...

to lunch planning—always an important cultural activity at Northwestern Mutual. Expansion placed some strain on the company's culture, but there were no major restructurings during the Schuenke years, and the character of the work force changed only gradually. Northwestern remained a statistical matriarchy, with a work force that was 70 percent female. What did change was the prominence of women in upper management. Madonna Hostetter, who had joined the firm in 1965 as an underwriter, became its first female executive officer in 1983, taking charge of the New Business Department. As the only woman (and one of the few non-golfers) in the firm's highest echelons, she was sometimes a lonely figure at executive planning rallies, but Hostetter eventually had company. By 1991, she headed the new Underwriting Standards Department, and three more women had

entered the executive officer ranks: Deborah Beck in New Business, Barbara Piehler in Corporate Services, and Martha Valerio in Policy Benefits. There were, in addition, sixty-two women officers. Deb Beck, who joined the company as an attorney in 1975, rose the highest. By the time she retired in 2006, Beck was an executive vice-president with ultimate responsibility for 1,500 employees—nearly a third of the entire work force. She was also the convener of an informal network of women in management whose members gathered periodically to socialize, share advice, and even, on occasion, play golf.

The glass ceiling had shattered in the field as well. In 1988, Beverly Chrisman became Northwestern's first female general agent, managing an operation in the far western reaches of Los Angeles. There were approximately 600 women in the field at the

Catherine Cleary

Patricia Graham

Kathryn Wriston

Beverly Chrisman

time—just over 10 percent of all agents but significantly more than the 100 who had sold Northwestern policies a decade earlier. On the board level, pioneer Catherine Cleary stepped down in 1987 after thirty-two years of service. Although she had first known Northwestern as the president's daughter, Cleary had become a prominent banker and lawyer in her own right. By the time she retired, two more women sat on the Board of Trustees: Patricia Graham and Kathryn Wriston. There was always room for improvement, but Northwestern had clearly made great progress. In 1993, the company received an EVE Award (Exemplary Volunteer Efforts) from the U.S. Department of Labor for its commitment to hiring and promoting women and minorities.

For the men and women of the investment departments—the nearly 300 employees who filled the top six floors of the new

North Building with their spreadsheets and ratings manuals—the Schuenke years were a time of steady growth and gradual change. Northwestern's assets more than tripled during the period, climbing from $14.6 billion in 1983 to $44.1 billion in 1993, and the company moved from tenth place to eighth in the industry rankings. Even though the threat of inflation was fading, the investment team lost none of its taste for equities. Bonds remained the base of the portfolio, doubling from 23 percent of assets in 1983 to 46 percent in 1993, but nearly all included some form of equity participation. In 1984, for instance, new investments carried a contract rate of 10.5 percent but an expected yield of 14.2 percent—a fairly typical spread for the period. The gap narrowed as market rates declined (taking Northwestern's dividend scale with them), but the constant infusion of new

... and became a significant force on the Board of Trustees as well. Beverly Chrisman was the pioneer among the general agents.

Investments of the 1980s included the tallest buildings in Honolulu (above) and Tampa (upper right) as well as apartment complexes across the country.

money pushed the pre-tax yield of the entire portfolio steadily upward, from 7.88 percent in 1983 to a new peak of 8.98 percent in 1989.

As one of the larger institutional investors in America, Northwestern developed a portfolio that was notable for its scope as well as its size. In the 1980s, the company owned the tallest buildings in Tampa and Honolulu, both of them anchoring downtown commercial centers valued in excess of $100 million. On the agricultural front, Northwestern's ventures ranged from a 1,700-acre vineyard in California's San Joaquin Valley to sprawling grapefruit groves near Florida's famed Indian River. The real estate portfolio, which was worth $4.5 billion in 1986, included shopping malls in Lansing, warehouses in Utah, parking structures in Chicago, and garden apartments in Orange County. Northwestern also continued to invest in oil and gas exploration. The spectacular results of the 1970s would not be repeated, but fossil-fuel holdings made this Midwestern life insurance company one of the thirty-five largest energy firms in America. Other investments defied classification. Policyowner dollars financed commercial jetliner fleets, a San Francisco newspaper, and a song catalog with 50,000 titles, including *Over the Rainbow* and *Singin' in the Rain*. One transaction might have caused the puritans of the company's past to roll over in their graves: a $100 million private placement in the distillery that made Jack Daniels and Southern Comfort.

The largest single investment of the period, and one of the most unusual in the company's history, gave Northwestern controlling interest of another insurance firm. The Mortgage Guaranty Insurance Corporation, founded in Milwaukee in 1957, was the largest private mortgage insurer in America. Better known as MGIC ("Magic"), it had enabled millions of moderate-income families to purchase their own homes even if they lacked the standard 20-percent down payment. During the recession of the early 1980s, when thousands of homeowners defaulted and its parent company went bankrupt, MGIC was in significant distress. Northwestern played the role of white knight, investing $250 million in the firm when others declined to step forward. The 1985 transaction had the potential, Don Schuenke maintained, to be "one of the most profitable investments the company has made," and it would also keep "a major Milwaukee employer remaining in the community." Conditions deteriorated after the purchase, but Schuenke and his colleagues were determined to turn the firm around. With a boost from stricter underwriting, new management, and a stronger economy, MGIC did indeed recover its old magic. Northwestern began to sell its stock in the reborn enterprise in 1991. By the time all the shares were gone, the company had realized a gain of nearly $1.4 billion on its original stake of $250 million.

The quarterback of the investment team during Schuenke's tenure was another Northwestern veteran: James Ericson. A native of bustling Hawarden, Iowa, and one of several home-office Scandinavians, Ericson had joined the company in 1965 as an investment lawyer. He became Francis Ferguson's assistant in 1972, and other promotions followed: head of Policy Benefits in 1975, general counsel in 1976 (succeeding Schuenke), and investment chief in 1980 (again following Schuenke). Jim Ericson made investment planning a central priority in his new position. The shift to equities had a disturbing impact on cash flow, and he instituted a system of reporting and projection that gave Northwestern the clearest possible picture of its position from one year to the next. As Ericson's departments continued to shine, one more promotion awaited him.

The Mortgage Guaranty Insurance Corporation (MGIC) was one of the period's largest, most demanding, and ultimately most profitable investments.

The Challenges of Diversification

In the 1980s, as the investment portfolio swelled, the home office expanded, and CompLife won new converts, a subplot had been developing. Slowly but steadily, Northwestern was moving toward a broader definition of its mission, branching out from life insurance to a significant number of related business lines. The trend was apparent in the very earliest days of Don Schuenke's administration. The theme of the 1983 executive planning rally—the first he led as CEO—was "The Challenges of Diversification." Before they discussed how and when to diversify, however, the executive officers, in true Northwestern fashion, tried to identify their company's "givens"—the irreducible elements of its identity. Don Schuenke reported the group's findings at the agents' 1983 annual meeting. "We want to continue putting the policyowner first," he said, "which we call trusteeship; mutuality and equity play a big part here." But trusteeship and mutuality, the executives decided, could apply to a multitude of products. Schuenke went on to announce that Northwestern would soon be selling Variable Life, group life and health insurance, and a wider array of pension products. He hinted that the actuaries had "other things on the drawing board" that were soon to come.

The company was, in fact, no stranger to multiple product lines. Individual life insurance had always been its centerpiece, but Northwestern was a major player in two other fields: disability insurance and annuities. Since offering its first disability income policy in 1969, the firm had quietly climbed into first place among the country's mutual insurers. Three-fourths of Northwestern's agents sold at least one policy each year, and they tended to target medical professionals: nearly 40 percent of the firm's DI policyowners in 1984 were doctors. Claims experience deteriorated later in the decade, prompting an extensive retooling of the contract, but disability insurance remained a core business line. Northwestern issued its one-millionth policy in 1993.

Annuities were the third leg of the product tripod. The 1968 decision to sell stock-based variable annuities had been made with some trepidation. Robert Dineen warned that, since buyers bore the risk of loss, the annuities represented "a very important and fundamental move." With the stock market still on the rise, Northwestern decided to move forward anyway, but first there were some regulatory hurdles to clear. A subsidiary (NML Equity Services) was formed to advise the fund and train the field force, agents were required to register with the Securities and Exchange Commission, and separate accounts were established to isolate the variable assets from the rest of the company's funds. Actual sales of the annuities ebbed and flowed with changes in the economy and federal tax law, but the spadework of the 1960s created much of the infrastructure for later expansion on the investment side.

More radical ideas were at least discussed. Although he was an ardent defender of the specialist's faith, Edmund Fitzgerald had seriously considered buying a group life insurance company in the early 1950s; he pulled back only after concluding that Northwestern could not spare the executive talent necessary to run the firm. Francis Ferguson explored a fee-based "executive estate planning service" in 1971, hoping to capitalize on his agents' expertise. That idea came to nothing at the time, but ten years later Ferguson took a proposal for group health insurance all the way to the board. The trustees discouraged further development work, and the 1981 Policyowners' Examining Committee concurred, stating that a group health product might be "dilutive of the company's excellence." Northwestern restricted its focus to three areas—life insurance, annuities, and disability insurance—that offered protection against the financial consequences of dying too soon, living too long, or suffering the "economic death" of disability.

It was in the 1980s—on Don Schuenke's watch—that the three-course meal began to resemble a smorgasbord, and it was Northwestern's agents who set the table.

Agents have always been the company's finger on the pulse of the marketplace; they know from one day to the next precisely what will sell and precisely what won't. In the 1970s and '80s, what they began to sell in ever-increasing volume was the products of other companies. A 1979 study showed that, of all the premium dollars generated by Northwestern agents, 39 percent went elsewhere. Some went to companies willing to accept applicants who couldn't meet Northwestern's strict underwriting standards. Others went to purveyors of dirt-cheap term. But a substantial proportion of the agents' outside business involved products that their firm did not sell, particularly group health and life policies, mutual funds, and tax-sheltered investments, including real estate limited partnerships. The agents were doing what they had always done—trying to serve their clients, augment their incomes, and ward off competitors—but the 1979 study created a great deal of consternation in the home office. Of all the forces that fueled the first stage of diversification, the 39-percent outside business figure was undoubtedly the most important.

The mobile telephone with attached antenna was a precursor of the modern cell phone.

The decision to branch out was not made lightly. Northwestern had always maintained an almost-religious devotion to a clean, uncluttered product line and the sharp focus it fostered in both home office and field. But there were some real-world hazards involved in doing nothing. The company's general agents were already feeling the pressure. Their incomes were absolutely dependent on the Northwestern sales of the agents they managed. They recruited the agents, housed them, paid the utility bills, hired the support staff, and shared in training expenses. Many were disheartened to find their field workers spending a substantial portion of each day on sales activity that contributed absolutely nothing to the agency. Some took direct action. By 1982, roughly 20 percent of Northwestern's general agents had formed agreements with other firms, typically for overriding compensation on cases placed by their sales representatives. They were functioning, in effect, as double agents.

The agreements gave home office executives even more reason to worry. Outside business threatened the very existence of the exclusive franchise that underpinned Northwestern's distribution system. The company had nurtured what many considered the finest field force in the nation, and the prospect of effectively losing it to "parasitic" competitors was chilling. Don Schuenke put the matter bluntly in a 1982 address to the field force: "Every time an agent sells a product outside of our system, it helps destroy that system." The same theme was sounded in speech after speech. "Do not," Schuenke implored the agents, "feed the hand that bites you." It was clear, however, that actions would have to accompany words.

New music for the field: agents trooped into the 1988 annual meeting, during a period of increasing product diversification for their company.

The company's leaders knew that, if the trends continued, there was an indeterminate point at which Northwestern's field force would no longer be Northwestern's.

The strategy that emerged in 1982 was one part defense and one part offense. The executive team concluded that diversification was necessary, but they saw it as a way to broaden the time-honored circle of success, to strengthen the bonds between agents, policyowners, and the home office. If the home office made more products available, agents would have less reason to do business with other companies, and policyowners would have less reason to seek the services of other agents. All concerned would receive more of what they needed. The company as a whole would be more efficient, more productive, and more interdependent. The result, looking ahead to 1992, was described as a "boutique," a company that offered a broader variety of products to meet a broader variety of needs. There was some resistance to the shift in direction, particularly among the more hardened traditionalists in the home office but, as the implications of the long-term trends became clearer, the prospect of dying on the barricades for a moribund ideal had less and less appeal.

Years of smoke finally erupted into flame in September 1982, when Northwestern announced a pair of strategic acquisitions: Standard of America Life Insurance Company and Robert W. Baird and Company. Standard of America, based in suburban Chicago, was a stock company specializing in group life and disability coverage for the employer market. Its seventy-five agents also sold group health insurance in concert with the Blue Cross and Blue Shield organizations in dozens of states.

Robert W. Baird, headquartered literally across the street from Northwestern Mutual's home office, was a regional brokerage firm with twenty-four branches in six Midwestern states, all of them offering a full range of stocks, bonds, mutual funds, and other investment products. In its annual report to policyowners, Northwestern was careful to put the two transactions in context:

> *These moves do not signal a change in our basic philosophy of concentrating on individual life insurance products. However, these two companies offer Northwestern Mutual unique opportunities to increase our future options in the rapidly emerging financial services market.*

The Standard and Baird purchases were, in other words, anchors to windward—transitional steps that presented a wealth of "future options" but, in the meantime, made perfect sense as investments.

Standard of America, it was hoped, would give Northwestern instant access to group insurance—an issue that had been hotly debated in the home office since at least the World War I era. In 1984, after further research and even more debate, the company decided to enter the group market through a different door. Rather than sell Standard's products or develop its own, Northwestern formed alliances with five reputable group life and health companies. These preferred providers competed for business on a case-by-case basis, submitting their proposals to Northwestern's agents through the LINK computer system. The company adapted its own annuities to the needs of the employer-sponsored pension market, and a group disability insurer joined the preferred-provider roster in 1988. The new arrangement enhanced the agents' ability to serve their small-business clients, providing them with access to a full range of group life, health, pension, and disability products without leaving the Northwestern umbrella. The agents did not, however, work alone. In 1982, the company hired Robert Carlson, former research director of the Life Insurance Marketing and Research Association (LIMRA), to head its marketing effort. Carlson led the campaign to build a network of group specialists in Northwestern's general agencies—trained experts who were always available to help the agents tailor individual solutions for their clients. "It was never intended," said Carlson, "that the agent was going to be a walking financial encyclopedia." The new senior vice-president worked closely with Walt Wojcik, Standard of America's former president, to craft Northwestern's approach to the employer-sponsored market. Trained as an actuary, Wojcik was an able executive who went on to serve as Northwestern's chief planner, chief financial officer, and chief information officer before he retired in 2002.

Growing from a seed that was first planted with the Standard of America purchase, group insurance blossomed in scores of agencies around the country, adding vitality to the three-way relationship between home office, field, and policyowner. In a long view, however, the Baird purchase was the more fateful of the two transactions, and it was certainly the more profitable. Northwestern bought Baird on the eve of the most breathtaking rise in the stock market's history. The Dow Jones Industrial Average climbed from an anemic 777 in August 1982, when the Baird agreement was in its final draft, to 2,701 in August 1987—a gain of 247 percent in five years. Common stocks languished for a time after the meltdown of October 19, 1987, but a "superbull" market

materialized three years later, carrying the Dow Jones from 2,810 in January 1990 to an undreamed-of 11,723 in January 2000. The rising market carried Robert W. Baird with it, generating consistently high returns for the brokerage firm's parent.

Double-digit profits are always welcome, but Baird had larger significance as Northwestern's foothold in the world of financial services—a foothold that has since broadened into a major niche. In its early stages, the "Baird experiment" had much in common with the group insurance initiative. Beginning in 1983, Northwestern placed Baird specialists in all of its general agencies. Their sole assignment was to work with individual agents whose clients wanted to buy mutual funds or tax shelters; the agents supplied the relationship, and the specialists supplied the expertise. For representatives who were already selling variable annuities, the move to direct investments was not particularly daunting. As the number of registered agents continued to grow, and as the stock market continued to rise, the volume of Baird products sold through the Northwestern channel soared from $4.1 million in 1984 to $87 million in 1986, and that was just the beginning. Before Baird, Northwestern's executives had watched with distinct anxiety as their agents entered the treacherous (and potentially litigious) waters of the investment world. As the Baird experiment became an established reality

New leadership: Bob Carlson (top) brought marketing expertise to Northwestern that was unmatched in the industry, and Walt Wojcik headed everything from Planning to Information Systems during his career.

Don Schuenke emphasized that Northwestern would stay true to its roots in life insurance even as the company offered a greater number of "ancillary" products.

A few years ago, it became clear that the needs of our target market were broadening. A good portion of our distribution system was providing additional products and services outside of our system to meet those client needs. Maybe we were a little late, but we are now providing many of those additional products and services ourselves. Let's call them ancillary products....

But the Northwestern is not providing these ancillary products as an end in themselves. They do not carry the same weight—the same value—as our primary products. And they never will. We offer additional products for a dual purpose. First, to strengthen the distribution system by enhancing client control and providing additional income to the agency force. And second, to sell more of our primary products, which are life insurance, disability insurance and annuities.

in the general agencies, everyone breathed easier. Agents had more to sell, policyowners had more reasons to buy from them, and the circle continued to grow within the sheltering confines of the Northwestern Mutual system.

Group life, group health, group disability, pension plans, mutual funds, and tax shelters were all important new arrows in the agents' quivers, but they were never intended to replace the long lance of life insurance. Northwestern's decision to diversify was made in the service of a broader goal. Addressing the agents in 1986, Don Schuenke spoke with absolute clarity about the genesis of the new products and their place in the larger corporate scheme:

The secondary products, in other words, supported Northwestern's primary mission, which was emphatically not financial services— at least as Don Schuenke understood the term:

The name "Financial Services" carries the wrong emphasis—it's the tail wagging the dog. The Northwestern is the premier life insurance company. We will continue to offer, and probably expand, our ancillary products. But our clients should know that they're dealing with the premier life insurance company.... The Northwestern meets fundamental needs, and the fundamentals don't change.

No one met fundamental needs better than Northwestern Mutual. It was ironic, therefore, and more than a little troubling, when the company's core products began to show signs of stress in the late 1980s, just as the "ancillary" strategy was gaining momentum. Northwestern's experience mirrored industry-wide trends. The convulsions of the previous decade—inflation, recession, and shifting public perceptions—had changed the life insurance business dramatically. As universal life waxed and waned, the industry entered a period of generalized stagnation and widespread distress. The financial press issued categorical pronouncements that permanent cash-value life insurance, in particular, had become a sunset industry, one whose demise was just over the horizon, and that career agents would vanish with it. Standard & Poor's, a firm known for its analytical expertise, concluded in 1987 that the "captive" field force epitomized by Northwestern Mutual was "an expensive, outmoded delivery system" whose days were numbered.

Northwestern, ever the epitome of independence, paid scant attention to the doomsayers. Year after year, the company outpaced its peers in policies sold, face amount issued, and premium received. The 1986 debut of CompLife was particularly well-timed, just as EOL's had been in 1968; when the market wanted flexibility, Northwestern had it in abundance. Within a few years, however, the company began to feel the same chilly wind that was blowing through the rest of the industry. Although insurance in force continued to grow, the firm's sales momentum slowed after 1987, and there was a series of year-to-year declines in policies issued or premiums received. In 1984, the agents had met Don Schuenke's $100 Billion Challenge with room to spare, pushing Northwestern's insurance in force into the twelve-figure range. Six years later, they were unable to answer his "80 in '90" call—an appeal for each representative to write at least eighty lives a year by the end of 1990. The effort was also known as the President's Enhanced Productivity Program, or PEPP. When it became obvious that PEPP had lost its energy, the program was quietly abandoned.

The significance of the trends, their likely duration, and Northwestern's proper response were all maddeningly open questions, but no one panicked. The company was an oasis of

The agents met Schuenke's $100 Billion Challenge in 1984, lifting the firm's insurance in force to a new peak.

would not be surpassed until 2001. Spurred by a variety of home office incentives, the agents made a concerted effort to increase term conversions, and the "Simply Select" program allowed new policyowners to buy more insurance without underwriting. The results for 1993 were, to say the least, heartening: across-the-board increases of 25 percent in new coverage, 19 percent in new life premium, and 13 percent in policies sold. Northwestern Mutual, under Don Schuenke's leadership, was vindicated once again.

And then it was time to go. The underlying issues were far from resolved and the way forward was by no means clear, but the next decisions belonged to Northwestern's next leader. At the age of sixty-four, with mandatory retirement on the horizon, Schuenke announced that he would step down as chief executive officer on October 1, 1993. His successor was already in the wings. James Ericson had capped his rise through Northwestern's ranks by becoming the company's president on January 1, 1990. After an apprenticeship that lasted nearly four years, he was more than ready to take the wheel as CEO.

With sales momentum on the rise again and no crises looming, the company could take a leisurely look back at its decade under Don Schuenke. In an unquiet time, he had been a wellspring of calm, a sure and steady hand even when the wind seemed to blow the hardest. Under his leadership, Northwestern

stability and success—still the most-admired firm in its field and still gaining market share from its competitors. Northwestern had weathered temporary slowdowns before, and there was no reason to believe that conditions of the late 1980s and early 1990s were anything different. The immediate challenge was to get growing again. With a confidence born of experience, that's precisely the task Schuenke and his team embraced. Aggressive recruiting pushed the number of full-time agents to 5,797 in 1993—a peak that had met the challenge of universal life with flying colors, and it was beginning to take on the challenges of diversification as well. Through it all, Schuenke had maintained an unswerving fidelity to the company's deepest traditions and his own fervently held beliefs. What his colleagues remember most vividly about Schuenke is the unmistakable moral dimension he brought to virtually every decision he made. That perspective was clear in his emotion-filled valedictory address to the agents:

> *It has been my undiluted pleasure to be a member of this family for the last thirty years, and to serve as its leader for the last ten. Working here has been not a job, but a joy ... not an occupation, but a vocation. With absolute confidence in those who follow, I leave you with these words: Do the right thing. Fight the good fight. Keep the faith.*

Don Schuenke had indeed kept the faith during his ten-year tenure, and with superior results. That faith would endure, but it was now the task of a new generation to reinterpret and refresh Northwestern's credo, to ensure its continued vitality in a world that seemed to be growing more volatile by the day. 🔹

Home office and field ran together in the 1993 Roots and Wings race, an annual celebration of company spirit that began in 1978.

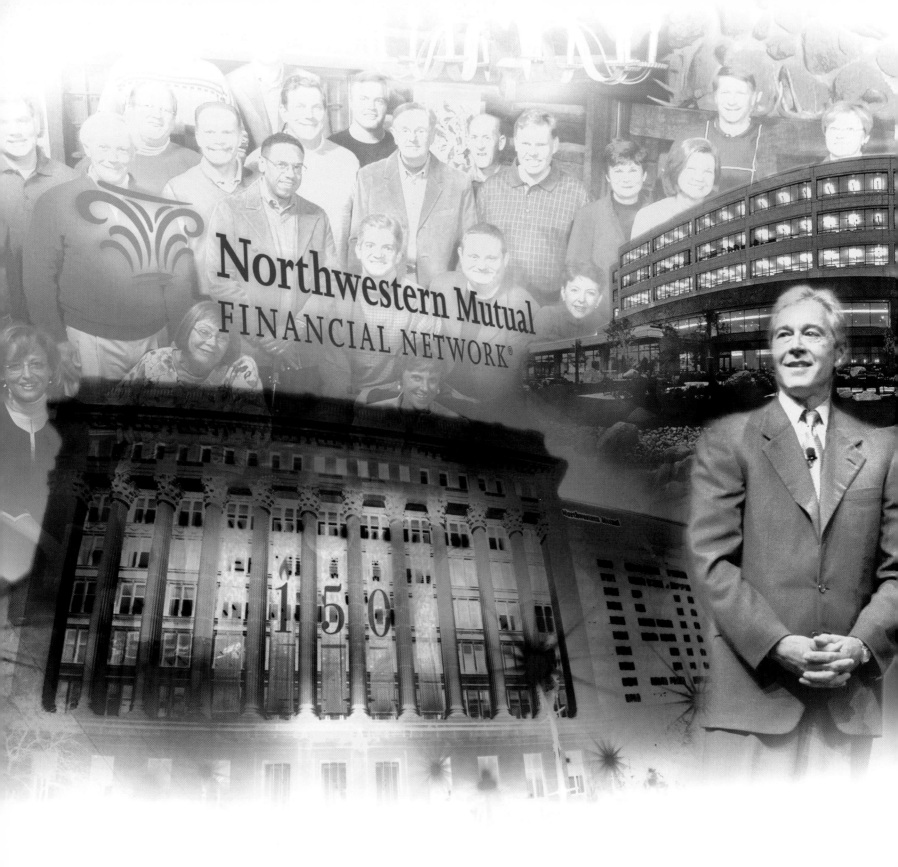

Northwestern Mutual
FINANCIAL NETWORK®

150

LARGER THAN LIFE

In the chronicle of any business enterprise that has weathered 150 years of change, the recent past inevitably appears as a work in progress. The events of earlier periods are already set in stone, while those of the last decade or two seem more like shifting sands—a jumbled assortment of decisions and details whose broader significance has yet to emerge. That may be true of any enterprise, but "work in progress" is an especially apt description of Northwestern Mutual at its 150th anniversary. No period in the firm's long history has witnessed a more sweeping transformation than the years since 1993. Steadily, purposefully, and inexorably, the company has moved from the relative simplicity of its traditions to a view of financial security that encompasses much more than life insurance. Northwestern, in a single phrase, has become larger than life. The implications of that shift for the company's present operations and future identity are still unclear, but they have already made the 1993-2007 period perhaps the most significant since Northwestern's rise to prominence in the mid-1800s.

Two chief executives—James Ericson and Edward Zore—have guided this work in progress on both sides of the millennium's turn. Despite pronounced differences in background and

Jim Ericson was a visionary leader who orchestrated Northwestern's response to dramatic change in the insurance industry.

temperament, they have played strongly complementary roles, exemplifying once again Northwestern's knack for choosing the right leader at the right time. The pair made a compelling combination: a visionary and a pragmatist. Jim Ericson took the broad view as his team shaped Northwestern Mutual's response to systemic change in its environment, while Ed Zore has focused with laser-like intensity on making that response a sustainable reality. Together Ericson and Zore have maintained Northwestern's superiority in every measure of performance, and together they have kept the firm moving, even as it changes, toward the goals its founders set in the nineteenth century.

Entering the New World

As much as he cherished his small-town roots, Jim Ericson always knew that life would lead him beyond the limits of Hawarden, Iowa. In 1965, after a Phi Beta Kappa career at the University of Iowa and a three-year stint with an Omaha law firm, Ericson found his larger world at Northwestern Mutual. The assignments of his first decade demonstrated the range of both his interests and his skills. At one time or another, the young attorney worked on offshore oil leases, agent contracts,

the corporate airplane purchase, and the agreement that brought the Milwaukee Brewers baseball team to town. He was a conspicuous success on every front. After graduating to executive posts on both the insurance and the investment sides, Ericson moved up to the company's top job in 1993.

If the new leader's early assignments demonstrated the breadth of his interests, they also reveal a certain native restlessness. That quality made Jim Ericson perhaps the most visionary chief executive in Northwestern Mutual's history. He was constantly looking at problems from new perspectives, never content with the obvious solutions, and he generated ideas in the same way a Roman candle throws off sparks. Like Francis Ferguson—a major influence on his early career—Ericson had an inborn desire to see things freshly and to act accordingly, but he out-Fergusoned Ferguson, launching more initiatives in eight years than his predecessor had in fifteen.

Jim Ericson was much more, however, than an idea factory. He was firmly rooted in Northwestern's values—most of them not so different, after all, from those he had learned back home in Hawarden—and he took an intensely personal interest in the company's agents. Addressing the field soon after he became president, Ericson said, "I want to learn how you think, work and feel," and he was as good as his word. The new leader spent his first year on a grand tour of the general agencies, visiting seventy-five in all, including fifteen during one memorable twenty-five-day stretch. He learned the names of hundreds of agents, and then he learned their children's names. It was Ericson's habit to take pictures of the agents he met and then send them prints after he'd returned to the home office—a practice that endeared him to many in the field.

Ericson's ongoing conversations with the agents confirmed something he already knew: Northwestern was competing in a new world. Cracks that first opened during Don Schuenke's tenure became fault lines under Jim Ericson; trends that surfaced in the 1980s became the fixed realities of the 1990s. The company's own performance indicated that something had changed. The sharp upturn that closed Don Schuenke's decade in office proved to be temporary. After rising 25 percent in 1993, the face amount of insurance sold actually fell 1.7 percent in 1994—Ericson's first full year as CEO. That was the first decline in new business since 1961. Recruiting of full-time agents sagged during the same period, dropping from 1,490 in 1991 to 1,169 in 1995—a 22-percent slide in just four years. Northwestern was not in the slightest financial trouble—its assets continued to grow nicely—but the trends were troubling. The scale of the challenge and the need for a commensurate response were both self-evident.

Northwestern competed in a new world, but it was rooted, as always, in an older world. By the time Ericson took charge, it was fairly easy to reconstruct the events that were causing such radical changes in such a seemingly impregnable industry. Viewed in hindsight, the 1970s and early 1980s were the watershed in the modern history of American life insurance—the dividing line between before and after. The rampant inflation and sky-high interest rates of the period pushed the market in two directions at once: away from whole life insurance and toward accumulation products. Stirred by earnest pronouncements from consumer advocates and even from their own government, the American public became extraordinarily rate-conscious. Inflation bred a new cynicism about long-term guarantees of any kind, and

Ericson took an intensely personal interest in the company's field force, getting to know hundreds of agents by name.

high interest rates created a new appetite for yields. There had been a time, and not many years earlier, when consumers focused exclusively on the dollars their insurance would provide if they died; now they paid as much attention to the dollars their premiums earned while they were still alive. The result was a dramatic unbundling of the insurance contract—into protection and investment.

Enter universal life, the unbundled product supreme. Promising the best of both worlds, universal life succeeded spectacularly in changing public attitudes toward life insurance. Never again would consumers remain blithely unaware of what companies did with their premium dollars. As actual returns matched the new policy's lofty illustrations—for the time being—traditional products went into eclipse. Agents pushing whole life insurance were like parents serving broccoli at the dinner table: it might be good for them, but the kids simply weren't buying it. Northwestern responded, and just in time, with its groundbreaking CompLife product. Powered by one of the highest dividend scales in the industry—a distinction the firm openly promoted—CompLife offered a level-premium alternative to the blandishments of the universal life sellers. The new policy helped stem the tide, but Northwestern's emphasis on its own rate of return—a company first— only encouraged the trend to unbundling. The odds of putting Humpty Dumpty together again grew more remote each year.

Conditions changed in the late 1980s. When the hurricane of runaway inflation and record-high interest rates finally blew itself out, a sort of calm prevailed. Northwestern, with many others, entertained hopes that the insurance industry was at long last returning to normal. As the wind died down, however, it became apparent that the levee had broken wide open and the water was rising fast. Swelled by forces that had nothing to do with inflation or interest rates, a torrent of change inundated the industry, flooding it with unfamiliar products and even less familiar competitors. Although the forces were different, the result was the same: a widening gulf between protection and accumulation.

The familiar dynamics of push and pull were hard at work. Universal life had been the industry's darling for nearly a decade. When it foundered in the late 1980s and early 1990s, sinking under the weight of its own unrealistic assumptions, there was nothing of comparable glamour to replace it—nothing, at least, that the financial press could endorse. The entire subject of life insurance began to seem dull and unappealing, a trend that was accelerated by the proliferation of low-cost, mass-marketed term plans. Computers allowed even small-scale competitors to design and administer their own products, reducing life insurance, in the public's mind, to a commodity that could be purchased through the Internet, bulk mail, or even matchbook covers. Consumers were pushed still farther away by a series of scandals that rocked the industry in the early 1990s. Some of America's largest firms admitted marketing abuses that hadn't been seen in nearly a century, among them policy-churning and blatant misrepresentation; the largest offender ultimately paid $2 billion to settle a class-action lawsuit.

As public trust in life insurance eroded, confidence in the investment sector rose with every uptick in the Dow Jones Average. The red-hot stock market of the 1990s exerted a powerful pull on even the most casual investors, and picking stocks seemed as effortless as throwing darts. Billions of dollars that might have gone to mitigating human losses went instead to pursuing capital gains. A constellation of other forces intensified the pull of the investment side. As defined-benefit pension plans went the way of the buffalo and as faith in the Social Security system plummeted, there was a growing awareness that financial independence in old age was fast becoming an individual responsibility. The proliferation of self-directed 401(k) plans amounted to a sea change in public assumptions. Technology, too, played a role. By enabling financial specialists to gather and manipulate data in ways never before imaginable, computers virtually created the mutual fund industry, money market funds, and a host of other consumer-friendly investment options. Mutual funds

eventually outnumbered individual stocks by a margin of three to one, and they offered a smorgasbord of choices for every type of investor, including those who were building their own retirement plans.

Demographic trends were yet another agent of change. The first baby-boomers entered middle age in the 1980s, and millions more passed their fortieth birthdays in the following decade. Raised in a climate of peace and prosperity, many had grown up with greater expectations than their parents had ever entertained—expectations that a rising market did nothing to diminish. As the baby-boomers' incomes rose with age, the lure of present gains frequently outweighed the fear of future losses, and agents were just as prone to such hopeful thinking as their potential customers. Federal and state regulators added a final layer of complexity to the picture. Years of legislative action chipped away at the once-impervious dikes that had long separated banks, brokerages, and insurance companies. By the 1990s, the dikes were down and previously separate companies were swimming in the same waters. As banks sold life insurance, life insurers sold mutual funds, and brokerages

Modern laptop computers pack as much power as the mainframes of the 1950s.

Jim Ericson spoke frequently and fervently of the enduring need for life insurance.

offered checking accounts, the safely sequestered financial services markets of times past became a competitive free-for-all.

All these factors—economic, demographic, technological, political, competitive—converged in the 1990s to create a perfect storm. Never before, not even during the upheavals of the Armstrong era, had the insurance industry faced such a stunning array of forces. Any one of them alone would have made a difference, but together they were transformative. The post-Armstrong reforms had basically restored

the industry to its previous equilibrium. The wave of change that crested in the 1990s swept away business as usual; it ripped the industry from its moorings and left in its wake a significantly altered landscape. At some point during the decade, America's life insurance executives came to the same conclusion: our world has changed. Growth in both sales and insurance in force slowed to a single-digit pace and sometimes lapsed into negative territory. Costs seemed to be rising out of control at the same time that recruiting of new agents dropped to historic lows.

With so many challenges on their doorsteps, life insurance executives were forced to make some hard decisions. Firms with weaker cultures and less robust balance sheets than Northwestern Mutual's began to head for the exits. Dozens of old-line competitors, convinced that the changes in their field were structural and permanent, set sail on the broad and treacherous waters of "financial services." They changed their names, altered their brands, and offered life insurance as one choice among many on a broad menu of products and services. Other firms, including giants like Prudential, Metropolitan, and John Hancock, traded in their mutual charters for stock status, hoping to raise capital for expansion, acquisition, and executive bonuses. Still others replaced their career agents with independent brokers, who cost nothing to train and little to maintain; the number of full-time agents representing single firms thinned from 250,000 in 1985 to 190,000 in 1999. Some companies took all of the above steps and still hit the rocks. A rash of insolvencies swept the industry in the early 1990s, and some firms vanished through the more civilized expedient of mergers. The number of life insurance companies in America sank from 2,195 in 1990 to 1,268 in 2000, and those that survived were not necessarily in sound condition. Companies that had survived a century or more of change found their financial ratings downgraded, their stock prices stagnant, and their futures in jeopardy.

Into this minefield, strewn with the wreckage of old competitors, walked Northwestern Mutual. Since its days as a frontier upstart in the 1850s, Northwestern had always been a conspicuous contrarian—the major firm least likely to jump on the latest bandwagon or follow the newest trend. The same instinct prevailed in the 1990s. If other companies changed their names, revamped their product lines, and jettisoned their agents, well, maybe they didn't have much to lose in the first place. They didn't have Northwestern's dividend scale, they didn't have Northwestern's cost structure, and they certainly didn't have Northwestern's agents. Quietly but forcefully, The Quiet Company resolved to continue going its own way.

What gave Jim Ericson and his team the courage to stay the course was their unshakable confidence in their core product. Life insurance might be unfashionable for the time being, but it would never become unnecessary; in any age, under any conditions, it provided the bedrock of protection for any human being with responsibilities. "The need for life insurance is as sure as the sun, the wind and the rain," Ericson declared at the 1995 annual meeting. He was just as convinced of the need for the informed counsel of experienced agents. "People need life insurance," he continued, "they admit they need life insurance, and they say they won't buy life insurance unless someone explains it to them." At its core, Northwestern was a life insurance company built around a career agency system, and that is precisely what Northwestern intended to remain.

One consequence of this fierce independence was a certain degree of isolation. As other firms diversified, demutualized, consolidated, or disappeared, Northwestern Mutual was practically the last of the Mohicans—again. In the early 1900s and once more in the 1920s, the company had stood virtually alone in its industry, on issues ranging from corporate ethics in the first case to group and disability insurance in the second. The 1990s were no different. As Northwestern kept rolling along while other firms careened into the ditches, the Milwaukee giant was the exception to every rule. "The sad and painful truth," Jim Ericson said in a memorable 1996 speech, "is that we are a silver lining surrounded by a cloud." Northwestern was still the most-admired life insurance firm in *Fortune's* annual survey, but it seemed to be the best of a vanishing breed. By the time Ericson stepped down in 2001, Northwestern Mutual was the last of the top ten firms still specializing in individual life insurance, the only one that had not reduced its workforce, one of two (with New York Life) that was still a mutual company, and one of three firms in the entire industry that could still claim the highest possible marks from all four ratings agencies.

"Secure the Base and Grow around It"

Although it was a glaring exception to the norms, Northwestern was emphatically never a world apart. The same perfect storm that transformed the entire industry swept through Milwaukee, challenging the company's assumptions and significantly impairing its performance. In the early years of Jim Ericson's tenure, sales were anemic, recruiting was off, and a generalized malaise seemed to have settled over the enterprise. Although CompLife still anchored the insurance line, there was a steady shift to lower-commissioned term and annuity products, creating an "income squeeze" for agents accustomed to healthier margins. The greatest area of growth was clearly on the investment side. Sales of Baird products, especially mutual funds, passed the $500 million mark in 1995 and surged ahead to $3.2 billion just five years later—an average annual growth rate of 45 percent. The number of agents licensed to sell investment products swelled from a relative handful in the 1980s to 4,200 in 2000—nearly 75 percent of the field force. The agents were simply following their clients, moving with the tide as the market's emphasis shifted from protection to accumulation.

The world changed for Northwestern Mutual as much as it had for every other insurance firm, presenting some obvious problems and some opportunities as well. No one took comfort in the firm's excellent competitive showing; superior results in a distressed industry were no cause for celebration. Northwestern, as always, benchmarked itself. If results failed to measure up to expectations, the company would take heroic steps to improve them. Standing pat was hardly a sound survival strategy in the new world of financial services; with a CEO as restless and creative as Jim Ericson at the helm, standing pat was not even considered.

It was against this backdrop that Ericson began to reposition Northwestern for continued success in the changed environment of the 1990s and beyond. His first initiative, somewhat surprisingly, focused on the home office. In 1991, even before he became CEO, Ericson launched a program he called Quiet Quality, informally known as Q2. The new program was the life-insurance equivalent of the quality efforts sweeping America's manufacturing sector at the time, and its goal was the same: continuous improvement of all key processes. In announcing the program, Ericson articulated a goal that would become a central theme of his administration: "to make the best even better." The new president was certain that "a common focus on customer service" was absolutely necessary to create "a lot of distance between Northwestern Mutual and its competitors." "The key competitive issues of the next few years," he insisted, "will be service, service, and service." Every employee received two days of training focused on the customer-supplier relationship in the workplace. Quiet Quality helped Northwestern's employees realize, many for the first time, that each of them had customers, whether they were across the hall in Milwaukee or across the country in one of the general agencies.

With the Quiet Quality program declared a success, Jim Ericson moved on to the signature effort of his administration: growth. He had been beating the drum for expansion since his first years as president, but it was in 1996 that Northwestern made growth the centerpiece of a formal, full-scale campaign. Ericson chose the 1996 eastern regional meeting—the first major event on the company's annual calendar—to announce his new initiative:

The Quiet Quality program, or Q2, focused the attention of Northwestern's employees on customer relationships, both internal and external.

We absolutely need to grow.... Growth is our only source of new capital, including the capital to support the exclusive agency system. It's growth—and only growth—that will keep our system healthy, keep it strong, and keep it alive. Growth is the fuel that drives our engine.... If we want to remain the company we are now—the Northwestern Mutual we know and love—we must grow.

In building his case for change, Ericson stressed the psychological benefits of expansion as well as the economic advantages: "Growth brings excitement, enthusiasm, challenge and drama to our lives." Nearly eighteen years earlier, Francis Ferguson had expressed precisely the same

sentiments: "Growth brings excitement and a heightened sense of destiny in home office and agency operations alike." Jim Ericson was invoking the same spirit of enterprise that Ferguson—the last growth-oriented CEO—had summoned in 1968.

Ericson may have been treading familiar ground, but he added something new to his growth rationale: a fresh interpretation of the 1888 Executive Committee statement. Taken out of context, Northwestern's credo could be read as a prescription for maintaining the status quo; any company, after all, whose stated goal was "less to be large than to be safe" and who embraced "certain salutary restrictions" might have seemed conservative to the point of catatonia. Ericson put the statement in its proper historical framework. Northwestern had in fact been growing like a prairie fire in the decade before the statement was written; new business increased an average of 25 percent each year in the 1880s. The whole point of the report, in fact, was to showcase the company's "thirty years of steady and successful growth" and to "congratulate its policy holders and friends on the remarkable results attained." The 1888 statement, then, was hardly a proscription *against* growth but rather a prescription for *how* growth should take place. Jim Ericson drew the obvious conclusion: ""We must grow the Northwestern Mutual Way." What that meant, in his view, was a clear and consistent focus on safety, quality and, above all, value to the policyowner. Too many people, he argued, made a false distinction between the dictates of tradition and the need to grow, as if the two were somehow mutually exclusive. Without compromising Northwestern's value proposition in the least, Ericson hoped to overcome what he termed "the tyranny of the 'or.'" "We don't have to choose growth or quality," he said. "We don't have to choose good service or low operating costs. We can have growth *and* quality and good service *and* low costs."

The gospel of growth with quality was something Jim Ericson could have preached seven days a week, but putting it into practice took much more than proselytizing. In a career company like Northwestern Mutual, growing the business meant growing the field force; it was only by adding "feet on the street" that the firm could hope to add policyowners. The company appointed a new field general to lead the charge: Bill Beckley. Beckley had joined Northwestern as a special agent in 1976, working in Santa Fe, New Mexico, and he showed such a knack for management that in 1986 he moved up to Chicago as successor to a Northwestern legend: O. Alfred Granum. In his twenty-three years as general agent in Chicago, Al Granum and his associates had put $3.1 billion of insurance on the books and ranked first among Northwestern's agencies in volume and/or premium thirty-seven times. Bill Beckley, effectively combining his native geniality with a hard-driving dynamism,

was a conspicuous success as Granum's successor. At the end of 1995, he moved ninety miles north to take charge of the entire agency system, working in the home office with another company legend—Dennis Tamcsin—until Tamcsin's retirement in 1999.

Northwestern's field system soon began to show signs of change. The number of general agencies decreased steadily, dropping from 103 in 1995 to 98 in 2003 and 90 in 2006, but the individual agencies were uniformly larger. The company relied more heavily on district agencies, most housing fewer than a dozen representatives, to develop its smaller territories, particularly in the Sunbelt. The standard general agent's contract was reworked with recruiting in mind; commissions were increased on new business and decreased on renewals, a clear

Beckley posed with the two Northwestern legends he succeeded in his career: Dennis Tamcsin (left) *and Al Granum.*

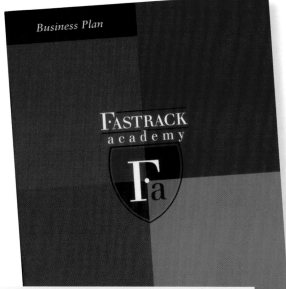

Fastrack Academy replaced Career School as the premier training program for new agents ...

signal that Northwestern wanted to reward growth rather than longevity. Recruiting and retention were a never-ending battle. The number of new agent appointments rose from a trough of 1,169 in 1995 to a historic peak of 1,787 in 2002—a gain of 53 percent— but the number of full-time representatives in the field grew more slowly, rising just 9 percent during the same years, from 5,624 to 6,149. Although the challenges were obvious, Northwestern was more than holding its own during a period of dramatic erosion in the ranks of America's insurance agents.

Whether they were fresh recruits or seasoned veterans, all Northwestern representatives benefited from a new emphasis on field support—an effort that involved Bob Carlson, Northwestern's marketing guru since 1982, as well as Bill Beckley and his team. Brand-new agents received five weeks of basic training and hands-on supervision, including help in developing effective business plans, and those who showed particular promise moved on to Fastrack Academy, an intensive one-week seminar held in Milwaukee. For the most

productive veterans—the elite of the elite—the company created the Northwestern Forum in 1998; membership was a distinct honor, but it also meant priority treatment on their larger, more complex cases. Agents at every level could choose from an impressive variety of sales aids. One of the most widely used was the Personal Planning Analysis, a high-tech and highly sophisticated version of the fact-finder interview Northwestern agents had been conducting since the early 1900s. Specific marketing programs helped agents reach groups as diverse as Generation Xers (those born in the decade or two after 1965) and new Americans from India, while training programs covered everything from agency administration to selling group life and health insurance. The goal, said Bill Beckley, was "to help every agent be more productive at every stage of his or her career." Such a broad-based approach was not inexpensive; by 1998, Northwestern had nearly doubled its annual investment in each full-time agent.

All the field initiatives were designed with growth in mind, and none required the addition of a single new product. In some ways, it seemed, nothing at all was changing. Northwestern's 1997 strategic plan—the first one openly shared with agents and employees—expressed the firm's most important objective in a single, unequivocal phrase: "Secure and expand our base of life insurance policyowners by growing our exclusive career general agency system." Life insurance and career agents—those were the twin foundations on which Northwestern based its hopes for continued success. "We will not change our focus on life insurance," Jim Ericson told the field in 1998. "Life insurance always has been—and always will be—our bedrock." But life insurance alone was not enough in the new world of financial services. As the walls came tumbling down and the dikes burst wide open, any company that insisted on such narrow specialization was courting disaster. From its decision to "Secure the base," therefore, Northwestern moved on to its second commandment: "Expand around that base." The result was a constantly growing array of products designed to ensure the health of the field and the future of the enterprise by meeting more of each client's needs.

Given the continuing boom in the stock market, it came as no surprise that the first new arrow in Northwestern's quiver was an investment product. In 1997, the company introduced Mason Street Funds, a proprietary line of mutual funds. Agents were already selling the products of highly regarded firms like American Funds and Capital Guardian; Mason Street Funds, named for the thoroughfare that bisects the Milwaukee campus, gave customers access to the investment expertise of Northwestern Mutual as well. Some policyowners responded immediately, but the company's hope was to establish a three-

year track record of solid performance and then market the funds more aggressively.

The second arrow was in some ways a logical extension of much earlier product developments. In 1998, the company unveiled QuietCare, a long-term care contract that reimbursed policyowners for skilled care they received in nursing homes, assisted-living facilities, or their own residences. Like a retirement annuity, QuietCare protected policyowners against the risks of living too long. Like disability insurance, it helped support them when they were no longer able to support themselves. Northwestern was obviously following demographic trends. Fifty years earlier, the firm's agents had sold policies that often helped the families of baby-boomers pay for college. In 1998, they began to sell policies that would one day help the same boomers pay for nursing-home care. Although the product was a logical

… while the Northwestern Forum offered activities for successful veterans, including top-level briefings from company officials.

response to the graying of America, long-term care was still a new field, and Northwestern proceeded with characteristic caution. QuietCare was sold through a wholly owned subsidiary (the reincorporated Standard of America Company), administered by a third-party specialist based in Minnesota, and priced significantly higher than competing plans. As the company and its agents gained experience with the new product, it became both more flexible and more affordable. The breakthrough came in 2002, when QuietCare became a dividend-paying contract. Sales increased 42 percent in a year, and Northwestern was on its way to becoming the sixth-largest provider of long-term care coverage in America.

Another new development grew out of a different generational dynamic. As the ranks of the nation's World War II veterans thinned, life insurance claims totaling billions of dollars were filed each year, and nearly a fifth of the proceeds was paid into trusts established for beneficiaries. Jim Ericson sensed a golden opportunity for Northwestern Mutual. In 1999, hoping to establish a new competitive front, develop relationships with the heirs of old policyowners and, not incidentally, fend off the incursions of banks and trust firms who were only too glad to sell those heirs life insurance, Ericson announced that Northwestern would start a trust company of its own. The effort developed slowly—the

subsidiary was not operational until 2001, and then only in three Midwestern states—but Ericson had high hopes for his latest creation. "Make no mistake," he told the agents. "This is a landmark for your company…. In adding trust services, we should become a powerful force in inter-generational marketing."

Mason Street Funds, QuietCare, and the trust company were all independent creations of the home office, steps that Northwestern could take without consulting any other organization. The larger trend of the period was toward mergers and acquisitions. Everyone, it seemed, was combining with everyone else in the 1990s: Connecticut Mutual with Mass Mutual, Travelers Group with Citicorp, US Life with American General and then American General with AIG. In 1997 alone, the life insurance industry recorded fifty-one transactions worth a total of $12.3 billion. Northwestern Mutual was alert to the trend. The company had made acquisitions before, notably Baird and Standard of America in 1982, but those deals represented little more than a toe in the water. In the mid-1990s, Northwestern entered serious merger negotiations with two mutual firms that had traditionally been part of its peer group. Those talks came to nothing, but Jim Ericson's team continued to test the waters. In 1998, they jumped in with both feet, taking a $1.2 billion plunge by purchasing the Frank Russell Company. Russell was a well-respected institutional

Northwestern Long Term Care Insurance Company™

A Northwestern Mutual Company

Northwestern Mutual Trust Company™

New products of the Ericson years included the Mason Street family of mutual funds, QuietCare long-term care insurance, and trust services.

Russell

AGGRESSIVE / CONSERVATIVE

Russell Aggressive Equity

Russell Non-U.S.

Russell Multi-Style Equity

Russell Real Estate Securities

Russell Core Bond

STEWART HOPKINS © 2001

The 1998 acquisition of the Frank Russell Co., a Tacoma-based mutual fund giant, gave Northwestern a major presence in the investment products sphere.

money manager that offered nearly 100 mutual funds and advised more than half the major pension plans in America. The company was perhaps most widely known for its market indexes, including the broad-based Russell 3000. Russell's main office was a sleek twelve-story tower in the heart of Tacoma, Washington—its hometown since Frank Russell founded the enterprise in 1936—but the firm had a robust international business, with nine offices and 1,400 employees on four continents.

In 1998, when George Russell, the founder's grandson and successor, neared retirement, he began to look for a buyer who could help the business grow—particularly on the retail side—without compromising its day-to-day independence. Northwestern, in the meantime, was looking for a money manager who could give it instant access to new markets. The match made perfect sense, and the cultural fit between the two companies could hardly have been better. Every Russell fund was advised by a team of outside managers chosen for their diversity of styles as well as their track records. This "manager of managers" approach reflected a concern for quality, an emphasis on consistent long-term performance, and a desire to meet needs rather than simply sell products—the same qualities that had endeared Northwestern Mutual to generations of policyowners. Although its bid was not the highest, the Russell family chose the Milwaukee firm over all other suitors. "We selected Northwestern Mutual for our future based on its unparalleled strength," said George Russell. The company, he continued, was "a strong fit with Russell, both strategically and culturally." On January 1, 1999, the Frank Russell Company became a wholly owned but independently operated subsidiary of Northwestern Mutual.

Practically overnight, the Russell purchase gave Northwestern a meaningful presence in the financial services world. "The major impact on our company, employees and agents," wrote Jim Ericson, "will be new opportunities for growth." Russell funds gave the agents a variety of new arrows for their individual quivers, and the same funds filled out the investment choices underpinning Variable Life and annuity policies. Other synergies were explored, but Frank Russell remained a "bolt-on" acquisition that required minimal supervision from Milwaukee. It was, in the meantime, a superlative investment. Russell's assets under management soared from roughly $42 billion at the time of the 1998 discussions to nearly $200 billion in 2006—a fivefold increase in just eight years—and the firm's profitability exceeded Northwestern's most optimistic projections.

With the addition of Russell, the company achieved critical mass in the investment products arena. In 2000, accordingly, Northwestern established

the Investment Products and Services Department, generally known as IPS, to bring what Jim Ericson called "a finer sense of order" to its family of accumulation products: annuities, Mason Street Funds, broker-dealer operations, trust services, and the Frank Russell relationship. More deliberately than ever, Northwestern was running on two tracks at once: insurance and investments, protection and accumulation, risk and reward. That distinction, in turn, played a critical role in one of the most widely discussed developments of Jim Ericson's tenure: changing the company's brand name. Addressing the agents' annual meeting in July 2000, Ericson said, "From now on we will be known, simply and broadly, as Northwestern Mutual." Dropping "Life" from the letterhead was not the only thunderclap. The salespeople formerly known as agents became "financial representatives" who worked inside a reimagined entity called the "Northwestern Mutual Financial Network," and other changes followed in due course: general agents were rechristened "managing partners," district agents became "managing directors," and NML was truncated to "NM."

To the half-informed observer, and to hundreds of Northwestern retirees, it might have appeared that the company's world was being turned upside down. Deleting "Life" from Northwestern's name, in particular, seemed equivalent to shaking the granite pillars and rattling the stained-glass

Northwestern Mutual
FINANCIAL NETWORK®

windows of the home office. The changes in nomenclature were, in reality, far less earth-shaking than they first appeared. Northwestern was altering its brand, not its identity. On one level, the company needed a new name to reflect its growing portfolio of products, particularly on the investment side. On a more strategic level, the name change reflected a conscious decision to reposition Northwestern in the marketplace. "Life" was not only too narrow a term for the company's product lines, but it also conjured up, for younger consumers in particular, an image of their grandfather's Oldsmobile. However essential it was to anyone with responsibilities, life insurance lacked the allure of other financial products, for all the push-and-pull reasons cited earlier. Most Northwestern representatives had already accommodated the shift in public tastes. By the late 1990s, relatively few still advertised themselves as life insurance agents who sold primarily life insurance products. Names like "Stone Financial" and "The Columns Resource Group" were far more typical, and conversations with new clients might just as easily have started with mutual funds or retirement plans as with life insurance. The same aversion to insurance affected potential representatives;

managing partners reported that the lines at career fairs got longer as soon as Northwestern Mutual Life became the Northwestern Mutual Financial Network.

As the new names gained currency, Jim Ericson was careful to focus on what *hadn't* changed. Interviewed in 2000, he emphasized the constants:

> While we're dropping the word "Life," this doesn't mean there is any change in our focus on life insurance. The real message is that we are the finest life insurance company in the world and we are a company that meets other needs.... As we make strategic moves, like the purchase of the Frank Russell Company, or the move into trust services, or the creation of high-end financial planning services, we make these moves with an unwavering eye toward making us a stronger life insurance company. Life insurance is the foundation of any sound financial plan.

In the end, the only casualty of the name change involved a telephone number. As the proliferation of cell phones drained the available inventory of numbers in Milwaukee and elsewhere, Northwestern reserved a new prefix—665—for its home office network simply because the numbers spelled out "NML." With "L" consigned to history, the number stayed, but the point was lost.

Picking up the Pace

Northwestern's determination to "secure the base and grow around it" took the company in some novel directions, but Jim Ericson looked even farther afield between 1993 and 2001. International expansion was one "evolutionary idea" he found especially intriguing. Surely there were other countries that could benefit from Northwestern Mutual's expertise, and Ericson believed that the global experts at Frank Russell could help establish a beachhead. Northwestern went so far as to organize international holding companies in Delaware, Bermuda, and Ireland, awaiting a time when they had something to hold. The firm also explored the concept of a mutual holding company— a mutual parent that can own operating stock subsidiaries. Wisconsin passed the enabling legislation in 1999, but the idea was purely defensive. As its one-time peers vanished, merged, or converted to stock companies, Northwestern looked ahead to a day when it might be the last purely mutual life insurer still standing, without allies to help fend off calamitous changes in tax laws or regulations. Until that day came, however, the company embraced its mutuality as not only the core of its identity but also a clear competitive advantage. Jim Ericson had little sympathy for firms who found it necessary to demutualize in order to raise capital. "We pay more dividends

than any other company," he said flatly. "We do not need additional capital." The beauty of a mutual insurance firm, and the one characteristic that sets it apart from virtually every other business, was, and is, that its customers and its shareholders are precisely the same people. There is no possibility of divided attention and no doubt whatsoever about whose interests take precedence. Northwestern may have become larger than life, but it was still determinedly mutual.

There is no question that matters of strategy—the growth initiative, product innovations, the Russell acquisition, the rebranding, and a fresh look at the very nature of the business—took center stage during Jim Ericson's years as CEO. They tended to overshadow other developments, but Ericson's insistence on taking a fresh look applied to the home office as well as the marketplace. With the same restless energy he showed in repositioning the field, Northwestern's leader tinkered constantly with the company's organizational chart, realigning people and priorities to meet the challenges of the new world. In 1997, for instance, the executive team's focus shifted from administrative functions to product-line responsibilities, a change that Ericson believed would make Northwestern "better aligned to penetrate each of our markets." In 2000, he established a new Marketing Department,

The "smart phone" serves many Northwesterners as a pocket-sized office assistant, combining e-mail, calendar, contact, and Internet features with cellular telephone service.

Three key executives of the Ericson years: (l. to r.) Ed Zore, Peter Bruce, and John Bremer

Gary (Skip) Poliner became a major figure on the financial side of the business.

and the New Business Department moved by degrees from a regional emphasis to a "customized" approach, with different staff units handling different types of applications. Some worked on "jumbo" cases submitted by leading representatives, while others stepped up their efforts to expedite the treatment of more typical policies. The point was to relieve financial representatives of unnecessary paperwork. "Our future growth—and yours," Ericson told the field in 1998, "depends on helping you spend more time on productive sales activity."

Each reorganization brought a reshuffling of executive responsibilities; Northwestern's leaders engaged in a lively game of musical chairs whose ultimate point was management succession. Three executives emerged as particularly central figures during the 1990s: Ed Zore, Peter Bruce, and John Bremer. In 1990, Zore capped his career on the investment side of the business by becoming Northwestern's chief investment officer,

executing a strategy he had helped develop in the previous decade: total return. The company's emphasis shifted from trophy properties— downtown office towers, oil and gas leases, destination resorts—to the portfolio as a whole. Asset classes were systematically balanced, risks were carefully analyzed, and results were rigorously measured. "We focused on the puzzle instead of the individual pieces," Zore summarized. That puzzle was heavily weighted to equities—20 percent of assets in most years, at a time when more traditional firms limited their exposure to 5 percent. Ed Zore's team proved adept at managing the risks of the equity markets. Northwestern's capital gains approached or exceeded the $1 billion mark repeatedly in the 1990s, helping to swell total assets from $44.1 billion in 1993 to $98.4 billion in 2001. The team may have produced more singles than home runs, but its batting average was impressive indeed; Northwestern moved up in the industry's asset rankings from eighth place to fifth between 1993 and 2000. When Ed Zore transferred to the insurance side in 1998—part of his training as a possible successor to Ericson—the reins of the investment operation passed first to Mason Ross and then, in 2007, to Gary (Skip) Poliner. Ross was a Milwaukee native who had made his mark on the real estate side of the business, while Poliner was a Pennsylvania-born attorney who spent the first thirteen years of his career in the Law Department. Both men continued the emphasis on total return with an equity slant that had earned such handsome returns in previous years.

Peter Bruce was just as busy on the operational side of the company. Since joining Northwestern as a newly minted attorney in 1970, Bruce had risen steadily through the ranks, earning a promotion to general counsel in 1980 (the youngest in company history) and then taking charge of a constantly growing cluster of departments that ranged from Policy Benefits to Corporate Services to Human Resources. In 1998, as a potential prelude to even higher office, he began to manage accumulation products and the new long-term care line. In every assignment he accepted, Pete Bruce earned a reputation for openness, fairness, and a willingness to question the established way of doing things—a habit he had acquired as a philosophy major at the University of Wisconsin. Like Michael Cleary and Edmund Fitzgerald before him, Bruce was an executive of exceptional human warmth, and he won nearly universal respect and affection from both home office and field.

John Bremer followed much the same career path as Pete Bruce. Born in Connecticut and educated at Fordham University (in economics rather than philosophy), he came to the home office in 1974, shortly after graduating from Duke University's law school. Beginning as a tax attorney, Bremer moved up to the general counsel's post in 1990 and then took charge of an expanding portfolio of operating departments. Known for his clear intelligence, sound judgment, and searching attention to detail, John Bremer emerged as an indispensable figure in the ranks of upper management.

For everyone in the home office—Zore, Bruce, and Bremer included—the pace of life quickened perceptibly in the 1990s. Growth in sales added new pressures, and growth in product lines added new layers of complexity. The number of full-time employees rose from 2,983 in 1993 to 3,832 in 2001—a 28-percent gain in eight years. New employees found that Northwestern remained an exceptional place to work, and in some ways it kept getting better. In 1998, the company introduced variable pay—an annual bonus plan that took effect when certain key measures of corporate performance were met. Originally developed for management, variable pay was extended to all classes of employees in 2004. The message was clear: if you help your company succeed, you will share in your company's success. Other workplace amenities of the Ericson years included a "business casual" dress code, lactation facilities for nursing mothers, and even chair massage, available at fifteen dollars for each fifteen-minute session. Paradoxically, however, most employees

What the comfortably dressed Northwesterner will wear: a "business casual" dress code took effect in 1999.

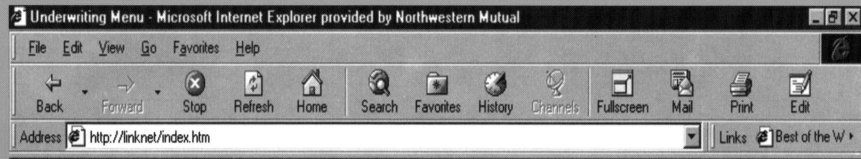

File   Edit   View   Go   Favorites   Help

Back   Forward   Stop   Refresh   Home   Search   Favorites   History   Channels   Fullscreen   Mail   Print   Edit

Address   http://linknet/index.htm   Links   Best of the W

LINKnet

News & Events

Marketing

Products

Underwriting

Computers & LINK

Contacts & Catalogs

Agent's Business

Field Management

Service

Search

LINKnet Help

Comments

Greg Oberland took charge of Information Systems after a stand-out career in insurance operations.

found themselves working significantly harder in the 1990s; fewer people were expected to accomplish more in less time than any previous generation—part of the same acceleration that was being felt virtually everywhere in corporate America.

There is no doubt that technology played a pivotal role in that acceleration. Doing more work and doing it faster than ever before, computers challenged their human masters to keep pace; as the mountains of data accumulated, employees had no choice but to climb them. If the 1980s were the decade that took digital technology from the data center to the desktop, the 1990s completed the transformation. Some sections of the insurance departments became virtually paperless, and investment specialists who had once generated piles of documents for a single trade could buy securities with the click of a mouse. Northwestern launched one of the industry's first websites in 1995; within four years, customers could view their policy values online, and managing partners could use the Internet for help in "e-cruiting" new representatives. The Information Systems

Department directed Northwestern's digital evolution, under the guidance of Walt Wojcik until 2002, then Barbara Piehler, and finally, in 2006, Greg Oberland. Piehler was a certified public accountant (and former Schlitz Brewing controller) who joined the company in 1983 and rose steadily on its administrative side. Oberland came to Northwestern in 1982 as an attorney and compiled a sterling résumé as head of Policy Benefits, Disability Income, New Business, and then insurance operations.

Although the resident experts worked in IS, Northwestern did all it could to encourage computer literacy at every level of the organization. In 1996, MutualNet began to replace the water cooler and the copy machine as a channel for home office communication—the same role LINKnet played in the field. Employees who wanted to buy PCs for home use received $500 rebates from the company, and in 2000 a CyberCafé allowed them to surf the Web during breaks at work. The rush to electronic living was not without its hazards. For many employees, seeing "Systems Up" or "Systems Down" on one of the small electronic billboards posted throughout the home office could mean the difference between a good day and a prolonged exercise in frustration.

The dangers of digital dependence were brought home most vividly, if only temporarily, during the Y2K scare. Because some computer languages identified years by their last two numerals instead of all four, various experts predicted that electronic chaos would ensue the instant that 1999 became 2000. Northwestern seemed especially vulnerable. Since life insurance policies stay on the books for literally a lifetime, the company was obligated to maintain the software supporting all of them—system upon system upon system, some dating back to the 1950s. All were different, and most seemed defenseless against the Y2K bug. In an effort that began in 1996, required hundreds of thousands of hours of labor, and cost nearly $30 million, Northwestern tested every line of its code and made all necessary corrections. Despite some anxious moments on New Year's Eve in 1999, the company turned the corner to 2000 without missing a step.

Passing the Y2K test involved a bit of serendipity. The project was far too massive for Northwestern to manage with the staff on hand. It so happened that, during a round-the-world trip sponsored by *Time* Magazine in 1995, Jim Ericson had stopped in Bangalore, India, the home of Infosys, an information systems giant hoping to expand its presence in North America. Impressed with the company's obvious technical expertise, Ericson arranged for Infosys to help with the Y2K project—the beginning of a partnership that has flourished ever since. Although much of the work is done offshore, both Infosys and Wipro, another Indian IS giant, have sent rotating crews of computer

Workplace amenities of the 21st century include CyberCafés for all employees.

The presence of highly skilled contract workers from India, most of them in Information Systems, has added a global dimension to the home office.

specialists to Milwaukee as Northwestern contractors. Those workers, who typically stay for a year or two and then return to India, have added a definite international flavor to the home office—and prompted a wider range of vegetarian choices on the cafeteria menus.

By 2001, the growing number of contractors and the burgeoning regular payroll had pushed Northwestern's work force to the 5,000 mark—well beyond the capacity of the downtown campus. In 1990, members of the Information Systems Department had left the West, or 611, Building for new quarters in the North

Office Building. By the late 1990s, they were moving back, and IS took over the entire 611 structure in 2001. Still there was a shortage of space. Northwestern rented entire floors in a pair of buildings just west of the original home office, but it was clear that a more permanent solution would soon be necessary.

And then it was Jim Ericson's turn to leave the building. On June 1, 2001, Ericson stepped down as CEO, turning the keys over to Ed Zore. Few tenures of comparable length had been half as eventful. In his eight years at the helm, Ericson, with substantial help, had launched an aggressive growth campaign, realigned the field, filled out the product line, purchased Frank Russell, rebranded the entire enterprise, and reorganized the home office—initiatives that touched every aspect of life at Northwestern. The results were, in a word, gratifying. New life insurance revenue grew by an average of 8 percent per year between 1993 and 2000—a blistering pace in a mature industry—and in 1996 Northwestern became the largest individual life insurer in America, with $430 billion of coverage on the books. Led by dynamos like Ruble Hord and Paul Krasnow, the firm's financial representatives boosted Northwestern's share of the individual market from 4.5 percent in 1994 to 7.5 percent in 2001. Although investment products showed steady growth, more than 80 percent of the company's operating revenue still came from insurance sales.

During periods of rapid growth in practically any business, it is not unusual for quality to slip and for fiscal stability to suffer until new people and new products have been completely absorbed. Not at Northwestern Mutual. Persistency and mortality both improved through the 1990s. The firm's surplus—the most telling indicator of a mutual company's financial strength—increased from 9 percent of its legal reserve liability in 1993 to 14 percent in 2001. That was a historic high, a feat made all the more remarkable by the fact that the company's dividend payouts were the largest in the industry. How strong was Northwestern Mutual? In 1999, when the company wrote off $842 million as part of the Frank Russell purchase, its surplus *still* reached a record high. Industry experts were paying attention. Not only did Northwestern Mutual remain the most-admired insurance firm in *Fortune's* annual survey, but in 1999, when the survey added a global component, Northwestern emerged as the most-admired insurer in the world—even though it had no operations outside the United States.

Jim Ericson knew why his firm was such a conspicuous success. Even though he had ushered in some of the most sweeping changes in Northwestern's history, it was all done, Ericson said in his last annual meeting speech, to preserve and extend an enduring tradition:

Your company has so many great strengths, and the beauty of it is, they're all intertwined. We have the finest products, which attract the best financial representatives, who choose top clients, who produce great persistency, which provides us with steady cash flow, that drives superior investment results, which brings us back to the finest products. We've always called it the circle of success.

Jim Ericson guided Northwestern during a time of transformation for both the company and its industry. Under his leadership, and the momentous changes notwithstanding, the circle of success was as strong as it had been at any time in Northwestern Mutual's history.

"Now We Had to Execute"

Northwestern was still emphatically a work in progress when Jim Ericson retired, and the man who replaced him was amply qualified to carry the enterprise forward. Ed Zore's success had not been guaranteed from birth. Like Ericson, Ferguson, and Schuenke before him, he had started on the lower rungs of the economic ladder. Zore was the grandson of immigrants from Slovenia, a small nation in the northern region of the former Yugoslavia, and he spent his formative years in West Allis, an industrial suburb just west of Milwaukee. His father was a metal finisher who worked all day around toxic baths of liquid chrome,

When the annual Fortune *survey went international in 1999, Northwestern was named the most-admired insurance firm in the world.*

Ed Zore, the principled pragmatist who led Northwestern into a new millennium

brass, and acids at the General Electric X-ray plant. (One fringe benefit: a complete set of chrome-plated tools in his home workshop.) Ed Zore learned early the value of hard work and the importance of making his own way. "You want something?," his father instructed. "Then you work for it." Holding down two jobs while he attended Don Bosco High School, Zore earned enough money to buy his first car: a 1956 Ford that he and his friends promptly rebuilt. He never lost his passion for cars, but a latent interest in business led Zore to the University of Wisconsin-Milwaukee. He earned two degrees in economics at his hometown university and then, in 1969, took a job as a stock trader at Northwestern Mutual.

Zore remained true to his roots in the buttoned-down world of the home office, displaying a blue-collar steeliness that blended perfectly with the tenor of the investment departments. In the nineteenth century, Northwestern had chosen its leaders from the investment side because they represented caution and conservatism. In the late twentieth century, investors were more often distinguished by their willingness to take risks and their ability to make swift decisions. Ed Zore exemplified the pattern. Although he embraced Northwestern's values as his own, Zore developed the mindset of a true trader: gather the facts, make a decision,

accept the consequences, and move on to the next decision. He was, in brief, pragmatism personified. Throughout his career, Zore has carried himself with a brisk informality, a confidence bordering at times on bravado, and a healthy streak of iconoclasm. Those qualities, coupled with his sheer competence, earned him a series of promotions within the investment departments, then an executive post on the insurance side, and finally, in 2001, the top job in the entire company.

Few chief executives in Northwestern Mutual's history have had more dramatic, even traumatic, first years in office. On September 11, 2001—only a few months after Zore became CEO—death soared down from the skies above Manhattan and engulfed the World Trade Center. Of the nearly 3,000 people killed in the terrorist attack, 157 were Northwestern policyowners. Not since the *Titanic* sank in 1912 with thirteen insureds aboard had so many Northwestern lives been lost in a single tragic event. The company's response was absolutely in character. A team of senior claims specialists, accompanied by Ed Zore himself, flew out to New York as soon as air travel resumed. Their home office colleagues canceled vacations and worked weekends to process claims that ultimately totaled $125 million. Nearly all were settled without death certificates, and most were paid within five days. Ed Zore was in the middle of the action. "Being with our financial representatives at this time was one of the most moving experiences of my life," he wrote. "I have never been prouder of Northwestern Mutual, of our people and of how important our business is to people in need." All the long, involved discussions about direction and strategy and demographics suddenly resolved to a single, piercingly clear realization: we're in this business to pay claims; what Northwestern does makes a critical difference in people's lives. For anyone who doubted, the 9/11 tragedy was a conversion experience. It reinforced the enduring value of life insurance in general and the enduring values of Northwestern Mutual in particular.

The events of September 11 may have validated Northwestern's mission, but they practically decked an economy that was already on the ropes. A recession had started in March 2001—the first in a decade—and the favoring wind at Jim Ericson's back was gone by the time Ed Zore took office. The stock market tumbled, finally succumbing to the "irrational exuberance" Federal Reserve chairman Alan Greenspan had decried as early as 1996, and the decade-long "superbull" limped to its end. Ed Zore, for one, welcomed the return to normal. "Investing is back in the hands of the professionals," he told the agents in 2002. "You won't earn 20, 25, and 30 percent a year by throwing a dart at a list of stocks." After their prolonged foray into what he called "fantasyland," consumers were once again coming back to Northwestern's value proposition, and

Zore felt the same sense of vindication that Don Schuenke, Michael Cleary, and even Henry Palmer had experienced in earlier times. "This is our time to shine," Zore declared at the 2002 annual meeting:

> *When the financial world was spinning out of alignment, we never lost our focus on the things that help our constituents achieve financial security. I'm talking about terrific fundamentals, world-class products, strong values, and the finest field force in the United States. What I'm saying today is that we have followed the same straight path for 145 years, and the world is coming back to us again.*

The shift was evident in Northwestern's own sales patterns. Variable Life, an investment-based policy, was the company's hottest product in the late 1990s. Sales of Variable Life dropped 32 percent in 2001, while CompLife, the firm's old standby, posted a 23-percent gain.

The return to tradition proved less enduring than Northwestern might have preferred. As the economy continued to struggle, interest rates sank to lows not seen since the 1950s, and the Dow Jones Industrial Average plummeted from its historic high of 11,723 in January 2000 to 7,286 in October 2002. For Northwestern's investment team, the days of billion-dollar capital gains were over, at least for the time being. But market

Baptism by fire: one of Zore's first duties was to direct his company's response to the terrorist attacks of Sept. 11, 2001. He is shown with New York managing partner Todd Schoon, who became Northwestern's vice-president of agencies in 2006.

The executive officers at their 2005 planning rally

John Schlifske, a former summer intern, became head of Investment Products and Services in 2004.

performance was not the only concern. The frenzied pursuit of profit at all costs had prompted some firms to take ethical shortcuts in the 1990s, and those shortcuts led to catastrophic dead ends when the economy slumped. High flyers like WorldCom and Enron crashed in headline-grabbing scandals that diminished public faith in American business and brought increased scrutiny from public officials. Even as they continued to dismantle the walls between financial sectors, government regulators stepped up reporting requirements and drew an ever-sharper distinction between the proper roles of commissioned salespersons and fee-based advisors. The financial services industry bogged down in an atmosphere of cynicism, uncertainty, and downright confusion that was hardly conducive to the sale of life insurance.

Northwestern Mutual felt the pressures first-hand; sales tapered off, recruiting lagged, and there were fresh concerns about the long-term viability of the enterprise.

Ed Zore didn't panic. He never lost his composure, and he never even considered re-evaluating the company's core strategy. The task ahead, in his view, was crystal-clear. "We didn't need any new agendas," Zore recalled in a 2007 interview. "What we really had to do was execute." Some initiatives of the Ericson years had not progressed much beyond the idea stage, and others obviously needed a second look. It was Zore's job to adjust the vision of the 1990s to the realities of the 2000s. In pursuing that task, he relied heavily on a seasoned team of senior executives. John Bremer took responsibility for administration, functioning as a genuine chief operating officer rather than a CEO-in-waiting. On the product side, Peter Bruce was ultimately in charge of all insurance matters, and a relative newcomer to top management, John Schlifske, headed Investment Products and Services (IPS). Schlifske was a Milwaukee native who had first seen Northwestern as a summer intern in 1982. He became a full-time employee in 1987, rising steadily in the investment departments until switching over to IPS.

The management team as a whole showed significantly more diversity than its earlier incarnations. In 2003, when nine of the firm's thirty-three executive officers were women, Northwestern was one of only sixty Fortune

500 companies in which women held at least a quarter of the top jobs. Progress on the minority front was slower, but in 2005 *Black Professionals* Magazine named Northwestern one of its "Top 25 Companies for African Americans." Ed Zore earned uniformly positive feedback from his entire executive corps. Highly collegial, eager to delegate, and always willing to consider opposing views, he fostered a powerful sense of teamwork among Northwestern's senior managers.

For the executive officers and everyone below them, the task of execution involved, first of all, undoing some things that were already under way. A simple mathematical exercise spelled the end of the international initiative. When it was determined that there were more potential policyowners in suburban Los Angeles than there were in all of Chile, the company lost its appetite for foreign expansion. In 2005, the Northwestern Mutual Trust Company was rechristened Northwestern Mutual Wealth Management, reflecting a shift in its emphasis from trust services to high-end investment advice for high-end investors. In 2006, the Mason Street Funds were quietly reorganized out of existence. Not only had the line been overshadowed to some degree by the Frank Russell funds, but regulators were taking an increasingly dim view of proprietary investment products. Perhaps the most significant undoing occurred in 2004, when Robert W. Baird & Company, after twenty-two years as an operating

A sisterhood of talent: Northwestern's women executive officers in 2005

subsidiary, was sold back to its managers. Northwestern had moved its broker-dealer operations from Baird to Northwestern Mutual Investment Services (NMIS) two years earlier, and there was little need for overlapping platforms. On a more strategic level, the Baird sale signaled a new stage in the firm's approach to IPS. Not only had Northwestern developed the skills necessary to administer investment products on its own, but those products became central enough to merit a place inside the parent company.

As older initiatives were undone, the company did a number of new things as well. The entire insurance portfolio was updated in stages, and a number of new products were introduced. The most notable was certainly universal life, which debuted in 2005. With a minimum first-year premium of $25,000 and at least $1 million in coverage, it was obviously designed for upscale consumers. Twenty years earlier, a Northwestern-sponsored universal life product would have been considered the height of heresy—an underwriting oxymoron—but some clients obviously appreciated the portfolio-based policy's extreme flexibility; universal life accounted for 60 percent of the company's new premium growth in 2006.

Perhaps the most visible new development of Ed Zore's tenure was a second home office campus. Northwestern had already exhausted the cardinal points of the compass at its Wisconsin Avenue headquarters; between 1914 and 2001, the company had built or rebuilt the South, East, North, and West Buildings, and all were filled to capacity and beyond. Rather than expanding downtown, Northwestern decided to grow on the edge of the city. In 2001, the firm purchased seventy-five acres in suburban Franklin—a site that had most recently been the home of the 41 Twin Outdoor Theater. Located twelve minutes south of the home office, the parcel was immediately buildable and large enough to satisfy Northwestern's space requirements for years to come. It also met a need for business continuity (i.e., disaster recovery)—a more pressing concern in the post-9/11 world. One of the major priorities in the initial stage of construction was a backup data center.

Fully aware that employees being transferred from downtown might feel like exiles at first, Northwestern planned some

The 41 Twin Outdoor Theater in suburban Franklin came down in 2002 …

special amenities for its Franklin campus. Once as flat as a pancake, the site was rearranged to give it more relief—a process that involved moving nearly 10,000 truckloads of earth. The results included almost two miles of walking and jogging trails, an artificial river (complete with waterfall), and enough trees and flowers to fill an arboretum. Work began in June 2002, and the first building was completed, on time and within budget, in April 2004. The five-story structure resembled, in plan, an airplane with two swept-back wings connected by an elliptical entrance and conference tower. (The artwork on one floor of the tower featured, appropriately enough, historic photographs of Milwaukee movie theaters, including the 41 Twin.) By October, nearly 900 employees had moved to Franklin, including the entire disability insurance team and selected staff units from Information Systems, Policyowner Services, and New Business. Some transplants missed the energy of the downtown campus, but they tended to forget their homesickness after a few lunches on the sunlit patio beside the cascading river. Although the transition to a two-campus home office involved some cultural adjustments—video-conferencing became a way of life for some employees—Franklin was deemed an aesthetically pleasing and highly practical solution to Northwestern's space problems. In 2006, even before the first building was fully occupied, work began on the second installment of the new campus.

... and in its place Northwestern developed a state-of-the-art office complex, with jogging trails, a waterfall, and other 21st-century amenities.

Franklin was a highly visible symbol of the firm's growth in size and sophistication, but the more vital part of executing Northwestern's corporate strategy was far less tangible than bricks and mortar. Under Jim Ericson's leadership, the company had bent its energies toward securing the base, growing around it, and strengthening the field. Ed Zore believed firmly in those priorities—he had, after all, helped set them—but Zore added another commandment: do it all more efficiently. "Faster, better, cheaper" became his mantra, and home office managers found themselves being held to new and higher standards of fiscal accountability. But the larger challenge was cultural. For generations, Northwestern Mutual had been managed by consensus and ruled by committee—a predictable outcome of its focus on the long term. Some companies could test-market their breakfast cereals or mousetraps. If the results proved disappointing, they simply stopped making the product and moved on to the next prototype. Northwestern had no such luxury. The market it tested generally had a fifty-year horizon, and one executive's mistakes could easily outlast his or her career. As Ed Zore pursued his "faster, better, cheaper" initiative, the business needs of the twenty-first century threatened to collide with cultural imperatives rooted in the nineteenth. Zore addressed both the risks and the potential rewards in 2007:

What we had here was a machine that was working wonderfully; it's just that we had to soup it up. It was like my first car: we had to take that engine out and make it a whole different vehicle, but without wrecking it. That's what I've been really focused on since I became CEO: opening communication, getting people more engaged, empowering them, but without blowing the place up. If we push responsibilities down, we can do wonders.

In the 1970s, Francis Ferguson had tried to remake the company in his own entrepreneurial image. Thirty years later, Ed Zore tried to make Northwestern a company of entrepreneurs. Proceeding with caution but conviction, he worked to replace any lingering vestiges of complacency and entitlement with a new sense of dynamism and ownership. It helped that he was a first-rate communicator: clear, candid, and forthright. "Push it down, push it down," Zore told his managers, and year by year the massive ship gathered speed.

"Faster, better, cheaper" was a mantra that could have been adopted by virtually any business that wanted to thrive in the twenty-first century. Ed Zore and his colleagues faced a more basic challenge that was unique to Northwestern Mutual: corporate integration. The central challenge of Zore's tenure, and one that will certainly shape his legacy, has been to fuse the disparate elements of the company's vision—

particularly its dual emphasis on insurance and investment products—into a single coherent whole. Like every CEO before him, Zore has pledged allegiance to the primacy of life insurance. "This is our strength," he told the agents when he took office in 2001. "This is our core competency. This is our claim to fame. This is where we've been distinguishing ourselves in the marketplace for nearly 150 years. Our values haven't changed." But Zore believes just as firmly in the importance of investment products. In a deregulated world, Northwestern could hardly limit its representatives to one product line; consumers wanted choices, and they wanted them, if possible, from a single source. "To protect our insurance side," Zore summarized, "we had to sell investments."

And so Northwestern found itself in the middle of two different worlds, selling some products that addressed risk (life, disability, and long-term care insurance) and others oriented to gain (annuities, mutual funds, and fee-based advisory products). The two lines solved substantially different problems, were subject to completely different regulatory authorities, and had significantly different commission structures. Their relative importance was shifting as well. Although life insurance continued to generate at least 80 percent of Northwestern's operating revenue, IPS was gaining fast. Mutual fund sales reached the $6.3 billion mark in 2005—enough to make Northwestern

Mutual Investment Services the fifth-largest independent broker-dealer in America. The growing importance of IPS was reflected in the company's rhetoric. Investment products that had been "ancillary" under Don Schuenke became "complementary" during Jim Ericson's administration and earned a promotion to "integrated" on Ed Zore's watch. The question was obvious: How do you bridge the chasm between insurance and investment products? How do you make integration a matter of reality rather than just rhetoric? Those questions were so fundamental that they were assigned to a new executive vice-president. In 2007, Business Integration Services was established under the direction of Marcia Rimai, a Harvard-trained attorney who joined Northwestern as head of the litigation team in 1993.

The answer that emerged was locked up in a deceptively simple concept: financial security. Some observers noticed a parallel between life insurance in the twenty-first century and railroads in the twentieth. It has been famously observed that America's passenger railroads perished because they forgot they were in the transportation business. Instead of embracing new

Even as it embraced the new, Northwestern preserved the old. This Signagraph check-signing machine from the early 1900s is prominently displayed in the home office museum.

Expert Guidance
for a lifetime of financial needs

The shape of the future: Northwestern visualizes financial security as a "pyramid of needs" that includes protection, accumulation, and preservation.

Trust Services

Estate Analysis

Investment & Advisory Services

Comprehensive Financial Planning

Employee & Executive Benefits

Business Needs Analysis

Retirement Solutions

Education Funding

Asset & Income Protection

Personal Needs Analysis

Wealth Preservation & Distribution

Wealth Accumulation

Risk Management

Northwestern Mutual
FINANCIAL NETWORK

Marcia Rimai, once the company's lead litigator, became its lead integrator, working to bridge the gap between insurance and investment products.

technologies, particularly air travel, they rode their old ones to the very end of the line. Life insurance faced a similar sunset. With the regulatory walls all but down, the insurance industry as such had ceased to exist by 2000. Everyone sold everything, and a consumer could turn to a bank, a broker, or a so-called insurance firm for substantially the same types of products, from mutual funds to term policies. What those increasingly homogenized products had in common was an emphasis on financial security; they existed to promote the economic well-being of the consumer at different points in his or her lifetime. Here was the unifying principle Northwestern had been seeking. "'Financial security,'" said Deborah Beck, the senior executive in charge of planning, "seemed to be the right phrase to connote a mix of

insurance and investment products with the guidance that pulls them all together." Beck and her colleagues came to see financial security as a pyramid of needs, with risk management at its base, wealth accumulation in the middle, and wealth preservation and distribution at the top. The company's aim was to offer products that met the consumer's needs at every stage of life, from insurance protection in the early years to long-term care and trust services in the later.

Northwestern Mutual may not have been the first company to use the pyramid as a model for financial security, but its interpretation differed from everyone else's. What set the company apart was the point at which it entered the pyramid. Banks and brokerage houses generally began in the middle—at the wealth accumulation stage. Northwestern started at the very bottom. Its entire business philosophy was rooted in a frank acknowledgement of life's inescapable realities, beginning with the most obvious: we're all going to die. If we don't die prematurely, we're going to get old. Even if we live to an advanced age, we may become disabled along the way or outlive our resources. In any of those events— death, disability, or advanced age—we or someone we love will likely be exposed to want. Those were precisely the realities that Northwestern insured against. Addressing the field in 2004, Ed Zore established the company's baseline in no uncertain terms:

Remember, everything begins with Life, DI, and Long-Term Care. These are the drivers, the start of everything, the base of the financial security pyramid. They're the doors to your relationships. This is where our vision begins. This is what we do better than anyone else in the world. We can never forsake our core products—NEVER.

But Northwestern did not stop at those core products. The company took a holistic approach to financial security, moving from protection to accumulation and finally to preservation and distribution. It offered not just life products but life-cycle products. The additions of the Ericson years, then, particularly those on the investment side, were not accessories bolted on for the sake of growth but vital components of an integrated system of security vehicles that could take policyowners from cradle to grave, from their most basic needs to their wildest dreams. "This is not just about insurance," Zore told the field in 2006. "It is not just about investments. It's about how everything fits together to help people reach for financial security." Northwestern

was moving toward a new identity: neither one nor the other but both combined.

The pyramid of needs reflected a compelling logic; it brought a new conceptual unity to the entire universe of Northwestern's products and services. Execution, as always, was the rub. When Ed Zore and his colleagues took a fresh look at distribution, they returned, as all their predecessors had, to the primacy of the exclusive field force. Here, however, they faced another, more perplexing question: how could one financial representative possibly hope to sell all those products? As its portfolio filled out, Northwestern was competing, in effect, for shelf space in the minds of its own sales force. The mounting number of professional degree programs hinted at the scope of the problem. The Chartered Life Underwriter (CLU) designation, first offered in 1928, had been the pinnacle of professional achievement for generations. In the 1980s, credential programs began to multiply like rabbits: Certified Financial Planner (CFP), Chartered Financial Consultant (ChFC), Long-Term Care Professional (LTCP), Personal Financial Specialist (PFS), and a host of others. Some of Northwestern's more studious field personnel

As Northwestern's product line expanded, so did the number of professional certifications available to the field.

areas, but the focus was on the individual representative. Northwestern made room for both tortoises and hares: representatives who were thoroughly effective at using traditional methods to sell traditional products and others who wanted the latest wrinkle and the last word in investment products for their most sophisticated clients. Many did in fact stay near the base of the pyramid, but the summit was there for anyone to scale.

Northwestern's agencies evolved, over time, from loosely connected teams of general practitioners to full-service clinics staffed with specialists who could solve practically any financial problem. The transformation was in part cultural. Since no individual representative could be all things to all clients, all representatives collaborated to be all things to individual clients. The focus shifted from solitary effort to joint work, from entrepreneur to "intrapreneur." For many financial representatives, the transformation was nothing short of revolutionary. After years, even decades, of functional independence, they moved with the company as a whole in the direction of greater interdependence—not only between individual representatives but also between home office and field. What did not change was the fundamental importance of the relationship between the well-informed representative and the self-interested client. "It all starts with the one-on-one relationship," said Ed Zore in 2006, and everything else

What did not change was the fundamental relationship of trust between financial representatives and their clients.

had more letters *after* their names than *in* their names. The company encouraged its representatives to learn everything they could, but there were obvious limits to how much one human being could absorb. With so many products and services to sell, how could anyone intelligently present them all?

The answer was The Network. The Northwestern Mutual Financial Network was a creation of the Ericson years, and its genesis reflected the best thinking of the entire senior management team, but it was on Ed Zore's watch that the idea evolved into a day-to-day reality. If financial security was a pyramid, then each agency was visualized as a team of professionals who decided precisely where they wanted to work on that pyramid. Highly trained specialists were on hand to provide expertise in particular product paled in comparison. The company's whole and entire strategy—the growth initiatives, the training programs, the expanding product line, the endless conceptualizing—could be said to have a single object in mind: enhancing the representative's value to his or her client. Northwestern has shown a faith in its field force that is matched by no other firm in America, and that faith is based on the certain knowledge that the field and the home office are complementary halves of a comprehensive whole. They move through time like a stately sailing vessel, with the home office acting as the keel and the field force as the sail. One keeps the craft upright and on course while the other keeps it driving forward, but it is the field, always, who finds the wind.

And has it worked? The pyramid of needs and the full-clinic agency model are both fairly new developments, but the results, once again, have been gratifying. All the complexities and uncertainties aside, Northwestern Mutual is an unqualified success by virtually any standard imaginable. In 2006, on the eve of its 150th anniversary and at the five-year mark of Ed Zore's tenure, life insurance sales were up 12 percent, recruiting rose 32 percent, the surplus ratio hit a new peak of 14.7 percent, and the company's share of the individual life market approached 10 percent. Persistency reached its highest level in nearly forty years, and Northwestern continued to

boast the highest dividends and the lowest expense ratio in the industry. A rebounding economy helped, but the company had clearly positioned itself to succeed, turning in such a strong performance that Zore called 2006 "probably the best year in our history."

One milestone was particularly well-timed: in early 2007, Northwestern Mutual attained $1,000,000,000,000 of life insurance in force. One trillion dollars is a lot to celebrate, particularly in your 150th-anniversary year, but Zore and his colleagues paid nearly as much attention to another achievement. When the list of sales leaders on the insurance side was compared with the roster of leaders on the investment side, nearly 20 percent were the same people—an indication that the integration strategy was working. Zore permitted himself a rare moment of satisfaction. "Maybe," he said, "we've got this thing figured out." In the long view, of course, one year does not a happy ending make, and all solutions are provisional—truths that Zore knows better than anyone. "The one thing that's certain," he said, "is that five years from now it's all going to be different." The way ahead is never clear, but there is another certainty: wherever Northwestern sails in the foreseeable future, it will be plowing the seas on some variant of the course set during the Zore years.

With Ed Zore in charge, Northwestern stands at the threshold of dramatic change in its outlook and its operations.

When Northwestern Mutual entered the world in 1857, the odds of its survival, much less its success, were beyond calculation. The company was founded by an eccentric Easterner in a thinly settled frontier state during a major depression, with no power brokers to back it and no constituents to champion its cause. The firm could easily have slipped beneath the waves, like most newly launched enterprises, but Northwestern stayed afloat, surviving a power struggle and a palace revolt to become a major force first in its state, then in its region, and finally in the nation. It was during the 1880s, when Henry Palmer was in charge, that the company's fate was sealed. It was in that decade and under that president that Northwestern adopted the value proposition that has animated the enterprise ever since, ensuring its vitality as well as its survival.

One hundred and fifty years after its founding, the world in which Northwestern operates has changed almost beyond recognition. Employees and representatives of the twenty-first century can look back with amused wonder at those long-gone days when moderate drinkers were uninsurable, disability insurance was roundly condemned, and agents cheered the 1927 announcement that new policies would be delivered by air mail. Although the historical context has changed radically, Northwestern's underlying values and the culture they support have not, and therein lies one of the firm's most remarkable achievements. The company still pays homage to Henry Palmer and the Executive Committee of 1888, but it must be remembered that they led Northwestern at a time when assets were a scant $33 million, insurance in force

had yet to reach the $200 million mark, and the agents' annual meeting never drew more than 300 people. The growth in scale since that time has been nothing short of astounding. The company's assets exceed $145 billion, it has $1 trillion of insurance on the books, and attendance at the annual meeting approaches 10,000—with no drop-off in enthusiasm. There has been an artful, intentional alchemy in that transformation. The company has, in effect, taken a recipe created for a small family and adapted it to feed an army, without sacrificing an ounce of nutrition or a fraction of flavor. That's a rare, perhaps unparalleled, accomplishment in the business world. The not-so-secret ingredient is Northwestern's culture, and the root of Northwestern's culture is its values.

There is no question that the changes of the recent past have been the most sweeping in more than a century. Northwestern has become larger than life; it has modified its name, added a suburban address, and adopted a new corporate strategy—and it remains a work in progress. How far do you go?, ask some anxious insiders. How much change can the company tolerate before it becomes a different enterprise? The simple truth is that Northwestern Mutual has always been a work in progress. At every point in its history, the company has had to accommodate, however grudgingly, the realities of its marketplace—Henry Palmer adjusting the product line of the 1880s no less than Ed Zore integrating the product platforms of the early 2000s. It was Palmer, remember, who authorized tontine insurance in 1881—a policy that would be universally discredited, even outlawed, within twenty years. He was simply doing what every

hip,   hip,   hooray!

Celebrating
150 years
of quiet strength

Northwestern president has done: giving the company's representatives, within well-established parameters of principle, what they needed to prosper, to enable them to provide timely services in a timeless fashion. That long-standing practice has produced a paradoxical blend of change and continuity. Northwestern had the inordinate good fortune to develop, relatively early in its career, a sense of abiding mission, and its leaders have shown, over many decades, the inordinately good sense to maintain their commitment to that mission. The result is an enterprise that, when considered in any particular period, is both significantly different and fundamentally the same.

The question remains: how far do you go? It is extraordinary that the question can still be asked. Alone among its former peers, Northwestern still promotes its original product with its original conviction. Alone among its former peers, and regardless of how much the details have changed, Northwestern remains faithful to its founding

principles—principles so deeply held that they are practically imprinted in the company's DNA. If Henry Palmer were to return to Northwestern today, he would no doubt be shocked by its growth in scale and the revolution in its technology, but he would just as surely recognize the enterprise whose character he did so much to shape. Palmer would find a firm still intent on doing the right thing, and doing it well. He would find men and women committed to treating all policyowners and clients equitably, and to treating each other with respect. He would find an almost-religious devotion to competitive excellence, and a devout belief in the personalism and professionalism of a skilled career field force. Henry Palmer would find, in brief, the firm described in the 1888 Executive Committee statement. That firm has become large as well as safe, and its certain salutary restrictions have evolved with time, but Northwestern Mutual remains, after all these years, pre-eminently the policyowners' company. 🌱

INDEX

ABOUT THE AUTHOR

Mike Miller

John Gurda is a Milwaukee writer and historian with eighteen books to his credit, including *The Quiet Company,* a 1983 volume published for Northwestern Mutual's 125th anniversary. Gurda's other works range from histories of businesses, churches, and neighborhoods to *The Making of Milwaukee,* an award-winning general history of Northwestern's home community. In addition to his work as an author, Gurda is a lecturer, local history columnist, and eight-time winner of the Wisconsin Historical Society's Award of Merit. Although he has the highest regard for Northwestern Mutual, Gurda does not anticipate writing the company's 175th-anniversary history in 2032. But call anyway.

CREDITS

Unless otherwise credited, all photographs are from Northwestern Mutual's corporate archives and the photography unit.

Chapter 1 collage photos: cows by Sam Bassett; carriage courtesy Ogden & Company, Inc.